# The Formation of England
## 550–1042

# THE PALADIN HISTORY OF ENGLAND

*General Editor: Robert Blake*
*Advisory Editor: Cameron Hazlehurst*

Other titles in this series will be:

Pre-Roman and Roman Britain *by* Professor G. D. Barri Jones
Conquests and Conflicts 1042–1450 *by* John Prestwich
1450–1558 *by* Dr C. S. L. Davies
1558–1660 *by* Professor Robert Ashton
1660–1760 *by* Professor Stephen Baxter
1760–1865 *by* Dr F. B. Smith
The Crisis of Imperialism 1865–1915 *by* Dr R. T. Shannon
1915–1970 *by* Robert Blake

H. P. R. FINBERG

# THE FORMATION
# OF ENGLAND
# 550–1042

HART-DAVIS, MacGIBBON
LONDON

Granada Publishing Limited
First published in Great Britain 1974 by Hart-Davis, MacGibbon Ltd
in association with Paladin Books
Frogmore, St Albans, Hertfordshire AL2 2NF, and
3 Upper James Street, London W1R 4BP

ISBN 0 246 10777 4

Printed in Great Britain by
Richard Clay (The Chaucer Press) Ltd
Bungay, Suffolk

# FOREWORD

## *by Robert Blake*

History does not consist of a body of received opinion handed down by authority from the historiographical equivalent of the heights of Mount Sinai. It is a subject full of vigour, controversy, life – and sometimes strife. One of the purposes of the Paladin History of England is to convey not only what the authors believe to have happened but also why; to discuss evidence as well as facts; to give an idea and an evaluation of the controversies which surround so many episodes and interpretations of the past.

The last twenty years have seen important changes in the approach to history and to historical questions. There has also been much painstaking research which throws new light on old problems and brings new problems into the field of discussion. Little of all this has so far got through to the general reader because it has been, naturally, confined to specialist journals and monographs. A real need exists for a series of volumes to inform the wide public interested in the history of England, and this is what the Paladin volumes are intended to meet.

All history is in one sense contemporary history. These volumes inevitably and rightly reflect to some extent the outlook of those who, whatever their own age, are writing in the 1970s. But there are in any decade a wide variety of attitudes and schools of thought. The authors of this series are not chosen to represent a particular body of doctrine; conservative, liberal, Marxist – or whatever. They are scholars who are deeply involved in the historical questions of their particular fields, and who believe that it is possible to put across something of the challenges, puzzles and excitements of their theme to a large audience in a form which is readable, intelligible and concise.

5

All historical writing must in some measure be arbitrary as to dates and selective as to area. The dates chosen in this series do not depart far from convention but perhaps just enough to encourage both author and reader to take a fresh view. The decision to make this a history of England, rather than Britain, is quite deliberate. It does not mean omission of the important repercussions of events in Scotland, Ireland, Wales or the countries which later constituted the Empire and the Commonwealth; rather a recognition that, whether for good or ill, the English have been the dominant nation in what Tennyson called 'our rough island-story', and that a widening of the scope would lead to diffuseness and confusion.

Historical writing also has to be selective as to themes. Each author uses his own judgment here, but, although politics, ideas, art and literature must always be central features in any work of general history, economic background, social structure, demography, scientific and technical developments are no less important and must be given proper weight.

All sorts of reasons can be given for reading history, but the best of them has always seemed to me sheer pleasure. It is my hope as editor of this series that this enjoyment will be communicated to a large number of people who might otherwise perhaps have never experienced it.

# CONTENTS

# PREFACE

In its treatment of the political, and still more the social, history of the Anglo-Saxon period this book differs at a number of points from the orthodoxy of the textbooks. Much of the documentary evidence on which it is based lies in chronicles, laws, and charters which have long been available in modern English translations. What has changed is not the evidence but our interpretation of the evidence. My object has been to present the reader with the most recent thinking on the subject, including my own. But anyone who undertakes to cover half a millennium in one not too lengthy volume inevitably has to decide what to leave out. While never, I hope, disguising opinions as established facts, I have chosen to present conclusions rather than the detailed arguments on which they are based. For these arguments, which are sometimes complex, and for full references to the source-material, the interested student may consult the works listed in the Select Bibliography (p. 237), which also includes a number of books representing older opinions which not all scholars are as yet prepared to abandon. He may like to compare the differing views of Anglo-Saxon history and make up his own mind between them.

H. P. R. F.

# Chapter I

# BRITONS AT BAY

A Dick Turpin riding from London to York in the middle of the sixth century would not have thought of the country through which he was travelling as England. A long time would elapse before that name was applied to the southern portion of Britain. Far away in Constantinople the lawful heir of Rome, the emperor Justinian, preoccupied with the reconquest of Italy and Africa and the codifying of Roman law, had no thought to spare for the dim island in the northern seas. The lost province of Britannia lay in fragments, and no one at that time could foresee that the fragments would ever be reunited under a single crown.

British princes, regarding themselves as the legitimate inheritors of Roman sovereignty, contrived to maintain at least the rudiments of administrative and fiscal organization. They could put armies into the field. They still professed to be Christians, and from time to time made gifts to the church. But essentially they were barbaric local chieftains, each fighting for his own hand. They ruled as more or less successful war-lords, and their subjects were governed more by ancestral custom than by any vestiges of Roman law.

Against five of these rulers the contemporary preacher Gildas, writing presumably from a safe distance, launched a terrific diatribe. The first, named Constantine, reigned over a still powerful kingdom in Devon and Cornwall, the old Dumnonia. He is denounced by Gildas as the unclean whelp of the Dumnonian lioness, polluted by crimes which included sacrilege and parricide.

Aurelius Conanus, the next object of invective, is described as a man grown old in iniquity, the last survivor of a noble race.

Since Gildas names him after the king of Dumnonia and before the king of Dyfed in Wales, it is plausible to locate him in the region of the lower Severn, perhaps in the territory of the ancient Silures, which included large parts of Herefordshire and Monmouthshire. Its capital, Venta Silurum, the modern Caerwent, gave its name to the British kingdom of Gwent. On the other hand, since Aurelius does not figure in the traditional genealogy of the rulers of Gwent it may be that he reigned on the other side of the Severn.

Dyfed, latinized as Demetia, occupied a large area in southwest Wales. Its king, named Vortipor or Voteporix, according to Gildas the bad son of a good father, is nearing the end of a sinful life. His tombstone, which stood until 1895 in the churchyard of Castelldwyran on the western border of Carmarthenshire, is carved in Latin capitals with the inscription "Memoria Voteporigis protictoris." The title "protector," bestowed under the later Roman Empire upon notable barbarian chieftains, may have become hereditary in his family.

To the north, in central Wales and Shropshire, the former territory of the Cornovii, with its capital at Wroxeter, had evolved into the British kingdom of Powys. Here perhaps lay the dominion of Cinglas (Cuneglasus), the "grey butcher," accused by Gildas of warring against his Christian neighbours, violating the marriage tie, and oppressing the church.

Last, tallest in stature, and most powerful in this quintet of colourful sinners, is Maelgwynn (Maglocunus), king of Gwynedd, the Latin Venedotia. His kingdom included north-west Wales and was based on Anglesey. As the "island dragon" he is accused of murdering his wife and a nephew whose widow he then married. For a while he repented and withdrew to a monastic cell, but presently he resumed the reins of power. At his court, which tradition places at Degannwy on the shore of the Conway, a troop of bards extolled his exploits until he fell a victim to one of the plagues which devastated Europe in the middle of the century.

Gildas does not speak, and may not have known, of the other British kingdoms. One of them, the kingdom of Elmet, stretched westwards from the marshes at the head of the Humber into the district of Leeds, where its name is perpetuated at Sherburn and Barwick, both of which appear on maps even today as lying "in Elmet." It maintained its independence throughout the sixth century and into the seventh.

In Cumberland the British principality of Rheged, its centre at or near the old Roman city of Carlisle, extended west of the Solway Firth and perhaps south into Lancashire. In what is now Scotland the kingdom of Strathclyde, with its main stronghold at Dumbarton, was destined to remain at least nominally independent until the eleventh century. Argyll and the adjoining isles had been settled at an unknown date by colonists from Dalriada in the north of Antrim, to form a Scottish kingdom of Dalriada. In 563 St Columba established a monastery on the island of Iona, with far-reaching consequences for the political, and still more the religious, life of the north. Finally, the wild tribes of Caledonia whom the Romans called Picts, perhaps because they painted or tattooed their bodies, occupied the whole of the land-mass between the Forth and the Pentland Firth. They appear to have formed two distinct conglomerations, the northern and southern Picts, but they frequently combined into a single formidable power.

In the intervals of warring against each other, the British rulers occasionally formed coalitions when threatened by a common foe, but they were incapable of maintaining a united front for long. Generous to their friends, and dangerous to their rivals, they could offer only a fitful resistance, and in the long run it was not military prowess or political skill which delayed their extinction, but the facts of geography.

The population of the island was already mixed. All along the western seaboard, not only in Dalriada but also in Dyfed and Dumnonia, Irish colonists had settled in appreciable numbers, and for centuries the east coast had attracted immigrants from the coastlands of northern Europe. They had not always come as enemies. Far back in the time of imperial rule men of Germanic origin had served in units of the Roman army stationed here. Inscriptions record the presence at Housesteads in Northumberland of Frisian and German troops, and at Burgh-by-Sands of a German cohort, a thousand strong. In 278 the emperor Probus

removed Burgundians and Vandals, east Germans living beyond
the Oder, to Britain, where they settled and helped the government to quell an incipient revolt. In 306 Constantius Chlorus
brought a force of Alamanni from south Germany under their
own king to Britain as auxiliary troops, and when he died they
took a leading part in promoting the accession of his son Constantine the Great. In 371 a strong force of Alamanni already stationed
in Britain were placed by Valentinian I under the command of one
Fraomar, who had previously ruled over a tribe dwelling opposite
Mainz. It is very likely that some of these imported Germanic
soldiers married native women and remained in Britain when their
term of service expired.

Archaeology helps to supplement the picture. It has brought to
light early Germanic cemeteries in significant proximity to the
gates of such Roman towns as York, Malton, Ancaster, Cambridge, and Leicester. York was the most important military
centre of Roman Britain. Less than a mile from the centre of its
legionary fortress urn-burials have been found showing in their
pottery close affinity with urns from Germanic cemeteries on the
continent. Similar urns from Sancton, Broughton, and Elmswell
suggest the presence of Germanic auxiliaries who drew their
supplies from the rich corn-growing area of the Yorkshire Wolds.
On the hillside to the south-east of Caistor-by-Norwich many
hundreds of pots have been dug up, betraying by their form and
ornament obvious Germanic taste. Early Saxon burials at Dorchester-on-Thames, Frilford, and Long Wittenham occur in close
proximity to Romano-British settlements. The consensus of
archaeological opinion now interprets all these finds as testifying
to the presence of Germanic mercenaries officially installed by
Roman-British authority near walled towns and other Roman
sites.

Thus by the middle of the fifth century the population of the
island in all probability included an appreciable element of Germanic blood and speech, and, as a natural sequel, a hybrid Anglo-
British intermixture.

The British authorities who assumed control after the collapse
of imperial rule revived the Roman policy of hiring Germanic
mercenaries to defend the island. Gildas, writing in the second

quarter of the sixth century, states that in face of a serious threat from beyond the northern frontier they introduced a new force of Saxons. Three shiploads of Saxons arrived in answer to the call, and were soon followed by many others, who "fixed their terrible claws in the eastern part of the island." The Britons undertook to supply the newcomers with provisions, but presently failed to do so, and the failure lit a flame of revolt among the mercenaries which scorched the land from sea to sea. It was probably as a result of these convulsions that the invaders began the process of establishing Germanic kingdoms in Britain.

It is an open question which of these kingdoms arose first. Gildas states that the Saxons were brought in to repel the men of the north, meaning the Scots and Picts. It is reasonable to surmise that early in their revolt they seized the plain of York and much of the East Riding. From this beginning rose the kingdom of Deira. North of the Tees, possibly as an offshoot from Deira or some- where further south, a kingdom of Bernicia took shape, beginning with a few settlements which looked to the rock of Bamburgh as their stronghold. The obscure kingdom of Lindsey occupied the uplands of Lincolnshire. The name of one of its earliest kings, Caedbaed, has the British element *Cad*, meaning battle, for its first element. Lindsey made little mark on the history of the time, being overshadowed always by more powerful neighbours. On the south side of the Wash a king named Wehha is said to have been the first who reigned over Norfolk and Suffolk. From his son Wuffa the East Anglian dynasty came to be known as the Wuffings. All these monarchs claimed descent from Woden, the Germanic war-god. Ida of Bernicia is said to have begun his reign in 547, and Ælli, the first securely dated king of Deira, in 558. The dates of the others are quite uncertain.

In the south a tradition well established by the end of the seventh century looked back to another Ælli, a king of the South Saxons, as the first supreme war-lord among the English. We may suppose him to have acted as commander-in-chief of a great confederacy, a mixed force of Saxon, Frisian, Jutish, and Frankish adventurers who successfully established themselves all along the coast from Selsey to the Thames. On the east Ælli's kingdom was bounded by the forest of Andred, beyond which lay the kingdom of Kent, founded, it is said, by Oeric surnamed Oisc, son or grandson of Hengist, the reputed leader of the great revolt. From Oisc the dynasty reigning in Kent became known as the Oiscings. To the west of Sussex, round Southampton Water, according to the confused traditions preserved in the Anglo-Saxon Chronicle, an adventurer named Cerdic had founded the principality of the Gewisse. Cerdic may have been a renegade Briton, for his name is certainly British, but it seems that his war-band consisted mainly of Jutes. Their settlements occupied the valleys of the Meon and the Hamble, the Isle of Wight, and, on the other side of Southampton Water, the territory east of the Hampshire Avon.

The names Essex, Middlesex, Sussex, and Wessex perpetuate the memory of the East, Middle, South, and West Saxons. Alone among the English dynasties the royal house of Essex claimed descent not from Woden but from Seaxnot, a god still worshipped by the continental Saxons in the eighth century. London was the chief town of Essex, and it is likely that East Saxon authority at one time extended over Hertfordshire and Surrey as well as Middlesex; we hear nothing of any Middle Saxon ruling family. The West Saxons occupied the lands immediately south of the middle Thames, where a group of cemeteries, all within ten miles of Abingdon, indicates that they had been settled from the beginning of the fifth century, if not earlier. No one then could guess how brilliant a future lay before them.

In central England the East, Middle, and West Angles formed the counterpart of this threefold division. Of East Anglia something has already been said. The Middle Angles, like the Middle Saxons, have no tradition of a ruling house; and the West Angles represent a later phase of expansion. In the valley of the Trent the originally obscure Mercian people, at first politically dependent on Deira, were ruled by a line of kings, the Iclings, so called from an ancestor named Icel, through whom they traced their descent from Offa, king of Angeln in Schleswig-Holstein, and through Offa back to Woden. The Mercians were an Anglian people, as were also the Deirans and Bernicians. To the Celts they were all "Saxons." It is clear that behind blurred terminology lay an essentially Saxon south and an essentially Anglian north, but ultimately the English, more aware of their common Germanic stock than of

17

their original differences, called themselves indifferently either "Angles" or "Saxons."

Thus by 550 the Celts of the west and north faced an aggressive people, hungry for land and power, and emboldened by successes already won. Any ambitious Germanic chieftain inured to fighting and marked out for leadership by the prestige of noble birth had only to enlist a few hundred warriors, attracted by the hope of booty or conquest, and stake everything on the chance of carving out a kingdom for himself. On the field of battle it was reckoned a disgrace for him to be surpassed in valour by his followers and for them to be less valiant than their chief. Personal loyalty to a leader was the foundation-stone of Anglo-Saxon society.

The land, the subject of the great struggle between Celt and Saxon, offered opportunities in plenty for newcomers either to take over such British estates as were still in working order or to tackle the vast areas not yet exploited. It is difficult for us to appreciate how much of Britain remained densely wooded at the beginning of the Anglo-Saxon period. Wolves, boars, deer, and wild cats found ample cover in the still uncleared natural forests. Between the Tees and the Tyne lay a region almost uninhabited except by wild beasts. At the end of the seventh century the site of Beverley was still known as Inderauuda, "in the wood of the Deirans," a forest which covered the greater part of Holderness. Similarly Wychwood in north-west Oxfordshire represents the wood of the people known as the Hwicce. In the west midlands the forests of Dean, Wyre, Morfe, and Kinver, and in the east those of Rockingham and Sherwood, covered scores of miles. The boulder clay of East Anglia and the east midlands, much of it heavy impermeable soil, must have borne dense forests of oak and ash. The names of Newton Bromswold and Leighton Bromswold, eleven miles apart, commemorate the now vanished Bruneswald. Oak, hornbeam, ash, and thorn dominated the greater part of Essex. The northern edge of this forest sloped away from near the Suffolk border towards the thickly wooded Chilterns. In the south-east the great forest of Andred was described by an annalist, writing in the year 892, as 30 miles wide and stretching 120 miles from east to west. In Wessex the forest of Selwood, known to the Britons as Coit Maur, the "great wood," ran north and south from the western edge of Salisbury Plain and for a century or more presented a natural obstacle to the westward expansion of the West Saxon kingdom.

*Timber*, in Old English, meant building material of any kind, but its more restricted sense points to the general predominance of wood in house-building and fencing. For these purposes and for their supply of fuel, the Anglo-Saxons naturally drew upon the woodlands. There too they could gather the wild honey from which they brewed the mead that enlivened their festive gatherings. The woods served also as feeding-grounds for the Anglo-Saxon pig, and we shall see how vitally important a part the pig played in their rural economy.

Almost equally with the forests, marshland formed a striking feature of the landscape. The coast on both sides of the Thames estuary, Romney Marsh, and the Pevensey levels offered excellent pasturage for sheep, but until they were drained they could not house large numbers of men. Nor could the saltmarsh north of Bristol and the mosslands of Lancashire. The Somerset levels west of Mendip lay under water most of the year, only a few islands of higher ground and the long dry ridge of the Poldens offering sites for early settlement. ("Glastingai," the oldest English name for Glastonbury, means the island of Glast's people.) The first West Saxon colonists established themselves on the uplands, and year by year waited to move their flocks and herds down to the levels until those rich pastures had been dried out by the summer sun. Hence the name Somerset, originally *Sumorsaete*, the summer dwellers.

"There is in the midland district of Britain," says the biographer of St Guthlac, writing shortly before 730, "a most dismal fen of immense size, which begins at the banks of the river Granta not far from the camp which is called Cambridge, and stretches from the south as far north as the sea. It is a very long tract, now consisting of marshes, now of bogs, sometimes of black waters overhung by fog, sometimes studded with wooded islands and traversed by the windings of tortuous streams." The Fens extended beyond the Wash and up the coast of Lindsey. Another belt of marshland stretched for more than thirty miles north and south of the Great Ouse.

19

After the woods and marshes, the third most important feature of the landscape was the *feld*, land free from wood, lying on the downs and moors, or sometimes in the open spaces of the forest. The *feld* provided common pasture for the sheep and cattle. Every village needed such ground, and sometimes two or more villages would share one and the same area of rough grassland.

*Pascua*, pastures, are always distinguished in legal documents from *prata*, meadows. These, lying along the bank of a river, were mown for hay, and the aftermath provided grazing for the cattle. As a source of winter fodder meadowland was very highly valued, and in an age which knew no systematic cultivation of grassland as such there was never enough of it to provide all the hay that was needed.

Here was a land, then, rich in opportunities waiting to be grasped by willing hands. For the second phase of the English conquest Gildas fails us; in any case he was more of a moralist than a historian. Something can be gleaned from a later British writer, Nennius, who in the early ninth century heaped together a medley of confused traditions. Archaeological excavation can tell us much about the pattern of early settlement, and some of its findings have been quoted here, but it throws little light, if any, on political developments. We have to fall back on the Anglo-Saxon Chronicle, first put together, from older materials now lost, at the West Saxon court in the last decade of the ninth century. Its entries are brief and often enigmatic. They preserve dim memories of conquering heroes and of the places where their victories were gained; English defeats are never mentioned. The dates are at best approximate.

From these imperfect materials, which have been the subject of endless critical discussion, we must piece together as best we can the history of the next stage in the making of England.

Chapter I I

# THE STRUGGLE FOR SUPREMACY

In 552, according to the Anglo-Saxon Chronicle, Cynric fought against the Britons at the place which is called *Searoburh*. The same annal makes Cynric a son of Cerdic, but another genealogy recorded elsewhere in the Chronicle makes him Cerdic's grandson, and we have no means of deciding which is right. This is only one of the inconsistencies which make the early annals such a tricky source. Those relating to Cerdic are duplicated, one set bringing him to Britain in 495 and another in 519, so chronology does not help.

The site of the battle is probably to be located at or near the Iron Age hill-fort now known as Old Sarum, near Salisbury. The victory opened up to the Gewisse all the valleys of those delightful streams, the Bourne, the Avon, the Wylye, the Nadder, and the Ebble, which from the north and west converge on Salisbury. After the comparatively sterile sands and gravels of the Hampshire basin those lush valleys, clear streams, and smooth downs must have presented themselves to the Gewisse like the vision of a promised land.

They waited four years before their struggle with the Britons came to a head at *Beranbyrg*, another hill-fort, now called Barbury Castle, five miles south of Swindon. Barbury dominates the great prehistoric ridgeway connecting Salisbury Plain with the Berkshire Downs. And it was probably along this route that Ceawlin came, to share in the battle and the triumph. Ceawlin, who here makes his first appearance on the historic stage, led a war-band recruited from the settlers in the Thames valley, the West Saxons properly so called. During the next thirty years

21

Ceawlin's exploits caused him to be remembered as having occupied the position, next after Ælli of Sussex, of supreme war-lord among the English. At first the ally of the Gewisse, he may soon have become their rival; the annal which records his accession to the kingship of Wessex in 560 possibly conceals a more or less successful effort by Ceawlin to unite the West Saxons of the Thames valley and the Gewisse under his rule. None of the early annals names Ceawlin's father, but later genealogists, rightly or wrongly, made him a son of Cynric and so were conveniently able to trace the ancestry of the whole West Saxon royal house back to Cerdic. Under West Saxon domination the Gewisse lost their identity as a distinct people, remembered chiefly by the occasional use of their name in the titles of the bishops of Winchester and the kings of Wessex.

## The Rise of Ceawlin

We hear next of Ceawlin in 568, when he engaged in battle not this time with the Britons but with King Ethelbert of Kent. The encounter took place at *Wibbandune* (?Wimbledon), and Ethelbert was driven in flight back to his own kingdom. It is clear that Ceawlin was now too formidable to be safely challenged by any other English ruler. Three years later a certain Cuthwulf, whose relationship to Ceawlin is uncertain, captured – or perhaps more probably recaptured – Limbury on the Icknield Way near Luton, Aylesbury in Buckinghamshire, and Benson and Eynsham in Oxfordshire, which may have been briefly recovered by still militant Britons operating from a base in the recesses of the Chilterns.

In 577 Ceawlin turned against the Britons of the Severn valley. Three British leaders – the Chronicle calls them kings – lost their lives in a great battle fought at Dyrham, seven miles north of Bath, and three once important Roman cities, Bath, Cirencester, and Gloucester, fell to the victors. The ample Cotswold sheepwalks and many fertile ploughlands now lay at the disposal of the West Saxons. They may have contented themselves with laying the region under tribute; possibly Ceawlin rewarded his chief companions in arms with gifts of British estates. In any case the battle of Dyrham proved a turning-point in English history. It seriously weakened the Britons of the south-west by cutting off their landward connection with their fellow-Britons of the Midlands and Wales.

In 584 Ceawlin captured many villages and booty beyond reckoning in another campaign against the Britons of which the highlight was a battle at *Fethanleag*. If this place is correctly identified with a wood near Stoke Lyne in the north-east of Oxfordshire, called "Fethelée" in a document of 1196, the campaign was probably a sequel to the advance begun by Cuthwulf in 571. The annal recording the battle of Fethanleag, however, ends with the more than usually enigmatic statement that afterwards Ceawlin "returned in anger to his own." We are left wondering what had excited his wrath. Was it an attempted insurrection of the Gewisse? The supposition gains some colour from the record that in 592 there occurred a great slaughter – the Britons are not mentioned this time – at "Woden's barrow," a neolithic long barrow now called Adam's Grave in Alton Priors on the northern scarp of the Vale of Pewsey, and that Ceawlin was driven out, presumably from the territory won thirty-six years previously. He died the following year, and his supremacy passed to Ethelbert of Kent. Mighty in battle, Ceawlin had not known how to consolidate his gains.

### Æthelfrith of Bernicia

The scene now shifts to the north. In the year when Ceawlin perished, Æthelfrith, grandson of Ida, succeeded to the throne of Bernicia. His kingdom had survived a formidable British onslaught led by Urien of Rheged and Rhydderch of Strathclyde. His brother-in-law Edwin of Deira was driven into exile either by Æthelfrith's father Æthelric or by Æthelfrith himself, who now ruled a united kingdom of Northumbria. The Venerable Bede, who finished writing his *Ecclesiastical History of the English People* in 731, depicts Æthelfrith as a character typical of the heroic age, "a very brave king, most eager for glory." Recording traditions which are supported by Irish annals and Welsh poetry, Bede says that he conquered more British territory than any previous

English chieftain. He opened the way for further Anglian settlement in the north by slaughtering many of the inhabitants and laying the survivors under tribute. The Britons of Edinburgh and the border country launched a retaliatory expedition against him, only to be defeated at Catterick. A bardic poem, the *Gododdin*, commemorating this disaster, is a classic of early Welsh literature.

Alarmed by Æthelfrith's successes, Aidan, king of the Scottish Dalriada, attacked him at the head of a large army, but Æthelfrith routed him at *Degsastan*, a place not certainly identifiable but evidently in Anglian territory. This put an end to any threat from Dalriada. Some ten years later, between 613 and 616, Æthelfrith attacked the Britons of Powys and worsted them at the great battle of Chester. At the start of the battle he perceived a throng of British priests, most of them from the monastery of Bangor-is-Coed, standing in what they believed to be a safe place. On learning that they had come there, after a three-day fast, to pray for the success of the British arms, Æthelfrith with grim logic declined to treat them as non-combatants and put most of them to the sword. The massacre, from which barely fifty out of some two thousand are said to have escaped alive, made so painful and lasting an impression on the northern clergy that whenever afterwards they saw an Anglian war-band coming many of them fled in terror, leaving their churches and endowments to be taken over by the nascent church of the English.

Soon after his victory at Chester Æthelfrith came to grief. His brother-in-law and rival, Edwin of Deira, had spent the long years of exile at first with British hosts and latterly at the court of Rædwald, king of the East Angles, who had now succeeded Ethelbert of Kent as overlord of the southern English. Under

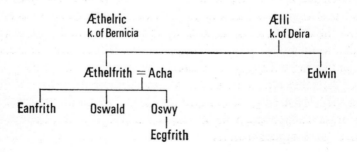

strong pressure from Æthelfrith Rædwald agreed to hand over or kill Edwin; but he was persuaded to change his mind. Anticipating the inevitable clash, he attacked Æthelfrith on his own ground before he could muster all his forces, and slew him in a battle on the east bank of the River Idle. Edwin thereupon returned to Northumbria and was accepted as monarch of both its kingdoms.

## The Reign of Edwin

A taciturn, proud, and reflective man, Edwin turned the lessons of exile to good account. His stay among the Britons had brought him into contact with Christianity and had so imbued him with the idea of Roman majesty that he determined to comport himself in all respects as a legitimate successor-king. A brilliantly conducted excavation at Yeavering in Northumberland, one of his chief residences, has revealed among other buildings a place of assembly with seating arrangements modelled on those of a Roman theatre. In time of war banners were carried before him, and when he walked the roads in peacetime he was always preceded by a standard of the kind which Roman writers called a *tufa*. For the refreshment of wayfarers Edwin caused bronze drinking-cups to be hung on posts wherever he noticed clear springs near the highway, and men stood so much in awe of him that no one dared to remove them. Generations after his death a proverb ran that in Edwin's time a woman with a newborn child could walk throughout the island from sea to sea and take no harm.

There is no record of any territory won from the Scottish peoples in his reign, but he is known to have expelled Cerdic, the last British king of Elmet, and incorporated Elmet into his own kingdom. In 626 he led an expedition against the West Saxons and destroyed five members of their royal house. In this campaign he can have met no active opposition from the Mercians, to whose kings he was related by his first marriage. Towards the end of his reign he took possession of the Isle of Man and drove Cadwallon, king of Gwynedd, out of Anglesey. No such powerful English monarch had ever been known in Britain. All the kingdoms of southern England acknowledged his supremacy except Kent, and to Kent he was allied by his second marriage to Ethelburh, a daughter of King Ethelbert.

His supremacy, however, rested on no organic basis. In 634 Cadwallon of Gwynedd, burning for revenge, led a mixed host of Britons and Mercian Angles across to the Northumbrian border. There, somewhere near Hatfield, he was met by Edwin. In the ensuing battle Edwin and his eldest son were killed, his army was scattered, and Northumbria immediately fell apart into its two component kingdoms.

### The Rise of Mercia

By this time a new power had arisen in the midlands. In 628 a member of the Mercian royal house, Penda, not yet king, assembled a war-band and fell upon a Wessex already weakened by Edwin's onslaught two years previously. At Cirencester he was able to impose terms of peace which involved the cession by the West Saxons of the Cotswold territory Ceawlin had won at Dyrham. The inhabitants, known as the Hwicce, whose name survives in the Oxfordshire Wychwood, were a British and Christian people with whom Anglo-Saxon settlers had begun to intermingle. They were now, apparently as a result of Penda's action, organized as a distinct political unit under a ruling house many of whose members bore distinctively Bernician names. After the defeat and death of King Æthelfrith seven of his sons, with a considerable following, had withdrawn to Scotland, and they remained in exile during the sixteen years of Edwin's reign. There was motive, time, and opportunity for some of them to join forces with Penda in a combined expedition against the West Saxons. If so, the principality or sub-kingdom of the Hwicce may have been Penda's reward for their assistance. Like their subjects, they were already Christians.

Penda was now king of Mercia, and had apparently succeeded in uniting under his sway the Mercians of the Trent valley and the congeries of small tribal units known collectively as the Middle Angles, who had earlier been governed by petty chieftains of their own styled ealdormen. In the campaign which brought about the overthrow of Edwin, Penda had led his war-band in alliance with Cadwallon of Gwynedd. For the rest of his life Penda never fought against the Welsh but always as their ally. They were linked by a common enmity to Northumbria. After the death of Edwin the sons of Æthelfrith returned to Bernicia. Eanfrith, the eldest, made a bid for his ancestral kingdom, but within a year was murdered when he visited Cadwallon to beg for peace. But in 635 his brother Oswald managed to defeat and kill Cadwallon, and was immediately recognized as king of all Northumbria. In 638 the Northumbrians captured Edinburgh and advanced their frontier to the Firth of Forth. But no king in Oswald's position could feel secure so long as the dangerous Welsh–Mercian coalition endured. In 643 he determined to break it up. His preventive campaign, which in the event proved fatal to himself, brought him to the Welsh border. There, on 5 August 643, he was defeated and killed. Penda ordered his head and hands to be severed from his body and hung on stakes. The place was then known to the English as *Maserfelth* and to the Welsh as *Cogwy*; tradition has long since identified it with Oswald's Tree, now Oswestry.

It is unlikely to be mere coincidence that not long after the battle we find a son of Penda named Merewalh reigning in Shropshire and Herefordshire with the title of king. Since the political history of Powys in this period is altogether blank, we cannot know how far its rulers acquiesced in this territorial loss. They may have considered that a small and relatively weak Anglian principality on their eastern frontier would be no danger to themselves but would ensure the continued assistance of Penda and his heirs against the still formidable Northumbrian enemy. The population over which King Merewalh ruled must have been predominantly Welsh in blood and speech, but Anglian settlers were planted among them, and were known as "Westerna," or, in one later text, West Angles. Merewalh's chief seat is believed to have been at Leominster. In 680 or thereabouts, having by then embraced Christianity, he provided a site at Much Wenlock for the foundation of a convent of monks and nuns, and in due time his daughter Mildburg became its abbess.

Penda's next campaign was provoked by the king of Wessex, Cenwalh, who had married and then repudiated Penda's sister. Cenwalh lost his throne in consequence, and spent the next three years in exile at the East Anglian court.

Thus in the course of thirty years Penda had made himself

master of central England. The principality or sub-kingdom of the Hwicce, comprising Gloucestershire east of the Severn, Worcestershire, and south-west Warwickshire, was ruled by a dynasty in close dependence on him. On the west the delectable country between the Wrekin and the Wye, bounded on the west by the forests of Clun and Radnor, acknowledged his son Merewalh as king; he set up another son, Peada, as king of the Middle Angles south of the Trent; and the original Mercia lay under his direct rule. It would remain for his successors to weld this loose confederation of principalities into a single formidable power.

### Northumbria under Oswy

In the meantime Oswald's brother Oswy (Oswiu) had succeeded him in Bernicia, still the object of implacable Welsh and Mercian hostility. In 656, after at least two previous raids, Penda resolved on his destruction. At the head of an immense army, which included contingents from Gwynedd and East Anglia, he again invaded the north. Oswy, in his extremity, tried to buy peace with a great treasure, but in vain. Faced with imminent destruction, he met his enemies with a very small force somewhere in the country round Leeds. The night before the encounter Cadafæl of Gwynedd, satisfied perhaps with his share of the spoil, stole away and sped ingloriously back to Wales. By one of those dramatic turns of fortune so characteristic of the period the battle ended in a complete victory for Oswy, leaving Penda and Æthelhere of East Anglia dead upon the field.

Never again did a British leader attempt to exterminate the English or to win back the sovereignty of Britain. The Welsh, divided by the expansion of Northumbria and Wessex from their fellow-Britons in Strathclyde and Dumnonia, were marked off as a separate people, self-contained within their western strongholds. Oswy's first marriage to a descendant of the princes of Rheged may have given him a legitimate hereditary claim to rule over southern Cumbria. Oswy's victory over Penda placed him on a height of power attained by no earlier English king. He annexed Deira to Bernicia, overawed the Picts and Scots, and for a time reigned as undisputed overlord of all the southern kingdoms.

## The "Bretwalda"

The English title given to such overlords was *Bretenanwealda*, *Brytenwealda*, or, in its contracted form, *Bretwalda*, meaning lord of Britain. As applied retrospectively to Ælli of Sussex, Ceawlin of Wessex, Ethelbert of Kent, and Rædwald of East Anglia, it signified at first the military leadership of a commander-in-chief whose victories led him to be hailed as the equal or superior of British princes. Later it meant the predominance of a king whose might overshadowed that of any other English king south of the Humber. But with the rise of Northumbria under Edwin, Oswald, and Oswy, this indeterminate hegemony began to assume a more imperial character. The biographer of St Columba states that after Oswald's defeat of Cadwallon in 635 he was "ordained" by God as emperor of all Britain. Columba himself had "ordained" Aidan as king of the Scottish Dalriada. The ceremony consisted in the laying-on of hands, not necessarily by a bishop, for Columba was a priest-abbot, not a bishop, and it was accompanied by the recital of a set form of blessing. This is the earliest mention in British history of a liturgical rite for the inauguration of a monarch. There was no crowning, and nothing is said of anointing. These features would be added later, to persist into the twentieth century.

The authority of the *bretwalda* was reinforced by matrimonial alliances and by the taking of hostages from the lesser kings. It enabled him to give safe-conduct to travellers through their territory. He could associate himself with them in grants of land, and exact tribute from them and their subjects. It was for him to settle disputes between them. In wartime he could require them to place themselves and their fighting men under his command. Always his supremacy depended in the last resort on military power, and it passed from one dynasty to another with the fluctuating fortunes of war.

The death of Penda left Mercia helpless under Oswy's control. At first he allowed Peada, now his son-in-law, to reign over the Middle Angles, but in 656 Peada was murdered. In 659 three Mercian ealdormen brought forward another son of Penda named Wulfhere whom they had kept in hiding, and proclaimed him king of all Mercia. During the next forty-five years, first under

Wulfhere (659–75), then under his brother Ethelred (675–704), Mercia regained the initiative. Fortified by the existence on their western flank of the two allied kingdoms of the Hwicce and the West Angles, the brothers appear to have maintained their father's good understanding with the Welsh. At no time did they behave as if there were any danger of a stab in the back from Wales, and neither of them was rash enough to engage in a war on two fronts.

They had still to reckon with Northumbria. In 671 Oswy seems to have performed the feat, unusual for a Northumbrian king, of dying in his bed. His son Ecgfrith succeeded him. In a campaign of which no details are recorded he checked an invasion by Wulfhere and detached Lindsey from the Mercian orbit; but in 679 Ethelred defeated him in a battle near the Trent, and Lindsey returned to its Mercian allegiance. Thereafter Ecgfrith left southern England to its own devices. This facilitated the growth of Mercian power, but Ecgfrith was much more concerned to maintain his father's power over the Picts and to extend Northumbrian supremacy over Strathclyde and Dalriada. In 684 he sent an expedition to Ireland which devastated part of Meath. Bede, looking back on this invasion, deplored it as an outrage against the Irish, a people, he says, who had always been very friendly to the English. Ecgfrith's intention may have been to forestall the possibility of Irish intervention in Scotland, into which he was planning further inroads. In the following year, against the advice of all his friends, he led a raiding party into Pictland. There the enemy lured him into some narrow passes in the midst of inaccessible mountains, and at Dunnichen Moss in Forfarshire he, with the greater part of his army, was overwhelmed and killed. Capture and slavery awaited the few who survived.

After this disaster the Picts, Scots, and Strathclyde Britons recovered much of the territory they had lost through Anglian aggression. They long continued to threaten the border of a Northumbria henceforth on the defensive. The Bernician dynasty survived, but no Bernician king could feel entirely secure, even among his own people. Never again would there be a Northumbrian *bretwalda*.

With Northumbria paralysed and Wales apparently acquiescent, the kings of Mercia turned their attention southward. In 675 Wulfhere carried war into the heart of Wessex. After harrying the Berkshire Downs he invaded Hampshire and annexed the Jutish territory east of Southampton Water, together with the Isle of Wight, to Sussex, at that time ruled by his godson King Aethelwalh. By 665 the kings of Essex had become his subjects. Ten years later he was again in action against Wessex. His brother Ethelred heralded his accession by ravaging Kent. Thus within twenty years from the death of Penda his sons had successfully established themselves as overlords of the southern English.

## The Westward Expansion of Wessex

The kings of Wessex, having lost Berkshire and the original territory of the Gewisse, were not content merely to lick their wounds. They could still try conclusions with their western neighbours. They had begun their westward drive as early as 614 with a massive attack which came to a head at Bindon, near Axmouth, in east Devon. For the next forty years they made no further advance, being fully engaged in the attempt to contain Mercian aggression. But in 658 Cenwalh, back in his kingdom from the exile into which Penda had driven him, took the field again and routed a force of Britons at *Peonnum*. This place was long identified with Penselwood on the border of Somerset and Wiltshire, but there is nothing to be said for this identification, and the most recent discussion locates the battle more plausibly at Pinhoe on the outskirts of Exeter. This implies that a contingent of Britons from Somerset took a prominent part in the resistance, for the annal records that Cenwalh drove them in flight all the way back to the Parret. The city of Exeter, the old Roman capital of Dumnonia, now lay in West Saxon hands. Three years later Cenwalh attacked again at Posbury, an Iron Age hill-fort seven miles to the north-west of Exeter. The victory – it must be remembered that the Anglo-Saxon Chronicle does not notice English defeats – left the West Saxons in control of the central corridor of Devon. The conquest seems to have been completed in 682, when King Centwine, Cenwalh's brother and successor, drove the Britons in flight to the Atlantic coast. The

British kingdom of Dumnonia shrank back into the recesses of Cornwall.

Centwine's contemporary Aldhelm states that he defeated his enemies in three great battles. We are not told who these enemies were; they are most likely to have been the Britons of Devon or Dorset. The inhospitable nature of the Dorset coast had precluded a massive invasion by sea, and entrance from the north was blocked by the defensive earthwork of Bokerley Dyke, stretching for six miles from the thickly wooded part of Cranborne Chase to the edge of the uninviting heathland of north-east Dorset. But with the West Saxons in command of both Wiltshire and Devon absorption could not long be delayed. By the reign of Centwine Dorset too was a West Saxon province.

The Saxon conquest of the south-west marks an important phase in the making of England. It would probably be a mistake to think of it in terms of a war between two modern states, like France and Germany, and of territorial annexation by the victor. Anglo-Saxon infiltration may well have begun and continued for some time before the first recorded clash of arms. The native Britons, who were certainly not all massacred, perhaps looked on at first with sullen acquiescence while bands of Saxon colonists established themselves on the rich red soils of central Devon and in the densely wooded combes. But sooner or later the process would give rise to what the jargon of diplomacy today styles incidents, and the stronger power would intervene to protect its colonists. Political annexation would follow as the aftermath of victory.

The chief sufferers from the Anglo-Saxon conquest, beyond any doubt, were the native aristocracy. Numbers of them must have fallen in battle; for the survivors nothing remained but to collect such movable wealth as had not been plundered and retire into Cornwall or Wales. Yet even here it is possible to paint too dark a picture. The Welsh *llys* or *lis*, meaning a chieftain's hall or court, survives not only in such Cornish place-names as Liskeard, but also at Liss in Hampshire and Liscard in Cheshire. As for British ploughmen and shepherds, a wholesale slaughter of the rural population would be difficult to compass even if it had been desired. Without their labour how could the conquerors make the most of their acquisitions? The place-name Walton – Welshmen's village – occurs in many parts of England.

The social and economic aspects of the conquest will be discussed later in more detail. Here we are concerned with its political results. By the end of the seventh century by far the greater part of southern Britain lay under Anglo-Saxon rule. Our older historians used the word Heptarchy as a collective name for the seven kingdoms of Northumbria, Mercia, East Anglia, Essex, Kent, Sussex, and Wessex. The name was misleading, for it ignored Lindsey, the Hwicce, and the West Angles, all of them fully equal in resources to a kingdom like Sussex, reckoned one of the major seven. We have seen now one, now another of the seven contending for supremacy, and we leave Mercia, the latest competitor, on the way to achieving a predominance in which lay the germ of a united kingdom of all England. That too would come in time, though not under a Mercian crown.

# Chapter III

# THE CONVERSION OF THE ENGLISH

As the provincials of the Roman world gave the names of their gods to the days of the week, making *mardi* the day of Mars, *mercredi* the day of Mercury, *jeudi* the day of Jove, and *vendredi* the day of Venus, so the Anglo-Saxons named Tuesday after Tiw, Wednesday after Woden, Thursday after Thunor, and Friday after Frig, deities whose cult they brought with them from their Germanic homelands. Tiw was a god of battles, less prominent in that capacity than Woden, the war-god from whom so many Anglo-Saxon dynasties liked to claim descent. Frig, like Venus, was a goddess of fertility, and Thunor, like Jove, the thunder-god. Little is known about the goddesses Hretha and Eostre; they would have been consigned to oblivion long since had not the name of Eostre been applied after the conversion to the greatest festival of the Christian year.

Anglo-Saxon heathenism was strongly enough entrenched to have left its mark on some fifty English place-names. Tiw is commemorated at Tysoe in Warwickshire, Thunor at Thundersley in Essex and Thunderfield in Surrey, Woden at Wednesbury and Wednesfield in Staffordshire, Woodnesborough in Kent, and a group of place-names in Wessex including Wansdyke or Woden's dyke. Heathen shrines or sanctuaries are represented by the element *weoh* in such names as Weedon, and by *hearg*, of which Harrow-on-the-Hill is the most conspicuous example. These latter appear not to have been dedicated to any one god in particular; they may well have contained altars to a number of deities. Elsewhere sacred groves, trees, wells, and stones figured largely as objects of popular veneration.

34

Bede speaks of the second month as the month of cakes, presumably a ritual offering; of the ninth as a month hallowed probably by some form of thanksgiving for the harvest; and the eleventh as the month when the Anglo-Saxons devoted to the gods the animals they were about to kill – an early reference to the practice of killing off superfluous livestock at the onset of winter. We may suppose these to have been cheerful occasions, but in general the Anglo-Saxon imagination was haunted by a doom-laden mythology of vengeful gods, preternatural monsters, dragons, and blood-drinking vampires.

### British Christianity

Since the reign of Constantine the Great Christianity had been the official religion of the empire. In Britain it was organized under a normal hierarchy of bishops, priests, and deacons. Down to the fifth century the British church remained keenly interested in theological argument and capable of such missionary effort as led Patrick, the grandson of a priest, to become the apostle of Ireland. Tradition preserved dim memories of Ninian, a bishop who had presided over a Christian community in Galloway with his see at Whithorn, and of Kentigern, perhaps the first bishop in Strathclyde. Among the reproaches which Gildas hurled at his compatriots there is no imputation of heathenism; he takes it for granted that they are all Christians, however unworthy of the name.

In 457 Pope Leo I altered the method of calculating the date of Easter, and the alteration was duly accepted in Britain. But thirty years later a further change took place, and by that time Anglo-Saxon heathenism had interposed a barrier across the natural lines of communication between Britain and the continent. There is not the faintest hint that the Anglo-Saxons ever attempted to impose the cult of Woden on their Christian subjects, but churches were plundered, the educated and the wealthy took to flight, and the native church, impoverished and largely isolated from its contacts with the European mainland, ceased to keep pace with continental reforms.

Throughout the Roman world bishoprics were normally established in cities. But there were then no cities in Ireland; there and in other Celtic lands religious leadership came to be largely exercised by monasteries, with bishops subordinate to abbots, some of whom ruled a whole chain of dependent communities. By far the most influential centre of this system in the British Isles was Iona. There, in 563, the Irish nobleman and saint, Columba, founded a monastery which presently commanded the obedience of numerous equally fervent and ascetic communities on both sides of the Irish Sea. Columba preached to the northern Picts, visited their king Bridei at his court near Inverness, and apparently made peace between the Picts and Scots. Under his rule Iona kindled a beacon-light of Christian culture which radiated far and wide over the north.

## Roman Missionaries

In 597, the year Columba died, the Roman missionary Augustine landed in Kent. Gregory the Great even before his election to the papacy had thought of attempting to convert the Anglo-Saxons, and he now determined to wean them from Germanic heathenism. The first step, obviously, was to win over the reigning kings.

We may reasonably surmise that political calculation as well as intellectual conviction helped to bring about the conversion of the English rulers. A religion with no theology worthy of the name confronted a system of belief elaborated by some of the subtlest thinkers of the Greco-Roman world. Their ancestral heathenism must have burdened the more intelligent English leaders with a sense of inferiority not unlike that of nineteenth-century African chiefs brought up against the sophistication of Europe. Some of them could perceive the moral grandeur of an asceticism which by stern self-discipline achieved triumphs of a different order from those won by the sword. At the same time their conversion might be applauded by their Christian subjects, giving as it did an air of legitimacy to their claim, against that of the British princes, to inherit the authority of Rome. The conversion of the English involved a deliberate acceptance of things Roman. The language of the church they entered was the language of the empire; the head of that church was the bishop of Rome, upon whom something of the imperial majesty had devolved. Thus, in becoming Christians, they also became, and meant to become, in more than one sense, Romans.

Kent, as the nearest kingdom to the continent, was naturally the first target of Pope Gregory and his missionaries. Its king, Ethelbert, may have owed something of his ascendancy as *bretwalda* to his marriage with a daughter of Charibert, the Frankish king reigning in Paris. It was a condition of the marriage that Queen Bertha should bring with her a Frankish bishop, Liudhard, and have liberty to practise her faith. The church of St Martin, on a hill just east of Canterbury, dating from the Roman period and still in use today, served as Bertha's oratory. Thus Christianity had already secured a foothold in Ethelbert's court, and he may himself have been predisposed in its favour. "It has come to our ears," wrote Gregory to the Frankish princes, "that the English race earnestly desires to be converted to the Christian faith." But it was necessary for Ethelbert to move circumspectly, and above all not to alienate the noble class on whom he depended for military support.

The man whom Pope Gregory had chosen as leader of the English mission was Augustine, prior of Gregory's own monastery of St Andrew on the Coelian hill in Rome. At some point in his journey through southern Gaul Augustine ran into difficulties and returned to discuss them with the pope. Gregory sent him back with the status of abbot, which gave him full authority over his companions. The pope may at first have contemplated only a preliminary exploration, but on learning, as he must soon have done, that there was already a bishop in Kent, he authorized Augustine to seek episcopal consecration in Gaul.

The missionaries landed in Thanet at some date in the spring or summer of 597 and sent to notify the king of their arrival. After a day or two Ethelbert came to meet them and listened while they expounded their beliefs. In reply he said that he himself could not forsake the religion of his ancestors but did not forbid them to make converts to their own, and in the meantime would supply them with provisions and lodge them suitably in his capital city. This was the Roman Dorovernium, later known as Canterbury, "the town of the Kentish people." Augustine and his companions began to celebrate the liturgy in St Martin's church, and by Christmas were able to report that converts in large numbers had been baptized. Ethelbert, while compelling no man to accept the new faith, showed them marked favour. As *bretwalda* he had much to give. Under his influence his nephew Saeberht, king of Essex, and Rædwald, king of East Anglia, became Christians, but Rædwald's conversion proved to be only skin-deep, for back at home he maintained, side by side with a Christian altar, one on which sacrifices continued to be offered to the heathen gods. Meanwhile Ethelbert allowed Augustine to repair dilapidated British churches and build new ones. After a prudent interval, perceiving no sign of a heathen reaction, he declared himself a Christian.

Encouraged by his initial success, Augustine asked the pope for more assistants. Thereupon Gregory sent a new band, led by Mellitus, Justus, Paulinus, and Rufinian, and accompanied by Laurence, a member of the original mission. He also wrote to Ethelbert and Bertha. Addressing Ethelbert as "rex Anglorum," he urged him to redouble his efforts for the conversion of his subjects. To Bertha he said that as an educated woman she might easily have won her husband over long before, but better late than never; she had acquired great merit by the help she had given to Augustine, and should now make good what she had neglected in the past.

By this time Gregory had drawn up an ambitious blueprint for the organization of the church in Britain. The country should be divided into two provinces, each with twelve bishops, with their metropolitan sees at London and York. He asked Augustine to consecrate a bishop for York, and signified that when this had been done he would send a pallium, the symbol of metropolitan jurisdiction, to the archbishop of York. Meanwhile he sent a pallium to Augustine, who was to hold the primacy during his lifetime; thereafter whichever archbishop had been ordained first should take precedence over the other.

The event showed this programme to have been over-optimistic. Ethelbert's authority over the East Saxons enabled him to build a church of St Paul in London and ensured the reception of

Mellitus as its first bishop. But Augustine so far depended on Ethelbert's support that Canterbury, not London, became the metropolitan see. Justus remained with him in Kent as bishop of Rochester, where Ethelbert built him a church dedicated to St Andrew. The king also provided endowments in land for the maintenance of the three bishops and their clergy.

Pope Gregory had urged Ethelbert to overthrow heathen temples, but on second thoughts he advised Augustine to leave them standing if they were substantially built and to consecrate them as churches, only destroying the idols. There was no need to deprive the people of their customary sacrifices of oxen; let ancient festivals be celebrated on appropriate days as religious feasts. (In conformity with this advice the spring festival of the goddess Eostre became the Christian Easter, and the great mid-winter festival of Yule was identified with that of Christ's Nativity.) For the bishop and his clergy Gregory prescribed a communal but not strictly monastic way of life, supported by the offerings of the people. If church property is stolen, the church must enquire whether the thief can support himself or not, and must in no case demand more than simple restitution. As to the laity, the marriage of first cousins and the heathen practice of marrying a stepmother are forbidden, but to the marriage of two brothers with two sisters not of their near kin there is no objection.

*Augustine and the Britons*

Gregory knew that the native British church departed in many of its usages from the normal practice of the West and had made no effort to convert the heathen English. But it had never renounced the idea of Catholic unity or failed in reverence for the see of Rome. The pope seems to have anticipated no great difficulty in forming a united Christian front in Britain. His mandate gave Augustine supreme authority over all the British clergy.

Thanks to the good offices of the *bretwalda* a meeting was arranged between Augustine and certain bishops and teachers of the nearest British province. They met somewhere on the frontier between the still heathen West Saxons and the Christian Hwicce, probably at a spot in Wychwood Forest. The Britons found no fault with Augustine's teaching, but, feeling themselves hardly competent to speak for the native church as a whole, they asked for a second and more representative conference.

The later gathering was attended by seven British bishops, most probably from Wales, and many learned men, chiefly from their renowned monastery of Bangor-is-Coed. We are not told where they met Augustine, but it is likely to have been at a place further north and west than the preliminary conference, and a good case has been made out for Abberley in Worcestershire, near the Herefordshire border. There was an ancient tree here called Apostle's Oak, famous enough to give its name to the parish of Rock, originally R(oak), in which Abberley was included until 1289. Augustine insisted on conformity in only two points, the date of Easter and the rite of baptism or confirmation; all other differences should be overlooked if they would join him in preaching the word of God to the English. It is said that Augustine, perhaps already a sick man, remained seated at the approach of the Britons. They took offence at this, rejected his proposals, and refused to acknowledge him as primate of Britain. The conference broke up, having only exacerbated a situation which demanded the greatest forbearance from both parties.

So much may be read between the lines of the story as it reached Bede more than a century later, not without some legendary accretions. It may be that Augustine's tone in the end was too authoritarian. On their side the Britons were less impressed by his papal commission than by his dependence on King Ethelbert. Rome was far away; the conquering English had already inflicted grievous losses on them, and threatened more.

By the end of his life – he died probably in 604 – Augustine had achieved a limited success in Kent and Essex, but little indeed outside the Kentish orbit. In Canterbury, with Ethelbert's help, he had established his cathedral on the site of a Roman church, and founded a monastery of SS. Peter and Paul (now known as St Augustine's) intending it to be a mausoleum for the kings of Kent and his own successors. Ethelbert outlived both Augustine and Bertha, dying in 618.

## A Heathen Reaction

His son Eadbald had not accepted Christianity. His accession gave the signal for the pent-up heathen reaction. The whole of Essex relapsed on the death of his cousin Sæberht, and Bishop Mellitus was driven out of London. He and Justus of Rochester withdrew to Gaul, and Laurence, whom Augustine had consecrated as his successor at Canterbury, was strongly tempted to follow them. He found means, however, to put the fear of God into Eadbald. The king at last accepted baptism, recalled the fugitive bishops, and restored Justus to Rochester. Like his father he married a Frankish princess, and for the remainder of his reign promoted Christianity as best he could, but his hold on Essex was not strong enough to restore Mellitus to the see of London.

The new archbishop, Laurence, wrote to the bishops and abbots of Ireland, deploring the breach between the churches and criticizing as unchristian the attitude of Dagan, a visiting Irish bishop who had refused to share meals with his Roman brethren or even to eat under the same roof. Laurence also made fresh overtures to the British church; but by now the battle of Chester and the massacre of the Bangor monks, which in retrospect appeared to Bede as a just retribution for their recalcitrant behaviour towards Augustine, had so embittered the native clergy as to wreck all chances of agreement.

## The Conversion of Northumbria

In 619 Laurence was succeeded as archbishop by Mellitus, and he five years later by Justus. This period was marked by an extension of the Roman mission into Northumbria. King Edwin may have been predisposed in favour of Christianity, but he followed Ethelbert's example in proceeding with caution. In 618 or early in 619, being now a widower, he married Ethelburh, a sister of Eadbald, promising to let her worship as a Christian and to consider the possibility of becoming one himself. On her northward journey Ethelburh was accompanied by Paulinus, who received episcopal consecration from Justus. Thus for the second time a royal marriage opened the way for the spread of Christianity among the English. Similar dynastic alliances would follow before long, with similar results.

Eadbald had been in correspondence with Pope Boniface V, who sent the pallium to Justus with an encouraging letter. The pope also wrote letters of exhortation to Edwin and Ethelburh, with presents of a gold-embroidered tunic for the king and a silver mirror and a comb of gilded ivory for the queen. On Easter Eve in 626 a daughter was born to the royal couple. With Edwin's consent she and eleven of her attendants were baptized at Pentecost. Soon after Edwin's return from his victorious campaign against the West Saxons he assembled his council at York. The ground had evidently been very well prepared. Coifi, the high-priest of Northumbrian paganism, opened the debate, asserting that his religion had neither virtue nor profit in it; it had certainly never done him much good with the king – a plain hint of gratitude for favours to come. He was followed by an unnamed nobleman, who delivered a moving and memorable speech comparing the life of man on earth to the flight of a sparrow into the hall where the king sits feasting with his thegns and ealdormen. "The fire is burning on the hearth, and all inside is warm, while outside the wintry storms of rain and snow are raging. The sparrow flies in at one door, and for a few moments the storm cannot touch it, but after a brief interval it flits out through the other door into the winter again. So this life of man appears but for a moment; what follows or what went before, we know not at all. If this new doctrine brings us more certain information, it seems right that we should accept it." After others had signified their agreement, it was the turn of Paulinus to be heard, and when he had said his say, Coifi set the example of abjuring heathenism. He said he would be the first to profane the sanctuaries of heathen worship, and he was as good as his word. Breaking the taboo which forbade a priest to carry weapons or to ride except on a mare, he borrowed a spear, a sword, and a stallion from the king, rode twelve miles to Goodmanham, threw his lance into the temple there, and ordered his companions to burn down the shrine and all its enclosures. On Easter Eve 628 Edwin was baptized at York in a temporary wooden church which he had built for the occasion.

Paulinus was long remembered in the north as an impressive figure, tall, slightly bent, with black hair, a slender aquiline nose, and an emaciated face. This description was given to Bede's informant by an old man who had been one of a crowd baptized by Paulinus in the Trent at Littleborough in the presence of King Edwin. On another occasion the bishop spent thirty-six days with the king and queen at Yeavering, baptizing converts in the River Glen, and he often stayed with Edwin at Catterick, baptizing in the Swale. It is a fair conjecture that among the crowds who availed themselves of his ministrations were British Christians whose own clergy had fled in terror before the conquering Angles. He built a church on a Roman site in the valley of the Don, and carried the gospel into the dependent kingdom of Lindsey, where his first converts were the reeve of Lincoln and his household. In that old Roman city he built a stone church of remarkable workmanship, and in it he consecrated Honorius, who in 627 succeeded Justus as archbishop of Canterbury.

Under Edwin's influence King Eorpwald of East Anglia had accepted baptism. His brother or half-brother Sigeberht, who succeeded him, had become a Christian while an exile in Gaul. A devout and learned man, Sigeberht determined on his accession that the whole of his kingdom should be won over to Christianity. His efforts were ably seconded by Felix, a Burgundian who had received episcopal consecration in Italy and was now sent into East Anglia by Archbishop Honorius. Felix established his see at Dunwich and toiled for seventeen years with marked success.

Edwin apparently expressed a wish that Paulinus should receive the pallium, which would have made him the first archbishop of York in accordance with the design of Gregory the Great. Pope Honorius complied with this request and sent two pallia, one for York, the other for Canterbury. His letter to Canterbury is dated 11 June 634. By the time it arrived Edwin had been killed in battle against Penda and Cadwallon. In pursuance, we may suppose, of instructions given by Edwin in case this disaster should occur, a trusty thegn saved much of Edwin's treasure and escaped by ship to Kent, taking with him Paulinus, the widowed queen, and her children. The see of Rochester was vacant at the time, and Paulinus was invited by the Kentish king and the archbishop to take charge of it. He remained there until his death twelve years later, and was succeeded by Ithamar, the first Englishman to hold episcopal office.

These dramatic changes did not ruin Christianity in the north, but they altered its complexion. The princes of Bernicia, sons of Ethelfrith, had been converted during their years of exile in Scotland, and Oswald in particular during the eight years of his reign (635–43) gave abundant proofs of Christian zeal. Secured on the Northumbrian throne by his victory over Cadwallon, he sent not to Canterbury but to Iona for a bishop, and before the end of 635 a company of monks under a leader named Aidan came to him and settled on the island of Lindisfarne, which became the Northumbrian counterpart of the Iona whence they came. In the ascetic rigours of their life, their indifference to the trappings of office, and their zeal for education, Aidan and his followers faithfully reflected the Celtic tradition in which they had been reared. Aidan himself, austere in his personal life, and stern in rebuking plutocratic sinners, was no fanatic. On his frequent preaching tours he travelled on foot, everywhere making a deep impression as much by his gentleness and moderation as by his teaching. When he received gifts of money he either passed them on at once to the poor or spent them in ransoming captives. King Oswald matched him in generosity. One Easter day, when Aidan sat at table with him, his almoner reported that a large crowd of beggars had collected outside. The king at once ordered that a silver dish heaped with choice food which had been set before him should be taken out, the food distributed, the dish broken up, and the pieces divided among the poor. When Aidan preached to the great men of his court Oswald often helped to clarify the bishop's imperfect English.

As *bretwalda* Oswald used his power to further the conversion of the southern English, especially the West Saxons. Pope Honorius had sent a missionary named Birinus who devoted himself to the evangelization of the Saxons in the Thames valley. When Kynegils, the reigning king, was baptized, Oswald stood godfather for him, and the two kings then gave Birinus the Roman town of Dorchester-on-Thames for his episcopal see.

In 643 Oswald fell in battle against Penda. He was heard to

pray for his enemies when they closed upon him, and his fame as a saint and martyr quickly spread all over western Christendom. His brother and successor Oswy had like him become a Christian in Scotland. Their arch-enemy, Penda, remained a heathen to the last, but even he felt that Christianity was a good religion if only its followers would live up to it. He placed no obstacle in the way of its propagation in Middle Anglia, where four missionaries, three of them English and one Irish, were already at work before his death. His son Peada, king of the Middle Angles, and Sige- berht II of Essex both received baptism at an estate near the Roman wall. Peada then married one of Oswy's daughters, and it was a condition of the alliance that his people should be Christian- ized. Thereupon the Irishman Finan, who had succeeded Aidan as bishop of Lindisfarne, consecrated Diuma, the Irish member of the original mission, as first bishop of the midlands.

## The Conversion of Mercia

By this time Penda's three other sons were all Christians. Merc- walh of the West Angles was converted by a Northumbrian missionary named Eadfrith, for whom he founded a church at Leominster. He and his brother Wulfhere, who from 659 to 675 reigned over all Mercia, were both married to brides from the royal house of Kent, and the youngest brother, Ethelred (675– 704), married Oswy's daughter Osthryth.

In 664 King Sighere, sharing with his brother the sovereignty of Essex, relapsed into heathenism, taking his people with him, but Wulfhere, his Mercian overlord, intervened with decisive effect. He sent his own bishop to win back the apostates and provided Sighere with a Christian wife, Osgith or Osyth, seem- ingly a princess of the Hwiccian ruling house. That same dynasty certainly provided a consort for Æthelwalh, king of Sussex, when he was baptized at Wulfhere's court.

Thus by 670 at the latest every reigning English king was a Christian. Eorcenbert of Kent, grandson of Ethelbert, was the first to enforce the destruction of heathen shrines and symbols. If the suppression had been less thorough in the rest of the country we should know more about Anglo-Saxon heathenism than we do.

Of opposition from the nobility we hear nothing. Many of the noble class, indeed, went further than to accept baptism; they enthusiastically embraced the monastic life. Benedict Biscop, a high-ranking thegn in King Oswy's service, abandoned all his worldly prospects at the age of twenty-five and embarked on a pilgrimage to Rome. A little later he took monastic vows and founded monasteries at Monkwearmouth and Jarrow which became famous intellectual centres. Devoted to learning, he built up a fine library of manuscripts and introduced music, wall-paintings, the whole panoply of Christian culture that he found in Rome and Gaul. But monasticism appealed not only to contemplative minds. Owine, an East Anglian nobleman by birth, gave up a brilliant position at the Northumbrian court to enter a monastery at Lastingham, and came to it carrying an axe and an adze to show that he expected manual labour to be his chief contribution to the work of the community. Others again devoted themselves to a solitary life in hermitages, as did Guthlac, a scion of the highest Mercian nobility, who took refuge from the world at Crowland in the midst of the dreary Fens.

## The Place of Women in the Church

Not the least of the benefits the new religion brought was that it opened a range of hitherto unknown opportunities for women who did not wish to marry and for widows. In the absence of facilities at home English girls were sent to school in Gaul, notably at Brie, Chelles, and Andelys; but under the influence of Aidan convents were founded at Hartlepool and Whitby. At the last-named a kinswoman of Oswy, the abbess Hilda, presided over a community which became renowned as a centre of scriptural studies. Whitby and similar foundations which arose elsewhere in England were all ruled by abbesses, but they also housed a staff of resident priests to administer the sacraments.

What did the common people think about it all? When some monks at Tynemouth got into difficulties with the wind and tide and their rafts looked like being carried out to sea, the country people watching from the shore said it served them right: they had robbed men of the old ways of worship, and now nobody knew where he stood. The authentic voice of the English grumbler! When we come in the next chapter to examine the social structure of early England it will be apparent that the lower ranks, however rebellious they might feel, were in no position to offer more than passive resistance. Heathenism, driven underground by the destruction of its images and temples, lived on in popular superstition, and the church found it necessary to appoint penances for those who sacrificed to devils, foretold the future with their aid, ate food that had been offered in sacrifice, and burned grain after a man was dead for the well-being of his household.

## The Conference of Whitby

In Northumbria the Celtic and the Roman strains in Anglo-Saxon Christianity met face to face, and in the long run they could not be reconciled. Minor variations of liturgical practice and clerical hair-styles could have been tolerated, but the difference in the mode of calculating the date of Easter was a chronic irritant. All agreed that this great festival should be celebrated on the Sunday of the third week of the month in which the full moon fell on or after the vernal equinox. The Celts took the equinox to be the 25th, the rest of Christendom the 21st of March. The discrepancy could produce two Easters as much as a month apart, as actually happened in 631, when the Roman Easter fell on 24 March, the Celtic on 21 April. It showed how rightly Augustine had insisted that the practice here should be made uniform. King Oswy's Kentish-born queen followed the Roman usage, and it naturally annoyed Oswy to see her still observing the Lenten fast while he himself, brought up in the tradition of Iona, was feasting on Easter Sunday. He summoned the most eminent spokesmen of both sides to debate the issue, and they met in fateful conference at Whitby in the autumn of 663 or the spring of 664. The debate was lengthy and at times acrimonious. It ended when Oswy declared that if he must choose between St Columba and St Peter, he would obey Peter, to whom Christ had given the keys of heaven. The adhesion of the most powerful monarch in Britain decided the question once and for all, giving the Roman party the upper hand. The bishop of Lindisfarne, Colman, withdrew discomfited, first to Iona, then to Ireland.

47

## Wilfrid and Theodore

Colman's departure left Northumbria without a bishop. The vacancy was filled by the appointment of Wilfrid, a Northumbrian priest who had been the most forceful spokesman on the Roman side at Whitby. He determined to fix his see at York, and as Canterbury was then vacant he went to Gaul and received episcopal consecration at Compiègne in a splendid ceremony attended by twelve bishops. In the meantime Oswy, in concert with the king of Kent, sent an English priest named Wighard to Rome for consecration to the see of Canterbury. But Wighard died soon after his arrival, and Pope Vitalian, taking the matter into his own hands, consecrated a sixty-six-year-old native of Asia Minor named Theodore, then living in Rome with a well-deserved reputation for learning, and sent him to rule the English church.

For the next quarter of a century the two great churchmen, Wilfrid and Theodore, dominated the ecclesiastical life of England. They soon found themselves involved in a delicate political situation. King Oswy's decision at Whitby may have been largely prompted by the fact that he was having some difficulty in holding Bernicia and Deira together. His son Alchfrith, governing Deira or part of it, was a close friend of Wilfrid, whom he made abbot of Ripon. But by the time Wilfrid reached Gaul as bishop-elect of York tension between father and son had reached breaking-point. Alchfrith was driven into exile or killed, and for two years Wilfrid judged it unsafe to show himself in Britain. Oswy secured the appointment of a new bishop of Lindisfarne, Tuda, but he died almost immediately, and the king accepted the decision to fix the Northumbrian see at York. In the absence of Wilfrid a disciple of Aidan named Chad was appointed to that see. When a reconciliation with Oswy allowed Wilfrid to return, a bishop without a bishopric, he retired to Ripon and spent the next three years there, from time to time discharging episcopal functions in Kent and Mercia. On Theodore's arrival Chad retired into monastic life, and Wilfrid took possession of the see of York.

While still a young man Wilfrid had visited Rome and spent three years with the archbishop of Lyons absorbing Mediterranean culture, the monuments of which lay all around him. In his episcopate he showed himself every inch a bishop in the Gallo-Roman style. He restored the church at York originally built for Paulinus, and built new churches at Ripon and Hexham of a size and architectural elaboration hitherto unknown in Britain. He took particular care to surround the liturgy with all the splendours of music, paintings, and gorgeous vestments. For Ripon he ordered a copy of the four Gospels to be written in letters of gold on parchment dyed purple. For the support of his churches he took over the endowments which had been abandoned by the fugitive British clergy. The heads of many monasteries placed themselves and the lands he had acquired for them under his protection, and his household became a school for young nobles. Ascetic in his personal life, his habits nevertheless differed widely from those of a saint like Cuthbert, who changed his clothes only once a year. Wilfrid took a cold bath every night, summer and winter, until in his old age Pope John VI advised him to be more careful. Throughout a long life he remained on the best of terms with the kings of Mercia, Kent, and Wessex. In Northumbria King Ecgfrith, who succeeded Oswy in 671, disliked his intimacy with the rising power of Mercia and resented his influence over the queen, Etheldreda, later abbess of Ely, a reluctant wife whom Wilfrid encouraged to remain a virgin. Ecgfrith's enmity was presently to embroil Wilfrid with the new archbishop.

Theodore, a cosmopolitan and tactful Greek, took a year to reach Britain, and in the course of his journey informed himself very fully on the state of the English church. He reached Canterbury on 27 May 669. Without delay he filled the vacant sees of Rochester, Dunwich, and Winchester. On Wilfrid's advice he fetched Chad out of his monastery and made him bishop of Mercia with his seat at Lichfield. By the autumn of 672 he was able to convoke a general assembly which met at Hertford, attended by the bishops of Rochester, Dunwich, Winchester, and Lichfield, Wilfrid of York being represented by his proxies. The council passed decrees forbidding bishops to exercise episcopal functions outside their own diocese or to oppress or despoil monasteries. Monks were not to wander from place to place without their abbot's leave, or priests without their bishop's. Incest, and divorce for any cause except adultery, were banned. Finally the council agreed to hold a yearly meeting every 1st of August at *Clofeshoh*, probably identifiable with Lubbanhoh, now Lubbenham, in Leicestershire, a conveniently central place accessible from Watling Street and adjoining Gumley, a residence of the Mercian kings.

A proposal to increase the number of bishoprics was mooted at Hertford, but ran into opposition. The prelate who had succeeded Chad at Lichfield proved recalcitrant and was removed from office for his pains. Wilfrid was not the man to be so easily put down, but under pressure from King Ecgfrith Theodore took the arbitrary step of dividing the Northumbrian diocese and displacing Wilfrid. He appointed Bosa, a monk of Whitby, bishop of York, and Eata, prior of Lindisfarne, bishop of Hexham, at the same time creating a new see for Lindsey. Thereupon Wilfrid appealed to Rome and left England to state his case.

The west wind drove him on to the coast of Frisia, and he spent the winter preaching to the heathen there. Resuming his journey, he stayed for a time with the king of the Austrasian Franks, then with the king of the Lombards, and finally arrived in time to appear before a council of fifty-three bishops under Pope Agatho. After hearing both sides, the council decided that the division of Northumbria should be upheld, but that Wilfrid should be restored to York, that the bishops who had supplanted him should be removed, and that Wilfrid should choose others in their place to be consecrated by Theodore. He returned to Britain with copies of the Roman decree and papal privileges for his monasteries at Hexham and Ripon.

It proved a hollow triumph. When he presented himself at Ecgfrith's court the angry king brushed aside his Roman documents and had Wilfrid flung into prison. Nine months elapsed before Ecgfrith was persuaded by his aunt Ebba, abbess of Coldingham, to release him. Exiled from Northumbria, Wilfrid stayed for some time in Mercia and Wessex, then visited the convert king of Sussex, Æthelwalh. He spent the next five years evangelizing that kingdom, which had been much enlarged by the action of Æthelwalh's godfather Wulfhere of Mercia in annexing to it the territory of the Gewisse in Hampshire and the Isle of

Wight. The king gave him Selsey for the seat of a monastery and bishopric.

The death of Ecgfrith in 685 removed Wilfrid's implacable enemy and left Archbishop Theodore, now an octogenarian, free to make overtures of peace. In the following year he and Wilfrid were reconciled at London in the presence of a company of bishops. Before the end of the year Wilfrid was back at Ripon, which he ruled as bishop for the next five years, postponing any attempt to regain York. Theodore hoped that he would succeed him as archbishop, but the last chapter of his stormy career still lay ahead.

Meanwhile Oshere, king of the Hwicce, had persuaded Theodore to create a new bishopric at Worcester. In the adjoining principality King Merewalh's son, Mildfrith, established one at Hereford. Theodore divided the diocese of East Anglia between Dunwich and a new see at Elmham, and created one at Leicester for the Middle Angles. For the Picts under Northumbrian rule he founded a see at Abercorn, which however became extinct after the defeat of Ecgfrith. By 690, when Theodore died, England formed a single ecclesiastical province with fourteen bishops all acknowledging the archbishop of Canterbury as their metropolitan. Bede sums up Theodore's achievement by remarking that he was the first archbishop whom the whole church in England agreed to obey. He had in fact created a united English church two and a half centuries before England was united as a single state.

Almost his last appointment happily exemplified the blend of Celtic asceticism with Roman discipline. St Cuthbert had been trained under one of Aidan's pupils. During his two years as bishop of Lindisfarne he spent weeks on end administering confirmation to the rough dwellers in the Northumbrian hills and comforting them in their misfortunes. Personally austere on the strictest model of Iona, he understood the necessity for order, and with his last breath urged his monks to maintain Catholic unity in their observance.

In cases of conscience Theodore showed himself a humane judge. He allowed a husband or wife to remarry after five years if their partner had been carried off into slavery, and he admitted several other causes of matrimonial breakdown. While disapproving in principle of the monasteries for both sexes which he encountered in Gaul and Britain, he made it clear that he would not interfere with the custom of the country. His decisions had an abiding influence on the penitential discipline as well of this country as of the churches that would be established later by English missionaries on the continent.

Bede remarks that in his own day some of Theodore's pupils were still living to whom Latin and Greek were as familiar as their native tongue. The archbishop made Canterbury a centre of learning which drew scholars from far afield to study scripture, astronomy, music, prosody, and Roman law. His legal sense caused him to bring a notary in his train, by whom the acts of the council of Hertford were recorded in writing. The use of formal charters, based on Roman practice, to accompany grants of land is traced back to his time. The English were becoming literate. But literacy implies books, and in an age when every book had to be laboriously copied out by hand, books could not be other than rare. Animal skins had to be scraped, dressed, and cut to size for the necessary parchment, lamp-black to be collected for the making of ink, reeds or goose-quills to be shaped as pens. In the conditions of the time the skill demanded for the art of writing could only be imparted in monasteries, and only monasteries provided the quiet necessary for concentrated work. Hence the multiplication of monasteries meant the multiplication of books. The monastic scribes of Ireland and Northumbria developed a large and beautifully legible handwriting, and with it a style of elaborately interlaced decoration. Both are displayed magnificently in the Lindisfarne Gospels, written and decorated seemingly by Eadfrith, bishop of Lindisfarne from 698 to 721, and now in the British Museum. A more workaday example is the copy of Jerome's commentary on Ecclesiastes which belonged to Cuthswith, an abbess to whom Oshere of the Hwicce in 693 granted an estate in Worcestershire for the building of a monastery. The book was afterwards taken to Germany by some Anglo-Saxon missionary; it is now in the university library at Würzburg.

During the vacancy at Canterbury of nearly two years from the death of Archbishop Theodore Wilfrid raised again the question of his status in Northumbria, to the intense displeasure of King Aldfrith, who had succeeded his half-brother Ecgfrith. Aldfrith expelled Wilfrid from Northumbria in 691, and Wilfrid spent the next eleven years in Mercia, where he founded a number of monasteries and was protected by the staunch friendship of King Ethelred. He appealed by proxy to Pope Sergius I, who in the meantime had appointed Berhtwald, abbot of Reculver, to the see of Canterbury. The pope referred the case to an English synod, and in 702 a council met at Austerfield, near Bawtry, attended by King Aldfrith, Archbishop Berhtwald, and other prelates. At first they tried to entrap Wilfrid into placing himself unconditionally in their hands. He demanded that they should first state a case against him. Then they required him to surrender all his monasteries and lands in Mercia, as well as those in Northumbria, to be dealt with at the archbishop's discretion. They cannot have seriously expected him to comply with so outrageous a demand, which in any case was beyond their power to enforce. He took his stand on the decision of Pope Agatho; they insisted on the settlement which Theodore under royal pressure had accepted in 696. "Let him stand condemned," they said, "for preferring the Roman judgement to ours."

Not surprisingly Wilfrid, with canon law wholly on his side, did prefer it. To Rome, accordingly, he now betook himself, appealing in person to the supreme authority. The pleading extended over four months in the early part of 704. Wilfrid and Berhtwald's representatives were questioned publicly, and all the documents on both sides were carefully examined. At length Pope John VI wrote commanding Berhtwald, whom he described, rather pointedly, as archbishop of the Kentishmen's church, either to convoke a synod and settle the matter once for all, or else to appear in person at Rome with Wilfrid's other opponents, on pain of excommunication. The pope also sent a letter to the two kings, Ethelred and Aldfrith, requesting their assistance. Aldfrith remained obstructive to the end, but his death removed the last obstacle to peace. Wilfrid recovered his two chief northern monasteries, Ripon and Hexham, with all their revenues, and did not press his claim to the bishopric of York. He was now past seventy years of age. In 709, after four peaceful years, he died at Oundle, one of the monasteries he had founded in Mercia.

The vitality of the English church at this time was largely concentrated in the monasteries. There men could receive a training which fitted them for episcopal office. The convents provided a dignified retreat for widows and a place of education for their children. In Ireland and Iona the monks lived in separate huts, assembling only for meals and worship. The buildings, including the church, the hospice where visitors were entertained, and the domestic offices, were all of timber and wattle, and the whole complex was surrounded by an earthen rampart. The inmates owed unquestioning obedience to their abbot, but easily obtained leave to wander abroad. At home they divided their time between prayer and work, either the work of study and writing or the labour of the farm. Some of them practised an asceticism of the utmost rigour; Cuthbert, for example, used to go out at dead of night and stand till daybreak up to his neck in the sea. Such extremes made little appeal to cultivated minds like Benedict Biscop, who for his foundations at Monkwearmouth and Jarrow compiled an eclectic rule of life based on his observation of seventeen different houses on the continent. Wilfrid adopted the moderate and sanely tempered rule drawn up by the great St Benedict for his monastery at Monte Cassino. This he introduced into all his own monasteries, and even into some of older foundation, such as Glastonbury. To ensure the appointment of suitable abbots and to safeguard their possessions from greedy laymen he either acted as abbot himself, as at Hexham and Ripon, or persuaded the head of the house to vest its property in him personally. It was his vast monastic connection, extending far beyond Northumbria, which exposed him to so much envy and hostility.

The bishops of Lindisfarne could not be accused of neglecting their public duties. Aidan and Cuthbert travelled incessantly, instructing candidates for baptism, administering that sacrament, and completing it by the rite of confirmation. But in establishing themselves on an offshore island they broke the rule that a bishop should govern his diocese from an urban centre. Outside the orbit of Iona this rule was generally observed. Canterbury, Rochester, London, Dorchester, Leicester, York, and Lincoln were all Roman towns where some degree of continuity with Roman-

British life persisted under English rule. When King Wulfhere annexed south-eastern Hampshire to Sussex, thereby cutting off the bishop of Dorchester from a large part of his West Saxon flock, Cenwalh of Wessex founded a new see at Winchester, another Roman town. It is not certain whether the original Mercian see was fixed at the Roman Letocetum (now Wall) or two miles away at the marshy spot known since Bede's time as Lichfield, which was certainly Chad's favourite retreat during his short episcopate. As a boy Wilfrid had spent two or three years at Lindisfarne, long enough to bring home to him its unsuitability as an episcopal see. In establishing himself at York he obeyed the ancient rule of the church and conformed to the example of Paulinus.

Wilfrid's precentor Eddius, surnamed Stephen, who accompanied him on many of his journeys, wrote a life of him not long after his death. His testimony, based on close personal observation, leaves no doubt that Wilfrid had many of the qualities of a saint and a great leader of men. He certainly showed heroic patience in his frequent times of trial. His was a vision bounded by no provincial or tribal horizon; from first to last it was inspired by a lofty conception of Christendom as a community cemented by loyalty to the papal see. With the single exception of Archbishop Theodore, the men who baited him were pygmies by comparison. Naturally this did not endear him to them, but the clergy and laymen who knew him intimately gave him their unstinted affection. His defeat of the Celtic party at Whitby, and the constant pressure from the papacy which he brought to bear on Theodore and Berhtwald, ensured that the English church should remain true to its Gregorian origins.

The Anglo-Saxons never forgot their debt to Gregory the Great. King Oswy had hoped to spend his last days in Rome, but death prevented him. Many another king formed the same intention and lived to carry it out. The see of Rome had so secure a place in English affections that a continental writer in the ninth century described the Anglo-Saxons as conspicuous above all other peoples for their devotion to the papacy. They had good reason. Under the guidance of the Roman church their leaders had emerged from barbarism into civilization.

Chapter IV

# THE SOCIAL STRUCTURE IN EARLY ENGLAND

Bede says that among the other benefits King Ethelbert conferred on the people of Kent, he established for them judicial decrees after the example of the Romans. He did indeed follow Roman example in committing his laws to writing, but they were written in English, not in Latin, and in substance they are a statement of Germanic custom rather than an echo of the imperial juris-prudence. Even the acceptance of Christianity appears only in the first clause, which recognizes the hierarchical gradation of bishop, priest, deacon, and clerk, and fixes penalties for wrong done to them in proportion to the rank of the aggrieved. Composed at some date between the arrival of St Augustine in 597 and Ethel-bert's death in 618, and still in force when Bede wrote more than a century later, the laws are our earliest source of information on the social structure of an English kingdom.

## The Slave

They reveal an elaborately graded society. In Kent, as through-out the western world, the lowest rank was filled by slaves. Some of the female slaves were employed as domestic servants. Here the word is *birele*, meaning cup-bearer, and penalties for raping her are appointed in proportion not to her feelings but to her master's rank: 12 shillings for a nobleman's; 6 shillings for a commoner's; 50 and 30 pence for women of still lower grades. Higher values are set on the honour of other slave women, pre-sumably employed not in the household but on the farm: 50

shillings for one belonging to the king, 25 and 12 shillings for women of the second and third class. The second-class or 25-shilling woman is described as a "grinding slave": evidently in seventh-century Kent, as in the Palestine of the New Testament, the grinding of corn was a task for women. To distinguish slaves from freeborn women, their hair was cropped.

The *theow*, or male slave, figures under that name only as the perpetrator or victim of robbery. If he steals, he is supposed to have means to pay twice the value of the stolen goods as compensation. More is said about the *esne*, who may be a married man, for one clause refers to his wife. Presumably he has a household of his own, not a mere lodging in the outbuildings of his master's farm. At a guess we may identify him with the *servus casatus* of the continent, a slave whose master has provided him with a hut to live in but reserves the right to call upon him for agricultural services. If so, he will probably spend much of his time working on his master's land, receiving food or perhaps money in return, and when not so engaged will be tilling his garden-plot or hiring himself out to his more prosperous neighbours.

## The "Laet"

A more problematic figure is the *laet*, who makes his first and last appearance under that name in Ethelbert's laws. The government of the later empire had planted Germans on Roman soil by the system of *laeti*. *Laetus* is a German word used to describe barbarian settlers either planted in tribal groups under the control of Roman prefects or assigned to individual landowners. They were primarily tillers of the soil, but with a liability for military service. It is not known whether they were settled in Britain under Roman rule as they certainly were on the other side of the English Channel, but the *litus*, *latus*, or *lazzus* reappears in the continental Germanic law-codes, occupying a position intermediate between freemen and slaves, and it is reasonable to equate him with the Kentish *laet*. Ethelbert distinguishes three classes of *laet*, and the three grades may represent, like the threefold grades of slaves and cup-bearers, a classification according to the rank of their masters, in which case the *laet* of the first class might be settled on the

57

king's land, of the second on that of a nobleman, of the third on that of a commoner.

### The "Ceorl"

The next person to be considered is the *ceorl*. Much has been written about the Kentish *ceorl*, much more indeed than the evidence warrants. The word means, first of all, a husband, "man" as correlative to "wife." Then, by extension, it comes to mean the head of a rustic household. The exact equivalent of his designation in modern English is not "churl," its lineal descendant, but "husbandman." The word tells us nothing about his racial origin, nor does it carry with it any connotation of either freedom or unfreedom. Ethelbert speaks of the *ceorl*'s "loaf-eaters," the children, domestic servants, and farm-hands who look to him for food. He is certainly a commoner, as distinguished from the *eorl* or nobleman. The clearest indication of his social status is his *mundbyrd*, the fine payable for an offence against one of his dependants. This is fixed at 6 shillings, that of a nobleman being 12 shillings, and the king's 50 shillings.

### The Freeman

Ethelbert speaks also of a class of freemen, seemingly distinct from the *ceorls*, but perhaps including some of them. In several clauses the freeman appears to stand in some kind of special relationship with the king. A penalty of 20 shillings is laid on anyone who attempts to deprive him of his freedom. For the rest he is liable to penalties if he breaks and enters another man's enclosure, and if he commits adultery he must provide the injured husband with a new wife at his own expense.

It costs money to purchase a wife, and the payment entitles the purchaser to expect a virgin bride. If she disappoints in this respect, the bridegroom can return her to her family and recover the bride-price. On the other hand, if all goes well on the wedding night he must give her a "morning-gift" next day. The morning-gift and any other property of a childless wife goes to her father's kin, but a wife who bears a living child and outlives her husband inherits half his property.

## The Nobleman

Twelve shillings is the penalty for slaying a man on the premises of a nobleman, and for seducing his domestic slave-woman. This is all that Ethelbert's laws have to say about the *eorl*: enough to show that he stands twice as high in social estimation as the *ceorl*.

Ethelbert's great-grandson Hlothhere issued a code of laws by way of supplement to those already in force. The code adds little to our knowledge of the social system. It speaks of the *esne* and his owner, who must surrender the *esne* if the latter has killed a man, and must in addition pay a *wergeld* or compensation for homicide proportionate to the rank of the victim. If the victim is a nobleman with a *wergeld* of 300 shillings, the additional payment will be the value of three men: that is, no doubt, three slaves. But if the victim is a freeman with a *wergeld* of 100 shillings, the additional payment is limited to the value of one slave. In view of frequent statements to the contrary by historians of repute, it is necessary to emphasize that neither Ethelbert's code nor Hlothhere's gives any specific information on the *wergeld* of a *ceorl*.

Of the freeman we are told that if he is accused of stealing a man, he must bring at least one witness from the village to which he belongs (*hyre*). Does this mean that some villages were populated by freemen who acknowledged no superior but the king? It may appear so when we remember that several of Ethelbert's laws imply or seem to imply a particularly close relationship between some freemen and the king. On the other hand, Ethelbert makes it clear that the nobleman has a village of his own. The verb *hyran*, implying some degree of subjection, may therefore point not to the king of Kent but to the noble lord of the village where the accused freeman lives.

## The Church and Slavery

We learn more than the contemporary secular laws tell us about Anglo-Saxon slavery from the *Penitential* of Archbishop Theodore. A father driven by poverty may sell his son as a slave, but if the boy is above the age of seven his consent is required. An invading army leads its prisoners away and enslaves them. If your wife is carried away by the enemy and you cannot buy her back, you may take another wife; and the wife also may remarry if she loses her husband in this way. If a free woman is sold into slavery when she is with child, the child goes free. If you allow a couple of your slaves to marry, and one of them is later bought into freedom, he or she may either buy out the other or contract a new marriage with a free partner; but the marriage of a freeman with a slave, if both parties are willing, cannot be dissolved. If you seduce your slave-girl you must set her free, but her child remains your slave. Theft, fornication, and the act of enticing a monk from his cloister may be punished by slavery. It is lawful for bishops and abbots to own men penally enslaved.

Perhaps the most important provision is one that relates either to the slave or to the servile *esne*, the man whose master has provided him with a dwelling and the means to support himself, but retains possessionary rights over his person and property. The church protects him by decreeing that his master may not lawfully deprive him of the money or livestock which he has earned by his own toil.

## Social Grades in the Laws of Wihtred

Manumission, the freeing of a slave, is now treated by the church as a religious act, one which may take place at the altar. This makes it necessary for the secular power to safeguard the position of the lord by decreeing that he who raises his man from slavery to serfdom under the church's auspices shall not lose any of the rights over him which he retained under the older system. Accordingly the code issued in 695 by Wihtred, king of Kent, provides that although a man freed at the altar shall be "folk-free," that is, free as against all men except his lord, the lord shall be the guardian of his household even if he is settled elsewhere than on the lord's estate, and when he dies his property and *wergeld* will belong to his lord. The reference to his household proves that he is now a *servus casatus*, one whom we have tentatively identified with the *esne* of the laws. He is found on royal, episcopal, and monastic estates, and doubtless also on those of lesser men. If he works on Sunday, he must pay a fine to his lord, unless he can plead the lord's command, and if he rides abroad on an errand of his own on that day, he must pay a heavier fine or be whipped if he cannot find the money. For the serf is still so far a slave that he remains liable to the flogging which in England, as in classical antiquity, is the slave's distinctive punishment. By contrast, the fully free man who works in the forbidden time only pays a fine. But if he is caught stealing, the king will decide whether he shall be put to death, or sold into slavery beyond the sea, or held to ransom for the price of his life.

In Wihtred's laws the nobleman, or *eorlcundman* of the earlier codes, is styled a *gesithcundman*. He owes his standing partly to his birth, no doubt, but the emphasis henceforth is on his position as a *gesith* or companion to the king. One clause refers to him as a "king's thegn." Between him and the slave stands the *ceorlisc man*, or commoner, a broadly inclusive term embracing small freemen, husbandmen, *laets*, and perhaps also the "folk-free" *esne*.

## Slavery in Sussex

Shortly before Wihtred began to reign in Kent the great Wilfrid spent five years preaching the gospel in the neighbouring kingdom of Sussex. His biographer records that King Æthelwalh gave him an estate in Selsey where the king himself resided, to be the seat of a bishopric, and subsequently endowed it with 87 hides of land. From a later document we gather that the 87 hides consisted of a group of villages in the promontory of Selsey, with seven more round Chichester and three between Arundel and Petworth. We may take it for granted that these villages were inhabited by all sorts and conditions of men, but Bede states that they included 250 male and female slaves, all of whom Wilfrid baptized and set free. Bede also says that Sussex at that time contained 7,000 hides. If the Selsey endowment was a representative cross-section of South Saxon society, this would give more than 20,000 slaves in Sussex as a whole. When we remember that in neighbouring Kent even a husbandman kept a slave or two, this large figure cannot be ruled out, but then the king was doubtless better off in that respect than most of his subjects.

## Slavery in Wessex

We meet the slave again in the laws of Ine, king of Wessex, issued at some date between 688 and 694. If the slave's master makes him work on Sunday, he is to be set free; but if he works of his own accord he must be whipped or pay a fine. The freeman who works on that day, however, may be reduced to slavery unless he can pay a heavy fine or plead his lord's command. It seems, then, that a Wessex freeman may have a lord set over him. If a freeman is found guilty of theft and sentenced to slavery, the accuser will have the right to flog him. It is a crime to sell one of your countrymen, whether slave or freeman, beyond the sea. This is the first of many enactments intended to discourage the export of slaves into foreign markets, an action which the Kentish law of Wihtred allowed in certain cases.

In 690 Ine appears to have led a campaign against the men of Kent. It would be usual on such occasions for a number of prisoners to be taken and enslaved. An interesting sidelight is thrown on this feature of Anglo-Saxon life by a letter from the archbishop of Canterbury asking the bishop of Sherborne to bring pressure to bear on the abbot of Glastonbury for the release of a captive Kentish girl. The archbishop had already intervened on her behalf without success. Her family were offering a ransom of 300 shillings, the *wergeld* of a Kentish nobleman, and the archbishop requests his colleague to obtain the abbot's acceptance of this offer so that the girl's brother, the bearer of the letter, may bring her back to home and freedom.

An earlier Anglo-Saxon captive, Bathildis or Baldhild, was more fortunate. After being sold as a slave to a Frankish magnate, she married Clovis II, king of Neustria, and bore him three sons, for one of whom she later acted as regent.

## Britons in Wessex

As might be expected in a kingdom that was still expanding westward into British territory, Ine's laws provide a definite place for Britons in the social scheme. The tariff of *wergelds* payable in compensation for taking a Welshman's life is arranged in a sevenfold gradation:

| | | | | |
|---|---|---|---|---|
| A Welsh slave | .. | .. 60 or in some cases | 50 | shillings |
| A landless Welshman | .. .. | .. .. | 60 | ,, |
| A landed Welshman with half a hide | .. | .. | 80 | ,, |
| The son of a Welsh rent-payer | .. | .. .. | 100 | ,, |
| A Welsh rent-payer .. | .. .. | .. .. | 120 | ,, |
| A landed Welshman with one hide .. | .. | .. | 120 | ,, |
| A Welsh horseman in the king's service .. | | .. | 200 | ,, |
| A landed Welshman with five hides | .. | .. | 600 | ,, |

The word for rent-payer is *gafolgelda*. *Gafol* is the rent paid to the king or to a lesser landlord, but when it is paid to the king it is not easily distinguishable to our eyes from a tax. The hide, which makes its first appearance in the documents here, is a unit of assessment for calculating the payments in money or kind due to the king or other landlord. Ine's laws throw no light on the method by which the assessment was imposed or the extent of land which lies behind it. One clause specifies the food-rent due from ten hides as 10 vats of honey, 300 loaves, 12 measures of Welsh ale, 30 measures of clear ale, 2 full-grown cows or 10 wethers, 10 geese, 20 hens, 10 cheeses, a full measure of butter, 5 salmon, 20 pounds of fodder, and 100 eels.

The Welshman with five hides of land is clearly a man of substance, but other men, probably English, hold as much as ten or twenty hides. For Ine's English subjects no comparably detailed tariff of *wergelds* is provided. Sums of 200, 600, and 1,200 shillings are mentioned. The 200-shilling man is clearly a commoner, for in one clause he is contrasted with a man of noble birth, and according to another you must pay his lord 30 shillings if you slay him.

### The "Geneat"

The laws also speak of the *geneat* and the thegn. *Geneat* means companion or retainer, and thegn originally meant servant. In poetry the two words are interchangeable. A *geneat* might have another master than the king, but the *wergeld* of a king's *geneat* may be as much as 1,200 shillings, the normal *wergeld* of a thegn.

63

In the later Saxon period the *geneat* will figure as the most dignified of rustics, and it is reasonable to conjecture that he owes that position to a gift of land made by an early lord to one of his retainers.

## The Wessex Nobleman

In Ine's code, as in Wihtred's, the nobleman is styled a *gesithcundman*, and is contrasted with the *ceorlisc man* or commoner. Normally, but not always, he is a landholder. He forfeits his land by neglecting military service and has to pay a fine of 120 shillings, twice as much as that paid by a landless man of his own class, and four times as much as a commoner for the same offence. The West Saxon conquest of Devon, completed in Ine's reign, provided the more enterprising *gesithcundmen* with opportunities for taking up forfeited or vacant lands in the newly-won territory, and Ine shows himself anxious that their original estates in the heartland of Wessex shall not be left to run down in consequence; if they were, the king would lose his food-rent. So a departing nobleman may take with him only his reeve, his smith, and his children's nurse, but if he has twenty hides, he must show twelve hides occupied by husbandmen; if ten, then six; and if three, then one and a half, before he leaves.

## The "Ceorl"

We have already seen that a *ceorlisc man* is liable for military service, and in a Mercian context we shall learn more presently about the nature of that service. He has a *wergeld*, the amount of which is not stated. The *ceorl* or husbandman who gives his name to this class appears to be occupying a farm which he is bound to keep fenced both summer and winter; if he fails to do this he has no claim on his neighbour's beast when it strays in and does damage. He may share ploughland or meadowland with others of his kind, and he may have occasion to hire a yoke of oxen from his neighbour. As a householder he is entitled to protection against brawling on his premises. In this clause he is described not as a

64

### OLD ENGLISH DESIGNATIONS
### OF SOCIAL CLASSES

*Note.* The categories in the following table are not mutually exclusive: e.g. a *gebur* might also be a *gafolgelda*, and every *ealdorman* would also be a thegn. Those marked * were probably all included in the genus *ceorl*.

| | Early Saxon *c.* 500–*c.* 650 | Middle Saxon *c.* 650–*c.* 850 |
|---|---|---|
| Slave | *theow* | *theow* |
| Unfree or half-free cottager | *?esne** | *?esnewyrhta** |
| Freedman occupying a farm | | *gebur** *?twyhynde* |
| Rent-paying tenant | *gafolgelda** | *gafolgelda** |
| Free farmer | *frigman* | *geneat* *?syxhynda* |
| Landed nobleman | *gesith* | *gesith* *thegn* *?twelfhynda* |
| Governor of a shire | *ealdorman* | *ealdorman* |

*ceorl* but as either a rent-payer or a *gebur*. This last word seems to denote a man of servile antecedents whose master has set him up on a sizeable farm and provided him with a house. In this connection we should note Ine's ruling that if the lord does not give him a dwelling the man who rents land and ploughs it may give up his tenancy should the lord try to exact service as well as rent. It seems to follow that given both land and house, he is tied to the land and owes labour-service to his lord. But if he surrenders the tenancy he cannot claim the value of the standing crops. This strongly suggests that the land had originally been sown with seed provided by the lord, a characteristic of the *gebur* as we shall find him more fully described in later texts.

When a lord turns a group of his slaves into serfs with domiciles of their own to which plots of land are attached, they are described in Latin texts as *coliberti*. A record of St Peter's abbey at Gloucester throws a vivid light on his condition. Early in the eighth century a certain Cynemaer, son of a *colibertus* named Wulfmaer, "oppressed by the work and the name," gave the abbey a fishery at Framilode in return for full emancipation. Thus three terms are used in different contexts to describe a freedman. As one of a half-free community he is a *colibertus*; as a cottager with little or no land he is still sometimes called an *esne* (a word which henceforth occurs very rarely in the laws); and as a householder farming a substantial acreage he is commonly called a *gebur*.

### The Position of the Lord

There is hardly any room for doubt that most if not all men of the *ceorlisc* class had a lord set over them, a lord who was by no means always the king. Any man who moves into another district stealthily without his lord's permission must come back when discovered and pay 60 shillings to the lord. The most significant clause of all is one decreeing that a *gesithcundman* who intercedes with the king, the ealdorman, or with his own lord, on behalf of his free or unfree dependants shall have no portion of the fine they have incurred, because he has not taken care to restrain them from evil-doing. In passing, we may note the implication that one *gesith* may be under another's lordship. More important, it is clear that the state imposes on every lord some responsibility for his men's good behaviour. Much as we should like to know how systematically and through what agents the West Saxon lord exercised his coercive power, Ine's code does not enlighten us on that subject; but the lord's right of jurisdiction, with the concomitant right in normal circumstances to take a portion of the misdoer's fine, is plainly visible here at least in germ.

The service which Ine forbids a landlord to exact unless he provides his tenant with a dwelling will obviously be performed on the lord's own land. It follows that some lords, if not all, keep at least a portion of their estate in hand as a demesne or home-farm, and do not rely exclusively on slave labour for its cultivation, but may require agricultural service from their tenant farmers.

## Social Grades in Mercia

The laws of Kent and Wessex, which have kept us lingering in the south of England, are our earliest and fullest sources of information on Anglo-Saxon society. Mercia too had laws of its own, but no Mercian code has survived. We turn for light to a compilation put together in the first quarter of the eleventh century. The compiler, who has been plausibly identified with Wulfstan, archbishop of York, based his work on careful antiquarian research. He reproduces accurately Ine's laws on the *wergelds* of one-hide and half-hide Welshmen. Probably, therefore, we may safely take his word for it that under Mercian law a husbandman's *wergeld* was 200 shillings and the thegn's 1,200 shillings. Thus a Mercian nobleman's life was six times as valuable as a husbandman's, and the same proportion is very likely to have held good in Wessex.

An incident related by Bede throws a ray of light on the military obligations of these two classes. In 679, when a great battle was fought between the armies of Northumbria and Mercia, a young Northumbrian thegn named Imma was left for dead on the field. Attached at one time to the household of Queen Etheldreda and more recently to that of the Northumbrian prince Ælfwine, he was evidently of high social standing. On the following day he began to revive and tried to make his escape, but was soon

67

captured by Mercian soldiers and brought to their lord, a *gesith* of the Mercian king. Fearing to invite the customary vengeance if he disclosed his rank, he declared that he was a *ceorl* ("rusticum") who had come on that campaign with others of his class to bring provisions to the troops. His face, bearing, and speech gave the lie to this pretence, and his captor questioned him again, promising to spare him if he would frankly declare the truth. When Imma did so, the Mercian kept his promise not to kill him, but sold him in London to a Frisian slave-trader, from whom Imma presently managed to buy back his freedom.

Throughout Anglo-Saxon history the typical warrior is the man of noble birth. The *ceorl* was indeed liable for military service, and in Ine's Wessex had to pay a substantial fine if he disregarded the summons, but the story of Imma shows conclusively that the husbandman's place was in the commissariat, not in the fighting line.

We may take it that what we have learnt about the slave-class from Theodore's *Penitential* holds good of Mercia and the other kingdoms, since Theodore was the first archbishop whom the whole church of the English obeyed. The biographer of St Werburg, a daughter of the Mercian royal house, tells us of a neatherd on her estate at Weedon, Alfnoth by name, a man "of holy life as far as might be for a man under the yoke of human slavery." This unfortunate somehow incurred the displeasure of the reeve, who gave him a cruel whipping, and would have flogged him to death if the saint had not worked a miracle to stay his hand.

### Northumbrian Society

Of the Northumbrian husbandman we learn from the eleventh-century compilation already cited that the price of his life was equivalent to that of his Mercian counterpart, 200 shillings. The life of a thegn was rather more than seven times as valuable. The Northumbrian nobleman of this period, like his peer in the southern kingdoms, is called a *gesith*, a companion of the king. A number of texts depict him as landlord of a village. On one occasion St Cuthbert goes to a village near the Tweed by invitation of its lord, a *gesith* of King Ecgfrith named Sibba. In the following reign a preaching tour brings Cuthbert to the village of a *gesith* named Hemma. St John of Beverley heals the wife of a *gesith* named Puch who had invited him to dedicate a church on his estate at Bishop Burton. This same nobleman is said to have given the neighbouring manor of Walkington to Beverley Minster when his daughter became a nun there. The bishop also dedicated a church at Cherry Burton at the request of a *gesith* named Addi. The parish of Cherry Burton originally included Leconfield and Scorbrough, an aggregate of more than 8,000 acres, and if it was co-extensive with Addi's manor, this nobleman was indeed handsomely endowed.

The lord of Bishop Burton could give a portion of his estate to the minster where his daughter became a nun. Does this mean that he was free to divide the rest among his other children or transmit Burton to one of them? By no means. All that is known of early England suggests that the church of Beverley would have been extremely ill-advised to accept the gift without confirmation by a royal charter. For the magnate owed his position to the king's favour and had only a life interest in the estate. Even when the lands passed from father to son, they did so as a mark of favour from the king. A younger son would serve in personal attendance on the king, hoping to be rewarded with a grant of land that would enable him to marry and support a family. If disappointed of this hope, he might retire into a monastery, as Benedict Biscop's cousin Eosterwine did at Wearmouth after spending some time in the service of King Ecgfrith. If the worst came to the worst he would leave the kingdom and seek his fortune elsewhere. The young Mercian nobleman Guthlac spent nine weary years in foreign service, part of the time among the Welsh. An Anglo-Saxon poem, *The Wanderer*, expresses in poignant terms the regret of one exiled from the splendours of the royal court.

> Where is the horse? Where the hero? Where the treasure-giving
>     prince?
> Where the seats at the feast, where the delights of the hall?
> Alas, bright goblet!

It was the need of the church for permanent endowments carrying full possessionary rights and not limited to the life of one beneficiary which led Anglo-Saxon rulers to grant land by 'book', that is, by charter solemnly attested by the magnates of church and state. Hence the long series of charters which, next to the laws, provide the most illuminating evidence on Old English history. The 'book-right' they conferred was at first known as church-right or minster-right. For a long time after the introduction of book-right it was confined to the churches; if a layman received a land-charter, as occasionally happened, it was always subject to the express or implied condition that the recipient would use it to found or endow a monastery. Not until the last quarter of the eighth century do we begin to find kings granting lands to laymen in hereditary possession.

Long before that Bede was in his grave. Almost with his last breath he complained in strong terms that scores of Northumbrian ealdormen, *gesiths*, and royal servants had been procuring land-charters by having themselves tonsured and calling their establishments monasteries, which they staffed with clerics of dubious character, so that there was not enough land left to provide for the class on whom the safety of the realm depended, and young warriors, unable to marry and settle down, either left the country or stayed at home and amused themselves by seducing nuns.

## The Other Kingdoms

On the social systems of Lindsey, East Anglia, and Essex the sources fail us, but there is no reason to suppose that they differed in any significant respect from the kingdoms already studied. The loose association of tribes collectively known as the Middle Angles may originally have been governed by ealdormen, for there is no record or tradition of a royal house. In the course of the seventh century they fell under Mercian domination, and their earlier social system, if in any way distinctive, must then have been assimilated to that of Mercia.

The impression left upon us by this survey is one of a highly class-conscious society ruled by powerful monarchs. Around the king stands a retinue of nobles whose main function is to fight his battles. If their service merits it, he will in time reward them with grants of land, and they will form a territorial aristocracy supported by the rents and services of the tillers of the soil, whom they are bound to protect and keep in order.

The modern study of place-names has reinforced this impression. The map is studded with personal names followed by the suffix -*ingas*, now -ing: Tooting, Havering, Ealing, Hickling, and the like. They constitute, not perhaps the earliest, but certainly a very early stratum of English place-names, and they signify the kinsmen or followers of the leader whose name they perpetuate. The expeditions which effected the conquest and colonization of Britain would seem to have involved an organization in which each detachment had its captain and was known by his name. If this organization was kept up after landing, the name would be transferred to the settlement when the leader received his share of the conquered land. We can only guess at such details: what is clear is that Tota, Haefer, and Hicel who gave their names to Tooting, Havering, and Hickling led bands of settlers over whom they wielded at least the kind of authority which leadership normally bestows.

At the other end of the social scale we find both predial and domestic slaves in considerable numbers. Some of them were Britons serving new masters, but the Anglo-Saxons did not scruple to enslave men and women of their own blood. The class was constantly recruited from prisoners of war, convicts, and hungry freemen who sold themselves for bread. At the same time, in England as on the continent the transition has begun from downright slavery to serfdom. It is cheaper to give your slave a plot of land and allow him some spare time in which to earn money than to bear the whole cost of his maintenance. It is also meritorious in the eyes of the church. But he remains your man, and in strict law his belongings are all yours. The road is still a long one that will lead him uphill to full freedom.

What of the intermediate class, the ordinary Anglo-Saxon farmer? For a century or more he has loomed large in our historical literature. The typical Anglo-Saxon husbandman is portrayed as a peasant proprietor tilling his own soil with his own labour, free by birth and condition, accustomed to speaking his mind in popular assemblies, and acknowledging no superior but the king. We are even assured that the free peasant community forms the starting-point of English social history.

This romantic figment finds little or no support in actual historical record. What in fact is the sum-total of the knowledge we have gleaned from the sources we have examined so far ? We may leave out of account the *geneat*, for his lord may not yet have settled him on a farm. Ine's code recognizes the Welsh *gafolgelda*, and there is no reason to doubt that this man had his Anglo-Saxon counterpart. The distinctive mark of the *gafolgelda*, Welsh or English, is that he pays rent for his land, with little or no labour service. The same code also mentions the *gebur*, without giving any details of his condition; he seems to be a man of servile origin whose master has helped him to start life on a holding of his own. To these we may perhaps add the Kentish *laet*. All of them, being commoners, will be included under the generic term *ceorl*, but we have no means of knowing which of them is typical of the class as a whole, nor is there any proof that, taken all together, they will outnumber the slaves. We do indeed hear of Kentish freemen living in a village. We also hear of the West Saxon *ceorl* who shares arable and meadow with some of his fellows. This communal husbandry must have involved a certain amount of discussion among rustic neighbours, for not every unforeseen problem of sowing and harvesting could be met by following customary practice. The discussions could, and probably did, take place in informal meetings at the village ale-house. Much has been made of the fact that the law makes no mention in this context of any supervision by the lord. But anyone who has lived in a closely knit agricultural community will testify that the wilful non-conformist stands little chance against the massed force of public opinion. Besides, it is ludicrous to suppose that a dispute about the fencing of a field at, say, Tichborne or Wootton Bassett will have to be referred to the king. The landlord may be in the background, but he is there, and when the law has enunciated a general principle he probably has means to enforce it if need be. We have to wait until the ninth century for any mention of a popular assembly, a folk-moot, and the context in which it is found then is one of fiscal administration and the punishment of serious crime; it is not concerned with petty agrarian disputes.

Legal freedom is one thing, economic independence another, and without economic independence freedom will be no very sturdy growth. The husbandman who must hire a yoke of oxen from his neighbour before he can plough his corn-plot is obviously a man of slender resources. A succession of bad harvests, an enemy raid, a cattle plague could soon reduce him to such poverty that he will sell himself and his offspring for bread. The law allows him to bargain with his lord, but it will be a very unequal bargain, for if he throws up his holding where is he to go? Against the lord who can fetch him back and fine him heavily if he absconds and seeks a change of masters, what is his legal freedom worth?

That the ranks of the Anglo-Saxons who migrated to Britain included a certain number of adventurers who could not boast of noble birth; that some of them secured substantial holdings in the former Roman province: these are reasonable surmises. If they and their descendants prospered, they would form an upper layer of the rural population, in course of time creating their own circle of dependants; if they failed, they would lose their freedom and become satellites of more powerful men. But all this is conjecture, incapable of proof. Evidence which cannot be gainsaid obliges us to think of the English countryside in the seventh century as largely dominated by an aristocratic, slave-owning class, with demesnes cultivated for them partly by slaves, partly by tenants with servile antecedents. For positive evidence of independent and self-governing village communities we search in vain.

73

Chapter V

# THE LAND

King Ine's code imposes a fine of 60 shillings upon the man who cuts down a tree big enough to shelter thirty swine. If he fells a large number of trees in a wood, he must pay thirty shillings for each of the first three but nothing for the rest, "because the axe is an informer, not a thief," but if he secretly destroys a tree by fire he must pay the full fine, "because fire is a thief." Nevertheless many place-names – Brentwood is the most obvious example – indicate that burning was a commonly practised method of clearance. The traveller in the western Cotswolds who comes upon a place called St Chloe may well wonder what the nymph so named was doing there and how she acquired her sainthood, but the place appears first in an eighth-century charter as *sengedleag*. This word, which in the neighbouring county of Worcester has become Syntley, is compounded of the Old English *senged*, meaning singed or burnt, and *leah*, which from its primary meaning of an open glade in a wood early developed the secondary sense of a woodland clearing. As *leigh* or *-ley* it is now one of the commonest elements in our place-names.

*Pig-keeping*

Thus laws and charters bear witness on the one hand to an energetic process of deforestation, and on the other to royal concern that the process should be kept under control. It was not in the king's interest or his people's that the feeding-grounds of their swine should be drastically reduced. Numerous place-names compounded from *swin* and *swine* prove how generally pigs were kept in Anglo-Saxon England. The oak and the beech, yielding acorns

74

and mast, kept the animals well fed throughout the autumn. In winter they fed chiefly on the roots of fern; in spring on fresh grasses; in summer, on berries and seeds. Nearly every wood included some patches of open ground which could provide such nutriment.

In 706, when an under-king of the Hwicce sold Ombersley in Worcestershire to Bishop Ecgwine for his newly founded monastery at Evesham, his charter included a proviso that if the island belonging to the estate should produce an unusually large crop of acorns, beechmast sufficient for one herd of swine should be reserved to the king. So active was the king's interest in swine-pastures that more than a century later a dispute about encroachments by his swine-reeve elsewhere in Worcestershire was brought before the great council of the realm. The bishop and clergy of Worcester successfully claimed two-thirds of the wood and mast, and refused to give up mast for more than 300 swine, declaring on oath that such had been the arrangement under King Ethelbald.

The Weald of Kent was probably the greatest swine-pasture in southern Britain. Portions of it could be and often were assigned by royal grant to particular estates in private hands, as when three separate pasture-grounds more than twenty miles away in the western Weald were attached to Islingham, north of the Medway. In order to shelter the pigs from beasts of prey and to collect them for slaughter, enclosures of some kind must have been provided. Loose, a village two and a half miles south of Maidstone, takes its name from the Old English word for a pig-sty, *hlose*, which also enters into such place-names as Loseley and Luscombe. Those remote wealden pastures, often many miles distant from the parent village, must have been looked after by resident swineherds and hence might in course of time develop a life of their own as independent settlements, as did Speldhurst near Tunbridge Wells, in the eighth century a swine-pasture belonging to Halling on the Medway.

## Sheep

The pig is much more prominent in early English husbandry than the sheep, although the sheep is an animal of more varied uses, providing milk and wool as well as meat, and contributing much to the fertility of the soil by its droppings. Ine's laws value a ewe with its lamb at a shilling until a fortnight before Easter, and provide that twopence shall be deducted from the price of a sheep if it is shorn before midsummer. Late as it seems to us, this was evidently the normal time for shearing.

A charter of King Wihtred, confirmed in 716, refers to a minster at Sheppey, which evidently engaged in sheep-farming, for the name means island of sheep. Across the water at Canvey a community of shepherds living in crude temporary shelters guarded large flocks of sheep from the recurrent dangers of the spring tides which flooded the open marsh pastures.

The bishop of Worcester is said to have purchased an estate by the River Stour "at the ford called Sheepwash." This is now Shipston-on-Stour, one of the many place-names recorded later which point to systematic sheep-farming in many parts of England, but especially on the Cotswolds, where it seems to have flourished during and beyond the Roman period. The early importance of Winchcombe, a royal manor lying at the base of the Cotswold scarp, is best explained by the fact that it controlled the northern approaches to the wold pastures. Early in the eighth century the abbess of Gloucester acquired Pinswell between Coberley and Withington expressly for a sheepwalk, and in the same period the abbess of Withington added to her property a tract of land east of the Coln, sloping gently from the river-bank up to a "common lea" adjoining another settlement, significantly named Shipton. Finally, a letter written in 796 by Charlemagne to Offa, asking the king to ensure that the *saga* – woollen cloaks or blankets – exported from his realm shall be of the same size as they used to be, points to a long-established commerce in the products of Mercian sheep-flocks.

## Oxen and Other Livestock

The ox was the normal plough-beast in England before and for some time after the Norman Conquest. One manuscript of Ine's laws shows that the "yoke" a husbandman may hire from another is a yoke of oxen, but it is not clear whether he needs them because he has none of his own or because his own are not strong enough for the work. Another law declares that an orphan child must have for its keep a cow in summer and an ox in winter. Ine's legislation includes the first of a long series of enactments, running through the whole of the Anglo-Saxon period, which impose heavy penalties on cattle thieves.

It is probable that cows were kept mainly to breed replacements for the plough-team, and after they had suckled their calves had little milk left for the dairy; hence the Anglo-Saxons looked to ewes and she-goats as their principal source of milk and cheese. We may note, however, that Archbishop Wulfred paid a high price for a tract of marshland between Faversham Creek and Graveney which was known as "the king's cow-land." Earlier the archbishop had purchased an estate enjoying the right of common pasture in the neighbouring wood. The land was known as *Hrithra leah*. This word for cattle or oxen, *hrither*, appears on the map today in such names as Rotherfield and Rotherhithe.

The goat, by nature a denizen of the woods, provided milk, hides, and the flesh of its kid for meat. There is no doubt that it was widely kept, but mention of it is rare in early records. Nor does documentary evidence of an interest in horses become plentiful until the tenth century, but the element *stod*, meaning a herd or stud of horses, occurs frequently in place-names, the earliest example being Stodmarsh, on the south bank of the Great Stour, which is mentioned in two seventh-century Kentish charters.

Enough has been said to show that livestock and pastoral husbandry loomed large in the rural economy of early England, larger than it would do when more of the forest had been cleared and more of the marshes drained. But there was never a time when men would go without bread and beer if they could help it. We must turn to the land on which they grew their crops.

## Units of Assessment

For a starting-point we may take this law of Ine: "If a man takes a yard of land, or more, at a fixed rent, and ploughs it, and the lord requires service as well as rent, the tenant need not take the land if the lord does not give him a dwelling." This law needs

77

to be read in the context of an expanding West Saxon kingdom. Its purpose is evidently to encourage new gains for the plough. The husbandman is not to be deterred from enlarging his plough-land by the fear that he will thereby incur a heavier liability for service on his lord's demesne. So the king attaches the liability for labour service to the house, the messuage, rather than to the arable holding. We have no reason to believe that the enactment was generally observed or lasting in its effects, but it may well have encouraged the colonizing movement which had already drawn men to take up land in Devon, land forfeited or left vacant by the defeated enemies they called the West-Welsh.

In this law we hear for the first time of the "yard of land." For centuries to come this unit, latinized commonly as *virgata*, virgate, will stand out as the normal holding of the typical husbandman. It is essentially an arable holding: the king takes it for granted that when a man applies to his lord for a new yardland his object is to plough it, with the tacit corollary that he will graze his livestock on the common pasture. The *gyrde*, the yard from which it takes its name, is not a length of thirty-six inches nor an area of nine square feet: these are not dimensions in which a plough can move. It is a measuring-rod laid across the furrows to determine their width and along them to determine their length. There is unlikely to have been a standard rod in Ine's day; there were certainly numberless local variations even a hundred years ago, despite the thirteenth-century ordinance of weights and measures which appointed a standard rod, pole, or perch of sixteen and a half feet or five and a half yards. By that time the ideal yardland is taken to be a parcel of thirty acres, each acre being 4,840 square yards, or forty statute rods in length and four in width. The acre is of that length because forty rods make a furlong ("furrow-long"), in theory the length of the furrow which oxen will plough if they are not turned round before they have gone as far as they can without undue effort.

The yardland meets us in a code which also speaks of hides. It tells us of the Welshman holding half a hide, a whole hide, or five hides, and of others, presumably though not certainly English, who may have as many as ten. From every ten hides the king expects a stated food-rent. Here the hide appears as a unit of assessment enabling the king to collect his dues. It is laid on the estate as a whole, with behind it some rough and ready notion of actual or potential value, without enquiring whether the value is derived mainly from pasture or ploughland. In the undeveloped state of the country at this early period there must have been many estates where pastoral husbandry was far more profitable than tillage. Arable or pasture, it is all one to the king so long as he gets his food-rent. We have seen reason to believe that the yardland was from the start an arable holding. There is no evidence and no likelihood that this was originally true of the hide, and it is futile to ask what was the acreage of the normal hide, or even if there was such a thing as the normal hide.

## The Arable

From these arid topics of assessment and measurement we turn with a sigh of relief to the fields themselves. Here too we have to consider one of Ine's laws. As the text is of fundamental importance for English agrarian history, it will be advisable to give it in full.

"If husbandmen have a common meadow or other share-land to enclose, and some have enclosed their share while others have not, and if cattle eat up their common crops or grass, then let those to whom the gap is due go and make amends to the others who have enclosed their share. The latter shall demand such reparation as is proper. If, however, any beast breaks fences and wanders at large therein, and its owner will not or cannot control it, he who finds it on his cornland shall take it and kill it. The owner shall take its hide and its flesh and suffer the loss of the rest."

The first thing to be noticed about this enactment is that it is conditional. The king does not take it for granted that arable share-land or a common meadow is attributable to all husbandmen. The man who applies to his lord for a yardland and ploughs it may well want it for his own sole use. Just such a one, in all probability, is the husbandman who is told that he will have no claim to a beast that strays in unless he keeps his farm properly fenced. His farm is not just a dwelling-place and its yard; the arable, and probably some pasture too, is enclosed within a ring-fence. In the broken country of the south-west, a landscape of innumerable little valleys nestling between steep hills and watered by springs and a plentiful rainfall, the isolated farmstead must have been very common indeed, a form of settlement perhaps already in existence long before the Saxon conquest.

Ine's famous reference to common meadows and arable share-lands is often quoted as proving that an 'open-field' system of farming existed in seventh-century Wessex. With certain necessary qualifications the statement can be accepted as true. In the first place, the term 'open' field is misleading. Every field in which crops were grown would need to be surrounded by a fence or wall or hedgebank or deep ditch if cattle were not to come and trample or eat the growing corn. Ine's law proves, if proof is needed, that the arable share-land of Wessex was so enclosed. The field is 'open' only in the sense that no obstacle separates one man's ploughland from his neighbour's. But there is no hint of communal ownership. The shares are clearly regarded as held by individuals, each of whom must be compensated for damage caused by his neighbour's default. We must think of these individuals as forming what has been aptly termed "a community of shareholders."

That one shareholder's ploughland lay in parcels intermixed with those of his neighbours – perhaps the most striking feature of the open-field system in later centuries – cannot safely be deduced from Ine's law. The law rather implies the contrary, that each man's holding extended to the edge of the field, and therefore he was held responsible for the adjacent part of the enclosing fence. Intermixture of parcels may come later from one cause or another. We may also guess that the furrows all lay in one direction. The pattern of a common field divided into small plots, with groups of furrows at right angles to one another, is familiar to those who have studied old field-maps, but in all probability it was not an original feature. In England, as in Germany, it seems to represent a later, more sophisticated plan.

Thus while Ine's law is good evidence that common meadows and ploughlands were already present in seventh-century Wessex, it does not entitle us to assume the complicated, fully matured system with which the textbooks have made us familiar. Nor does it tell us whether the system was new or old. We may guess, but we cannot prove, that it was known much earlier and in other parts of the country. Some historians believe that it goes back to the earliest days of Anglo-Saxon settlement, and was brought over by the Anglo-Saxons from their continental homes. But of late years archaeological evidence has been accumulating from the coastlands of northern Europe to prove that up to the time of their migration to Britain the field pattern familiar to the Anglo-Saxons was of exactly the same type as that prevailing at the time in Wessex, a pattern of small square fields and short furrows. There is in fact no ground for believing that the immigrants brought with them better ploughs or a more advanced agricultural technique than those they found when they arrived.

## The Crops

Wheat, rye, barley, and oats were the standard cereals of Anglo-Saxon England, but not all four were cultivated everywhere. Saint Cuthbert tried to grow wheat on the rocky island of Farne, but although he waited till midsummer it failed to germinate. Then he tried barley, with much better success, for, leaving miracles aside, barley will ripen farther north than any other grain. In his hermitage at Crowland Guthlac lived – naturally to no great age – on barley-bread and water.

Ground into meal for bread-making or converted into malt for brewing, barley easily eclipsed all other cereals. The Anglo-Saxons consumed beer on an oceanic scale. This will not surprise us when we bethink ourselves how much of their meat had to be salted for preservation through the winter months. The original meaning of *beretun* and *berewic* is 'barley-farm' in each case, but barley was so clearly taken to be the principal Anglo-Saxon grain that both words came to be used of establishments where corn of any kind was stored; hence the numerous Bartons and Berwicks to be found on the map today.

The importance of rye in the early English period is shown in the preamble to King Wihtred's laws which declares that they were drawn up by the Kentish royal council in an assembly held on the sixth day of *Rugern*, that is, in the month of the rye harvest, in 695. Ryarsh, the name of a village seven miles north-west of Maidstone, signifies 'rye field'.

Oats were fed to the calves and foals, and also provided porridge for human consumption. A document prescribing the quantities of food and drink to be distributed on certain anniversaries heads the list with 120 wheaten loaves and 30 "clean" loaves, the former presumably wholemeal, the latter fine white bread made from carefully sifted flour. Churchmen needed such bread for use at the altar.

Beans, always an important article in the diet of the poor, were probably grown in the fields as well as in garden plots: hence such names as Banstead and Binstead. Flax (*lin*), cultivated to provide linen fibres and lamp-wicks, has left its mark on several Linacres and Lintons; and pollen analysis has traced the cultivation of flax and hemp in East Anglia back to the Anglo-Saxon period. That woad (*wad*) was widely cultivated in that period for use as a dye is proved by numerous place-names, Waddon, Wadborough, and the like.

It can only be an assumption, though a reasonable one, that the Anglo-Saxons continued to harvest the wild and cultivated fruits which had been known in the Roman period, including apples, medlars, cherries, mulberries, plums, bullaces, and damsons.

## Mines

Under Roman rule gold had been mined in Wales, lead chiefly in the Mendips and Derbyshire, tin in Cornwall, coal in Somerset and the north, iron in the Forest of Dean and the Kentish Weald. There is no reason to believe that all this activity ceased with the advent of the Anglo-Saxons. In 689 the king of Kent granted one ploughland containing an iron-mine to the monks of Canterbury. His charter states that it had belonged to the hereditary royal estate administered from Lyminge, but gives no exact indication of its whereabouts. In 835 an abbess, presumably of Repton, granted Wirksworth in Derbyshire to an ealdorman, subject to an annual rent-charge of 300 shillings-worth of lead to Archbishop Ceolnoth for Christ Church, Canterbury. Some years later Lupus, abbot of Ferrières in Gaul, wrote to King Ethelwulf of Wessex asking him to send lead for the roofing of his church. A lead-mine figures in the boundary of Stoke Bishop near Bristol. Scattered references like these are all the evidence we have for mining operations in the Old English period.

## Forms of Settlement

A landscape so varied as that of England naturally produced a wide variety of practice. It also exerted a direct influence on the pattern of settlement. We may easily fall into the error of making the early village too populous. The midland settlement which appears on nineteenth-century maps as a large village may well have started life as a nucleus of one or two hardy pioneers, indistinguishable in point of numbers from the population of a south-western hamlet.

The *vicus*, the smallest unit which the Roman authorities had recognized for purposes of administration, might be a small town or a civil settlement outside a Roman fort. The Anglo-Saxons, when they found one, knew it for what it was. They borrowed the Latin word and turned it into *wic*. In the laws of Kent, London itself appears as *Lundenwic*, and the king has a reeve there called a *wic-gerefa*. The word *wic-ham*, a compound of *wic* and the Germanic element *ham*, seems to have been applied by early English settlers to places close to Roman roads and usually near Roman-British *vici*; hence a number of Wycombes and Wickhams. In the very common place-name Wick or Wyke, *wic* has its more general sense and means no more than a collection of buildings. In course of time it was associated with buildings used for special purposes, especially those connected with livestock and dairy produce: Shapwick (sheep-farm), Butterwick, Chiswick, and the like.

*Ham*, from its primary sense of home or dwelling, comes to mean a group of dwellings, a village, and finally an estate or manor. When *hams* and *tuns* occur in genuine charters of the seventh century, the former outnumber the latter by two to one. Thus both are ancient, but *ham* is relatively uncommon in the midlands and the west, and this suggests that its use in place-names was becoming obsolete as the tide of English conquest surged westward. By contrast, *tun* was used in name-making throughout the Old English period and for some time after the

Norman Conquest. In primitive German it seems to have denoted a fence or hedge. This leads naturally to the successive Old English meanings: an enclosed piece of ground; an enclosure containing a house; a farmstead. Then, as a *tun* expands from its original nucleus, it comes to mean first, a hamlet or village, later a whole estate. The laws of Ethelbert show that a king and a nobleman might each have his *tun*; those of Hlothhere and Eadric imply a village, for they rule that a freeman charged with theft shall bring at least one witness from the *tun* to which he himself belongs. The current meaning of *town* as an urban area was not developed until after the close of the Old English period.

Sometimes an ancient *ham* gave birth to a secondary settlement called a *tun*: thus Briningham and Brinton, Corringham and Carrington, Ovingham and Ovington, Nottingham and Sneinton, Wintringham and Winterton. We have already noted the daughter settlements which grew up on the swine-pastures of the Kentish weald. Dairy-farming led to a parallel development when the herdsmen of the parent village drove their cattle in summer to a low-lying and well-watered standing-place which they called a *stoc*. This in time grew up with an independent life of its own. Calstock, for example, begins as the *stoc* of Callington, Plymstock as the *stoc* of Plympton, and Basingstoke as the *stoc* of Basing.

The husbandman who is bidden by Ine's law to keep his *worthig* fenced both summer and winter clearly occupies a farm surrounded by a stockade. *Worth*, a simpler form of *worthig*, is common in the midlands, and the variant *worthign* especially so in the west midlands. All three are frequently compounded with personal names, suggesting that they begin as individual possessions; and all may end as substantial villages: Bayworth, Holsworthy, Bedwardine. Even the humblest form of dwelling, the *cot* or *cote*, can become the nucleus of a settlement named after its early occupant.

Villages are of all shapes and sizes. Modern industry and mining have given rise to settlements where the dwellings are dotted about at random by a stream or crowded on hillside terraces without any coherent plan. Setting these aside, three main types can be distinguished. Some villages are built round a green, as at Bledington in Gloucestershire, or a pond, as at Finchingfield in

Essex. Others are grouped round a central building, usually the church. In others again the houses are strung out along both sides of a roadway. On one occasion St Cuthbert was staying in a place called Hruringaham, apparently somewhere near Melrose, when a house at the east end caught fire, and as the wind was blowing from that quarter it looked as if the whole village would be destroyed; but the saint by his prayers brought about a change of wind and saved the situation. This sounds like a village built along a single street.

The core of Withington in Gloucestershire, a villa-estate under Roman rule and from the close of the seventh century the site of an Anglo-Saxon minster, is a compact rectangular nucleus of lanes and buildings, including the church, rectory, and manor house, with a street leading westward out of it and up to an ancient trackway from Corinium, the Roman Cirencester. But at some date before 774 the abbess of Withington acquired a tract of land on the other side of the little river Coln, and a new settlement grew up, of an entirely different pattern. Here the buildings, instead of forming a rectangular group, are strung out for more than a quarter of a mile along the road to Compton Abdale. The result is that side by side in what today forms one village are two different patterns, the one shown by documentary evidence to be appreciably older than the other. The example warns us that it is unsafe to construe the aspect of a mature village seen on the map or on the ground today as evidence of its original shape. Documents of very early date are needed to help us dissect it into its component parts, and such documents are rare. But intelligent fieldwork combined with documentary research has lately succeeded in isolating the original pattern of Linton in the West Riding, where two fields immediately adjoining the village on the east and west, of 72 and 70 acres respectively, are certainly older than Domesday Book and antedate the outer fields created by an extension of tillage in the twelfth and thirteenth centuries. There is room for much more analytical work of this kind.

## Huts, Farms, and Palaces

We are a little better informed about early Anglo-Saxon dwellings. Thirty-three buildings, occupied from about the end of the fifth century, were uncovered by E. T. Leeds on a deserted site between Drayton and Sutton Courtenay in Berkshire. On a floor about two feet below ground level a tent-like superstructure had been erected, supported by slanting posts secured to a central ridge-pole. The roof must have come down to the edge of the excavation. Two of the buildings appear to have been used as weaving sheds, and one as a potter's workshop.

The sunken hut, usually quite small, little more than $3 \times 2$ metres, and built over pits which vary in depth from 0.2 to 1 metre or more, was by far the most common type of Anglo-Saxon building. It is also found over large areas of continental Europe. Wijster, in north-east Holland, a settlement abandoned at the time of the migration to Britain, contained eighty sunken huts, apparently used as outbuildings by the occupants of large farmsteads. Of the latter, 72 out of 86 were long-houses, in which human beings and livestock were sheltered under one roof. The interior, with a length of more than twice the width, was divided by roof-posts into a wide gangway and two side aisles, one of which was used as a byre and the other as a dwelling by the farmer and his family.

Wijster is not the only European site where the sunken huts are associated with larger structures at ground level, and it has been suggested that at Sutton Courtenay and elsewhere in this country these larger buildings have simply been overlooked in the course of excavation. It is a possibility which must always be borne in mind, and if substantiated it may justify us in concluding that the sunken huts were used mainly as workshops, not dwellings. On the other hand, 101 sites in this country, ranging in date from c. 400 to c. 850, have yielded traces of only thirteen buildings at ground level as against twenty-four sunken huts. An excavation still in progress at the time of writing has brought to light sixty-eight such huts at Mucking in Essex, bearing signs of continuous occupation from the late Roman period to the first half of the sixth century, but so far there is no trace of other houses. At West Stow in Suffolk thirty-four sunken huts have been excavated, many of them used for weaving and other processes connected with wool, but only three buildings at ground level have been located as yet. In the present state of archaeological knowledge, therefore, it appears that in this early period comparatively few Anglo-Saxon countrymen occupied houses of any size; the majority lived rather squalid lives in sunken huts.

Since long-houses on the continent go back to the Bronze Age, and were known to the Anglo-Saxons at Wijster and elsewhere in their continental homelands, it is reasonable to suppose that they were also built on this side of the North Sea. They have in fact been found at Mawgan Porth in Cornwall and at Jarlshof in Shetland, but in the greater part of England they have yet to be proved older than the twelfth century.

Until quite late in the Old English period the use of stone as a building material was confined to churches and some fortified strongholds. With a few exceptions, every dwelling-house was built of wood, turf, or some form of unbaked earth. This is true not only of farmhouses but of manors and even royal palaces. When the royal manor of Cheddar was excavated, a farmhouse-like wooden structure, 78 feet long and 20 feet wide in the middle, dating from the eighth or ninth century, was the earliest recognizable feature of a site destined to be much enlarged later. Early in the seventh century a massive timber hall was built at Yeavering in Northumbria, with lesser halls set about it, probably dwellings for the king's companions in arms. One structure of more primitive type may have housed the native servants. There was also a grandstand for open-air assemblies. Later the grandstand was enlarged; additional small dwellings were built, and a hall of more ambitious design took the place of the original great hall. This phase is believed to have begun in the period when King Edwin held court there and entertained Paulinus for more than a month while he baptized converts in the River Glen. After a devastating fire buildings of lighter construction were put up, some of them with annexes or porches at the gable-ends, and a Christian church was added. A second fire made it necessary to rebuild the great hall, the church, and two smaller halls. The place was occupied until 670 at latest, then finally abandoned. Today silence reigns over Yeavering except when the wind rages through the valley where a *bretwalda* feasted his warriors and the mead-horn passed from hand to hand.

# Chapter VI

# THE MERCIAN SUPREMACY

Darwin, if he had thought of it, could have found an appropriate illustration of the survival of the fittest in the politics of the Heptarchy. In the early stages of Anglo-Saxon history the rulers of Sussex, Kent, and East Anglia had each in turn been acknowledged as *bretwalda*, but in each case a single reign saw the beginning and end of their supremacy. They never became quite negligible, but in the race for power they were soon left behind.

The inhabitants of Sussex were a primitive and ignorant folk whose acquaintance with the art of fishing was limited to the taking of eels until the great Wilfrid came among them to preach the gospel and instruct them in the rudiments of civilized living. Down to the time of Wilfrid's host, Æthelwahl, they seem to have obeyed only one monarch. Later kings are not known except as names in charters, and from these it appears that several kings might be reigning simultaneously, making Sussex an easy prey to aggressive neighbours.

Kent, more advanced in every way, was also subject to division between two or more princes of the reigning house. As the home of the primatial see it could never be negligible, but its influence was more ecclesiastical than political. In 695 King Wihtred issued a code of laws of which the most notable enactment was one freeing the churches of Kent from taxation. He followed this up with a charter guaranteeing the property of the churches against encroachment and exempting them from the obligation to supply provisions or labour at the behest of the king or any other layman. Wihtred granted this immunity to Canterbury, Rochester, and eight monasteries named in his charter, but later kings and

88

churchmen construed it as applying to churches in general and often invoked it in the inevitable struggles for and against ecclesiastical privilege.

Essex, a heavily wooded region, was subject to a dynasty which also controlled Middlesex and Hertfordshire. Its importance lay in the possession of London, "an emporium," says Bede, "for many nations who come to it by land and sea." But the heathen reaction which drove Bishop Mellitus away frustrated Pope Gregory's intention to make the city an archiepiscopal see. The kings of Essex were doomed to become satellites of stronger powers.

## Sutton Hoo

One of the most sensational finds of modern archaeology has focused attention on East Anglia. At Sutton Hoo, above the estuary of the Deben near Woodbridge, a mound was uncovered in which a ship some 85 feet long and 14 feet wide lay buried. There was no sign of a mast or sail. A chamber in the middle of the ship contained an assortment of precious and beautiful objects, the whole seemingly intended as a memorial to some seventh-century king or chieftain who had perished in battle or at sea. Bronze bowls, silver-mounted drinking-horns, a helmet, a shield, two silver spoons, a purse containing forty gold Frankish coins, a six-stringed lyre, a fluted bowl, a gold buckle, a jewelled clasp, and a great silver dish bearing the monogram of the Byzantine emperor Anastasius (491–518) astonish as much by the excellence of their workmanship as by their intrinsic value. The treasure of Sutton Hoo reveals the East Anglian kingdom as a maritime power with extensive trading contacts overseas. But three of its kings fell in battle against Penda, and a fourth, King Æthelhere, lost his life in Penda's final conflict with Northumbria, where he took part as Penda's more or less willing ally. After his time the kingdom sinks into such obscurity that even the succession of its kings is not certainly known.

## Bede

The eclipse of the lesser kingdoms in effect reduced the Heptarchy to a trinity of three considerable powers. In intellectual achievement Northumbria far outshone Mercia and Wessex. Mention has already been made of the great library which Benedict Biscop assembled for his twin foundations of Monkwearmouth and Jarrow. That collection enabled the Venerable Bede to become famous throughout Europe for the range and depth of his scholarship. From his admission as a child of seven to his death in 735 at the age of sixty-three Bede spent the whole of his working life at Jarrow. His long series of scientific treatises and biblical commentaries caused him to be ranked as one of the great doctors of the church. His influence as a master of chronology has endured to the present day. The fact that we reckon years from the nativity of Christ is due to him, for though he did not invent the system his reasoning and example led to its rapid adoption throughout Christendom.

Bede's greatest work, and the one most widely read today, is his *Ecclesiastical History of the English People*, completed in 731. Besides drawing on older writers, such as Gildas and the biographer of St Germanus, he obtained from Albinus, abbot of St Augustine's, Canterbury, information based on the records and traditions of that church concerning the activities of Augustine and the other early missionaries. Albinus, again, employed Nothelm, a priest of London, to search the Roman archives and furnish Bede with copies of letters from Gregory the Great and other popes. By correspondence Bede consulted the monks of Lastingham on the conversion of Mercia and the reconversion of Essex; Cyneberht, bishop of Lindsey, on the propagation of the faith in that kingdom; and Daniel, bishop of Winchester, on the early history of Wessex, Sussex, and the Isle of Wight. In his quest for trustworthy evidence, collected from responsible informants and where possible from original documents, Bede shows himself admirably sensitive to what he calls "the true law of history."

At the same time it is important to recognize his limitations. There are large blanks in his narrative. It is an ecclesiastical, not a political history. Saints and missionaries occupy the centre of the stage; the kings who favoured or opposed them receive only incidental notice. Concerned as he is mainly with his Anglo-Saxon fellow countrymen, he says virtually nothing about the Britons living under their domination, and not much that is favourable about those who still retained their independence. Discretion led him to omit or gloss over some awkward facts. Moreover, the kings, queens, bishops, and nobles who come to life in his pages are all persons of the highest social standing; the common people are notably absent. Nevertheless, without the *Ecclesiastical History* we should be woefully ill-informed about most of the events related in the foregoing pages.

## Northumbrian Eminence

After Bede's death the lamp of learning was kept alight by his pupils, and especially by Egbert, brother of the king who reigned over Northumbria from 737 to 758. Already bishop of York, Egbert received the pallium in 735, when the plan of Gregory the Great for a northern archbishopric at last took effect. His reputation attracted disciples, and York soon became the leading centre of English scholarship, equipped with one of the finest libraries in western Europe. So renowned was the school of York that in 782 Charlemagne invited its head, Alcuin, to take charge of the school attached to the Frankish court. Many of Alcuin's pupils joined him there. He became one of Charlemagne's principal advisers and his chief agent in executing the decree of 789 which enjoined the standardization of liturgical usage throughout the Frankish empire and the preparation of revised service-books to ensure uniformity. At Tours, where Alcuin spent the last eight years of his life, he made the abbey of St Martin illustrious for its learning and for the highly legible form of writing developed by its scribes. This Carolingian minuscule, to give it its technical name, was revived by the copyists of the Italian Renaissance in the fifteenth century and influenced the early printers in their choice of type-forms. It thus became the direct ancestor of the alphabet familiar to us on the printed page today.

Bede had grown to manhood in the reign of Aldfrith (685–704), the illegitimate half-brother of Ecgfrith, whom he succeeded as king after the disaster of Dunnichen Moss. Aldfrith proved sufficiently formidable to the enemies of Northumbria to ensure a peaceful reign, though within narrower boundaries than of old. The security he gave his kingdom provided a favourable setting for scholarship, and his patronage was all the more enlightened because having spent many years in study among the Irish before his unexpected accession to the throne, Aldfrith was himself one of the most learned men of his day.

After his death a series of palace revolutions shook the monarchy, but King Eadberht, brother of Archbishop Egbert, arrested the decay and during the twenty-one years of his reign played an effective part in northern politics. In 750 he wrested the plain of Kyle in what is now Ayrshire from the Britons of Strathclyde. A few years later he successfully attacked their capital, Dumbarton, in conjunction with the king of Pictland. But his son and successor, Oswulf, was killed by his own retainers, and thereafter the annals of Northumbrian kingship are a monotonous tale of treason, murder, and usurpation. The kingdom still extended as far northward as the Firth of Forth and held together in at least nominal unity, but the great barrier of the Pennines precluded easy travel between the eastern and the western halves and hindered royal attempts to suppress incipient revolt. Bede's last work, a letter to Bishop Egbert written the year before the pallium was sent to York, is heavy with foreboding. He deplored the profusion of land-grants which had left the kings without a reserve from which to maintain the class on which the safety of the realm depended, and he denounced in strong terms the connivance of church and state which permitted local magnates to turn their establishments into sham monasteries and thus to evade their public liabilities. The letter throws a searchlight on weaknesses which condemned Northumbria to political isolation.

## The Rise of Wessex

The rise to greatness of any Anglo-Saxon kingdom depended on the ability of its rulers to keep the loyalty of its warrior class and to dazzle them with the prospect of reward in the shape of land-grants. Here Wessex was fortunately placed. It is true that Mercia pressed hard upon its northern provinces, but only a sparsely populated British kingdom opposed its expansion into the south-west. Wessex was not yet a united kingdom. Any active member of the royal house could and sometimes did take the title of king;

it is said that five kings perished when Edwin of Northumbria invaded Wessex.

King Cenwahl and his brother Centwine, whose successful invasion of Devon has been described on an earlier page, traced their pedigree from Ceawlin and thus represented the dynasty which had originally reigned in the Thames valley. In 685, according to the Anglo-Saxon Chronicle, "Caedwalla began to contend for the kingdom." Bede describes Caedwalla as a young prince descended from the royal house of the Gewisse. His name, like that of Cerdic, the reputed founder of the family, points to a British or partly British ancestry, being an anglicized form of the Welsh Cadwallon. Refugees in the Chilterns and Andred enlisted in his war-band, and with their help he first set himself to reconquer the Gewissan territory in Hampshire and the Isle of Wight which Wulfhere of Mercia had given to the king of Sussex. He devastated Sussex, killed its king, and settled some of his followers in the Isle of Wight after giving a third of the island to St Wilfrid. He also made himself master, though briefly, of Kent, and of Surrey long enough to give the church a great estate at Farnham, where the bishops of Winchester continued to reside until 1927. Bede styles Caedwalla king of the Gewisse, but in another passage he implies that he was presently recognized as king of all Wessex. It seems that he displaced Centwine, who is said to have retired into a monastery. But he had been severely wounded while harrying the Isle of Wight, and though barely thirty years of age, a Christian but still unbaptized, he determined to end his days in Rome. On Easter Sunday 689 he was baptized in the presence of Pope Sergius. Ten days later he died.

## The Reign of Ine

Brief and violent as Caedwalla's reign had been, it ended the state of things in which princes of the royal house had been able to divide the kingdom between them. Henceforth no man in Wessex but the king himself could claim any higher rank than that of the ealdormen who governed the shires under him. In all probability this royal predominance emerged as a result not of Caedwalla's aggressive career, but of the policy of Ine, grandson of one of

Ceawlin's grandsons, who began to reign after the young man's abdication. A strong king, Ine made the Kentishmen pay dearly for their resistance to his predecessor. He kept Sussex and Surrey in subjection, and in 710 obliged the king of Sussex to join him in a campaign against King Geraint of Dumnonia. The victorious issue of this campaign probably led to the beginning of English settlement in Cornwall; it certainly left Ine in a position to grant land on the Cornish side of the Tamar to Glastonbury. But Welsh annals record that the Cornishmen won a victory in 722 somewhere on the estuary of the Camel, and the English advance, it seems, received a serious check.

On the whole, Ine contended very successfully against his enemies at home and abroad. In 715 the king of Mercia invaded Wessex, and a battle took place at *Wodensbeorg*, the scene of Ceawlin's defeat in 592. The Chronicle does not say who won, but Ine certainly held all the country south of the Thames, and may even have recovered territory north of the river which for a time the Mercians had made their own.

Ever since their conversion the kings of Wessex had been good friends to the church. When the Mercian invasion of Berkshire and east Hampshire made the original West Saxon bishopric of Dorchester-on-Thames untenable, King Cenwahl founded an episcopal see at Winchester. He enriched the British monasteries at Sherborne and Glastonbury while placing English abbots in charge of them. At Glastonbury Ine built a church dedicated to SS. Peter and Paul alongside the primitive wattle structure in which the earliest monks or hermits had worshipped. The westward expansion of the kingdom made it necessary to divide the diocese of Winchester, and in 705 Ine established a new bishopric at Sherborne with jurisdiction over all the English churches west of Selwood. He granted lands, woods, and fisheries to Malmesbury, Muchelney, and above all Glastonbury, his favourite church. In 704 he so far improved upon the example set by Wihtred of Kent as to exempt the churches and minsters of his kingdom from all taxation in perpetuity.

Quite early in his reign Ine issued the code of laws which has proved his most lasting memorial. In seventy-six articles the code touches upon nearly every aspect of social, religious, and agrarian life. As earlier chapters of this book have shown, it is a source of primary value for the historian. Ine's laws unmistakably reflect the ideas of a sage and far-sighted ruler. One cannot but admire the statesmanship which had brought Britons and Saxons together in an integrated society where the rights of both were legally safe-guarded. Nearly two centuries elapsed from their promulgation before any king of Wessex felt called upon to introduce further legislation.

### The Sons of Penda

After a reign of thirty-seven years Ine resigned his kingdom and spent the remainder of his days in Rome. His successors had to contend with the ever-growing power of Mercia. It has already been seen that within twenty years from the death of Penda his sons had established themselves as overlords of the southern English. Wulfhere's authority was paramount in Essex, where he intervened with a high hand when half the kingdom relapsed into heathenism. He could dispose of the bishopric of London. The king of Sussex became his godson and the beneficiary of Wulf-here's invasion of Hampshire. By his marriage to a Kentish princess Wulfhere secured the goodwill of that kingdom. But his attempt to subdue Northumbria was defeated by King Ecgfrith; Wulfhere took to flight and his power collapsed. For a short time his kingdom paid tribute to Ecgfrith, until his brother and suc-cessor Ethelred reversed the situation and put an end to Northum-brian pretensions in southern England. His victory over Ecgfrith at the battle of the Trent led, through the mediation of Arch-bishop Theodore, to a durable peace between the two kingdoms.

Historians have done something less than justice to Ethelred. In war he acquitted himself like a true son of Penda. After his victory over Ecgfrith Lindsey became and remained a Mercian dependency. He made his power felt in the south by harrying Kent, and by granting two estates on the Wiltshire–Gloucester-shire border to the monks of Malmesbury. Grants of land in the kingdoms of the Hwicce and the West Angles could not take effect without his consent. He seems to have maintained his father's good understanding with the Welsh, for we hear of no hostilities

95

on that front. It seems to have been in his time that the Mercians completed their occupation of Cheshire, which had begun late in the sixth century with the infiltration of small groups, possibly by leave of the Welsh authorities. (The place-name Tarvin, a Primitive Welsh word for boundary, has been thought to mark the frontier between Welsh and English along the River Gowy, stabilized for a while before the English achieved numerical preponderance.) There may have been unrecorded local conflicts, but by 689, when Ethelred founded the church of St John at Chester, the take-over was complete. All Cheshire had become a Mercian province.

Ethelred's friendship with St Wilfrid gained him respect at Rome. For twenty-nine years he maintained his position as the most powerful monarch in central and southern England. Then he abdicated of his own free will in favour of his nephew Coenred and retired into a monastery at Bardney in Lindsey, where he spent his last fourteen years, at first as a monk, later as abbot.

His withdrawal from the world let loose a series of devastating Welsh raids into Mercia. After a reign of only three years his successor abdicated, as also did Offa, king of Essex, and both kings retired to Rome. The next king fought Ine at *Wodensbeorg*, apparently without advantage to himself. In 716 a far more formidable character, Ethelbald, grandson of Penda's brother, succeeded to the Mercian throne.

### The Reign of Ethelbald

As a landless adventurer lurking in the Fens near Crowland, Ethelbald had been befriended by St Guthlac. After his accession he rose swiftly to power. In 731 Bede recorded at the close of his *Ecclesiastical History* that Ethelbald was now master of all England south of the Humber. At first he was content to let the scribes who drafted his charters call him simply "king of the Mercians," but after a while he claimed to be regarded as "king not only of the Mercians but of all the peoples of southern England." In his time London and Middlesex were finally detached from the East Saxon kingdom. In 733 he occupied Somerton, a royal domain in Somerset, and although King Cuthred of Wessex did not tamely submit he was obliged to join Ethelbald in a campaign against the Welsh, and he could not prevent the Mercian from disposing of estates in Somerset and Wiltshire at his pleasure.

In a letter to King Ethelbald the English-born apostle of Germany, St Boniface, complains bitterly that from the time of Ethelbald's predecessor lay magnates have been encroaching on the privileges of the church. They have treated monasteries and monastic estates as their own property, and Ethelbald himself has not respected the immunities which the churches have enjoyed ever since the conversion under Gregory the Great.

Ethelbald was prepared to go some way to meet such criticisms. In 742, in a council held at *Clofeshoh*, attended by the archbishop of Canterbury, fifteen bishops, three abbots, and eight ealdormen, the privilege by which Wihtred of Kent had exempted the churches from all secular burdens was read out and confirmed, primarily for the benefit of Canterbury, but with an implication that it should hold good for all England south of the Humber. Yet Bede's letter to the bishop of York had made it plain that the indiscriminate granting of land in church-right freed from every kind of earthly service was one of the main causes of Northumbrian decline. Ethelbald did not mean to make the same mistake. In 749 he held another council, a gathering of ealdormen at his manor of Gumley, where the bishops of Lichfield and Leicester were the only churchmen present. Here Ethelbald again declared the churches and minsters free from all secular burdens, but this time with the significant reservation that their lands would remain liable to provide man-power for bridge-building and the defence of fortified places. He added that kings and ealdormen would demand hospitality only as a free-will offering. It was no doubt as obvious to his subjects as to Ethelbald himself that favours asked by a strong ruler are not easily refused, but the council of Gumley marks the first formal breach of ecclesiastical privilege, and its effects were to be permanent.

Wat's Dyke, an earthwork between four and five feet high, running for thirty-eight miles from the estuary of the Dee at Basingwerk in Flintshire across Denbighshire to Newbridge near Oswestry in Shropshire, is attributed with great probability to Ethelbald. It set the seal on Mercian domination of Cheshire.

Ethelbald reigned for forty-one years. He never married, and his private life gave plentiful cause for scandal. In 756 he was murdered at Seckington near Tamworth by his own bodyguard. For a few months after his death civil war raged in Mercia, but before the end of the year Offa, descended like Ethelbald from Penda's brother, seized the throne. He was to prove an even more aggressively powerful king than his predecessor.

## Offa and the Mercian Supremacy

Not content with reserving bridge-work and fortress-work when granting land by charter, Offa added a third reservation. All occupants of bookland must in future provide a quota for military service when the king or the local ealdorman called out the host. The kings of Wessex followed suit. By 794 they were exacting military service; by 801 bridge-work; and by 842 fortress-work. These obligations, which it will be convenient to epitomize as the three common dues, together with a whole series of minor liabilities, had always been incumbent on lay holders of land, but henceforth, with rare if any exceptions, they were demanded from church lands as well. This meant that book-right ceased to be synonymous with church-right or minster-right, and laymen could satisfy their appetite for hereditary tenure without resorting to the more or less transparent subterfuges condemned by Bede. Once book-right was limited by the reservation of the three common dues there was no reason why laymen should not have it as well as churchmen, and in fact from Offa's time onwards land was granted to favoured laymen in perpetual inheritance without any religious implication, real or feigned.

With the other English kings Offa dealt in masterful fashion. The sons of Oshere still governed the Hwicce, but where their father had been styled *rex*, they had to content themselves with the title of *regulus* or *subregulus*; indeed in 777, when Offa granted Sedgebarrow to one of them, he styled him "my under-king, ealdorman, that is, of his own people." After 794 there are no more Hwiccian charters, and nothing more is heard of the local dynasty. In Herefordshire and Shropshire Mildfrith, son of King Merewahl, who founded the cathedral of Hereford and was buried there, seems to have been the last *regulus* of the family. The country over which they had reigned was thenceforth administered by Mercian ealdormen. A king of Lindsey who attested one of Offa's charters was the last recorded member of his ancient dynasty. In 794 Offa caused Ethelbert, king of East Anglia, to be beheaded, perhaps because he tried to assert his independence. Two princes in Sussex, at first entitled kings, appear later as ealdormen, and Sussex never again enjoyed the status of a kingdom. It was not empty grandiloquence when Offa styled himself in so many words "king of the English." He meant to be treated as sole monarch of England south of the Humber, with the other kingdoms reduced to mere shires in which no grant of land could take effect without his consent. He went so far as to revoke a grant by Egbert II of Kent on the ground that a client king had no authority to confer book-right. By claiming as his exclusive prerogative the power to create hereditary tenure Offa at once exalted his own regality and strengthened his hold on the military forces of the whole country.

In Northumbria Offa acquired a position of influence by giving one of his daughters in marriage to the reigning king. The Kentish dynasty founded by Oisc seems to have become extinct when the last of Wihtred's sons died, and its place was taken by obscure kings who were in no position to withstand the mighty Mercian. For the first half of his reign Offa asserted an effective overlordship in Kent, to the extent of making land-grants without reference to the local ruler, but in 776 rebellion broke out, and a clash of arms between Kentishmen and Mercians ensued at Otford. For the next ten years Offa is not known to have wielded any authority in Kent.

In his relationship with the Welsh Offa enjoyed varying success. Welsh annals record a battle at Hereford in 760, a harrying of Dyfed by Offa in 778, an expedition into Wales in 784, and a battle at Rhuddlan in 796. But in the intervals of hostilities, most probably during his last twelve years, Offa conceived the idea of a negotiated frontier, and marked it by the building of his famous Dyke. This massive earthwork covered some 120 miles as the crow flies from the estuary of the Dee at Prestatyn to the Severn estuary at Sedbury near Chepstow. It was broken only in places where dense woods precluded the movement of armies or where negotiation with the Welsh princes entailed the cession of territory which in earlier days the English had made their own. Its construction must have drawn upon huge resources of man-power and engineering experience. After twelve centuries it still impresses the beholder, a monument to Offa's flexible statecraft and inflexible will.

## Ecclesiastical Politics

In 786 two legates, George, bishop of Ostia, and Theophylact, bishop of Todi, arrived in England, sent by Pope Adrian I to review the state of the church. After visiting the archbishop of Canterbury, they came to Offa's court and presented their credentials. At a council attended by Offa and Cynewulf of Wessex they detailed the reforms which the pope judged necessary. Then they separated, the bishop of Todi taking Wales and southern England for his province while the bishop of Ostia went on to Northumbria. There, in a council attended by King Ælfwold, the archbishop of York, and all the magnates of the north, he promulgated a series of decrees to which they promised obedience. The first ten decrees referred to questions of faith and ecclesiastical discipline; the remainder were addressed to the laity. They prohibited irregular marriages and heathen practices, and required kings and princes not to exact more from the churches than was allowed by Roman law and the usage of ancient emperors: an obvious protest against the recent limitations of ecclesiastical immunity. Then the legate rejoined his colleague, the decrees were read out in Latin and English to a similar assembly convoked by Offa, and accepted by the whole council.

It is safe to assume that Offa seized the opportunity to discuss with the legates certain politico-ecclesiastical changes which he had in mind. The see of Canterbury, then occupied by Jaenbert, formerly abbot of St Augustine's and a Kentishman in sympathy, perhaps also by birth, had effective spiritual jurisdiction over all the southern English. Offa, in whose mind Kentish hostility rankled, determined to secure ecclesiastical autonomy for Mercia. He persuaded the pope to divide the province of Canterbury and to make Lichfield an archbishopric. Historians have written of this act as a kind of outrage. There is no doubt that it was dictated as much by political as by ecclesiastical considerations. On the other hand, there are few, if any, parallels in western Christendom to the huge province of Canterbury, and reason suggested that England could well find room for three metropolitans.

Offa had another boon to ask of Rome. He wanted to ensure that the kingship should remain in his own branch of the Mercian dynasty. He knew that in 781 two sons of Charlemagne had been anointed as kings by the pope in person, and he was bent on securing consecration for Ecgfrith, his only son. It is not known whether the ceremony was performed by the archbishop of Lichfield or by the legates, but it certainly included the rite of anointing; in their decrees the legates had spoken of kings as the Lord's anointed. The inauguration of a monarch by a religious ceremony goes back, as we have seen, at least to the time of St Oswald, when it took the form of a simple laying on of hands by a priest. Whether or not it had since been supplemented by the more solemn rite of anointing, performed by a bishop, it is certain that from the time of Offa anointing formed an essential part of the ceremony, as it has been ever since. The ordination of a son during his father's lifetime was a novelty in England. It created a precedent that would be remembered by at least one later king.

Pride of ancestry counted for much in Offa's dealings with the Frankish court. Himself the namesake and descendant of an Offa who had reigned in Schleswig well before the Anglian invasion of England, and who incidentally was held by tradition to have set the example of drawing a permanent boundary between his and the neighbouring kingdom, the great Mercian could with some justification regard the Carolingians as mere upstarts. Hence when Charlemagne, not yet emperor, but king of the Franks and Lombards and patrician of the Romans, proposed that his son should marry one of Offa's daughters, Offa refused unless a daughter of Charlemagne should be given to his son Ecgfrith. This led to a rupture between the two potentates, who until then had treated one another with careful courtesy. Charlemagne closed his ports to English traders, and Offa retaliated in kind. Earlier correspondence in which both parties had taken travelling merchants under their protection shows how brisk a two-way traffic was interrupted by the breach. In the earlier exchange Offa had asked that certain "black stones" – marble, perhaps, or the basaltic lava exported from Germany for use in grinding corn – should be cut to a specified length, and Charlemagne in return had asked that the English *saga* – woollen cloaks or blankets – should be of the same size as they used to be.

The Franks had reformed their currency, and here Offa was not above following their example. He made the silver penny the standard coin of southern England, and with many variations of design it remained so until well after the Norman Conquest. The penny showed the king's name on the obverse and the moneyer's name on the reverse. Gold coins were struck more rarely, but there is one example carrying the legend OFFA REX in roman capitals, and evidently designed for acceptance by Arab traders, for it imitates a dinar struck by the caliph Al-Mansur in 774. The 'mancus' of thirty silver pennies for which these gold pieces were often exchanged appears as a term of account in English documents. Offa, perhaps as a *quid pro quo* for the pope's acquiescence in his wishes, undertook to send 365 mancuses each year to Rome for the relief of the poor and the maintenance of lights.

## The Tribal Hidage

Part of Offa's wealth arose from the tribute which as *bretwalda* he collected from the dependent kingdoms. It is likely that the remarkable document known as the Tribal Hidage dates from his time. This is a list of peoples, beginning with the inhabitants of eighth-century Mercia, to whom it attributes 30,000 hides. Then follow the names of twenty-eight smaller peoples, with assessments ranging from 300 to 7,000 hides apiece. Between them they answer for 55,100 hides. Finally come the men of five whole kingdoms: East Anglia, Essex, Kent, Sussex, and Wessex, bringing the total up to 244,100 hides. All the figures are round figures: $x$ hundreds, $y$ thousands. Hence it does not pretend to be an enumeration of men or families or estates. It is a tribute-list, of transparently Mercian origin, but not limited to the peoples immediately subject to the Mercian king, for it includes five other kingdoms which in the eighth century had to recognize, however reluctantly or briefly, the Mercian king as their paramount lord. Behind it lay earlier antecedents. The system goes back to the age of Northumbrian supremacy, as is shown by the fact that in the pages of Bede as in the Tribal Hidage Sussex accounts for 7,000 hides. Bede also knows the hidation of Anglesey and the Isle of Man. Neither appears in the Tribal Hidage, but both had been subjugated by the Northumbrian *bretwalda* Edwin.

Offa drew up a code of laws which in the estimation of Alfred the Great ranked him as a legislator with Ethelbert of Kent and Ine of Wessex. Unfortunately no copy of his laws has been preserved. The story of his reign has to be pieced together from charters, letters, and brief annalistic entries. He died on 26 July 796, leaving behind the memory of a great and ruthless king. Alcuin, who kept in constant touch with English affairs, praised the good, moderate, and chaste customs which Offa established, but could not forget how much blood he shed to secure the kingship for his son, and judged that this was not a strengthening of his kingdom, but its ruin. To this well-informed observer it appeared very likely that the happiness of the English was nearly at an end.

## Mercia and Wessex

Wessex, though it appeared in the Tribal Hidage, never sank into complete dependence. Towards the close of King Ethelbald's reign King Cuthred routed him in battle, but Cynewulf, who reigned over Wessex from 757 to 786, had to attest a charter by which Ethelbald granted Tockenham in Wiltshire to an abbot of Malmesbury, and a grant by Cynewulf himself to Bath Abbey required Offa's consent. But when Cynewulf sold thirty acres south of the Avon to the abbey Offa disallowed the transaction; he also gave the great manor of Potterne in Wiltshire to the church of Sherborne. It looks as if Offa was trying to assert in Wessex as in Kent an exclusive right to grant land by charter. But if so his success was only partial, for Cynewulf made numerous grants in his own name without reference to the Mercian king. The king of Wessex was better able to hold his own, even against Offa, than any other king in the south. He fought great battles against the Britons of Cornwall, but in 779 Offa defeated him at Bensington in Oxfordshire. One night in 786, while visiting his mistress at *Meretun* (?Martin in Hampshire), Cynewulf was killed in a surprise attack by a band of eighty-four men led by a rival claimant to the throne. The affray continued until all the king's attendants lay dead, except one British hostage. In the morning the king's thegns arrived to find his adversary barricaded in the house. He offered them money and land on their own terms if they would recognize him as king, but they replied that they would sooner die than serve the slayer of their lord. Then they fought around the gates until they broke in and killed all but one of those within, including the leader. The incident stood out in marked contrast with the fates of Ethelbald of Mercia and Osred of Northumbria, both murdered by men of their own households. It showed that the ideals of the heroic age were not dead in Wessex. The success of the West Saxon kings in attracting and keeping the loyalty of their thegns through thick and thin would ensure the salvation of the kingdom and ultimately of all England in the ordeals that lay ahead.

Cynewulf was succeeded by one Beorhtric, in opposition to Egbert, a descendant of King Ine's brother. Beorhtric enjoyed the support of Offa, who gave him his daughter in marriage and helped him to drive Egbert into exile. Egbert took refuge at the Frankish court and bided his time.

The heir whose succession Offa had been at such pains to ensure survived his mighty father for less than five months. The kingship then passed first to Cenwulf (796–821), then to Ceolwulf I (821–3), two brothers who represented a collateral branch of the royal house.

The ruin which Alcuin had predicted did not ensue immediately. Under Cenwulf Mercia remained powerful. A Kentish revolt which had broken out shortly before Offa's death was crushed by Cenwulf, who also maintained his authority over Sussex, Essex, East Anglia, and Berkshire. His position was strengthened by the appointment of an abbot from Lindsey named Æthelheard to the see of Canterbury. But to be a friend of Mercia was to be treated as an enemy by the Kentish rebels, and for a while the archbishop

had to go into exile. At this juncture Cenwulf initiated a correspondence with Pope Leo III. The creation of an archbishopric
of Lichfield had been strongly resented by the southern clergy,
and Cenwulf, being now on good terms with their archbishop,
was prepared to undo Offa's action. He represented to the pope
that the elevation of Lichfield had been obtained by false pre-
tences, and that the two metropolitan sees planned by Gregory the
Great sufficed for England, though he would not object if the
southern metropolis were fixed at London instead of Canterbury.
In the event the suppression of the Kentish revolt opened the way
for Æthelheard's return; the pope was unwilling to deprive
Canterbury of its ancient dignity; and in 803, with the unanimous
consent of king, pope, and all the southern clergy, Lichfield
reverted to its original status as a bishopric in the province of
Canterbury.

According to the Anglo-Saxon Chronicle, in 796 Archbishop
Æthelheard had convoked a synod "and established and confirmed at the command of Pope Leo all the things relating to
God's monasteries which were appointed in the days of King
Wihtred and of other kings." If this implies that the churchmen
were endeavouring to regain the fullness of their ancient immunities, the event belied their hopes, for Cenwulf continued to reserve
the three common dues. But the actual record of the synod shows
that the bishops were really trying to curb the institution of proprietary churches. Kings and nobles, setting themselves up ostensibly as patrons and protectors of the monasteries, had begun to
treat their lands as part of their own domain. This practice contra-
vened the ancient canon law of the church, but the popes had to
allow and make the best of it. Offa established several monasteries,
all dedicated to St Peter, and he obtained from Adrian I a privilege
placing them under his lordship and that of his descendants. Leo
III gave Cenwulf a similar privilege with particular reference to
the monastery at Winchcombe, at the same time allowing him to
dispose of his other monasteries at will. The most remarkable of
these transactions was one by which Cenwulf, with the acquiescence of the feeble King Beorhtric, who was dominated by his
Mercian wife, contrived to turn Glastonbury, the most revered
monastery in Wessex and the mausoleum of its kings, into a

private family possession. In 798 he secured from Leo III a privilege which gave his son Kenelm the hereditary ownership of Glastonbury and all its scattered estates, amounting to 800 hides in all. The proprietary church, by now a regular feature of the ecclesiastical landscape, would be the target of reformers for centuries to come.

Cenwulf was not the man to waive what he conceived to be his rights. The archbishop of Canterbury, Wulfred, who succeeded Æthelheard in 805, resisted his claim to the ownership of certain monasteries, including those of Minster and Reculver in Thanet. Cenwulf denounced the archbishop at Rome, and for at least four years made it impossible for him to exercise his archiepiscopal functions. Finally he summoned Wulfred to London, and demanded that as the price of reconciliation the archbishop should surrender an estate of 300 hides and pay a fine of 120 pounds; failing this, he would be stripped of all his possessions and exiled from the country. He added that no intervention by pope or emperor would avail to secure his reinstatement. The archbishop, much against his will, had to accept these terms. No such violent dispute had troubled the peace of the English church within the memory of man.

The struggle against the Welsh, suspended by Offa, was resumed by Cenwulf. In 818 he harried the Welsh of Dyfed, and was probably making ready for another Welsh expedition in 821 when he died at Basingwerk. In the following year his brother Ceolwulf I captured Degannwy and nearly extinguished the ancient kingdom of Powys. But in 823 Ceolwulf was deposed, and with him the dynasty which had raised Mercia to greatness came to an end. For another half century the kingdom preserved its independence under kings of unknown ancestry, but the glory of Mercia had departed.

Its influence in Wessex ended with the death of King Beorhtric in 802, when his widow Eadburh, Offa's daughter, withdrew to the continent. Charlemagne made her abbess of a large convent, but she soon disgraced herself by sexual misconduct, and was reduced to beggary, ending her days in Pavia with only one attendant: a wretched end for a daughter of the great Offa. During her husband's reign she had made herself so odious to the West Saxons that they swore never again to accord the title of queen to a king's consort.

On Beorhtric's death his rival, Egbert, returned from exile and was accepted as king in Wessex. His accession marks a turning-point in Anglo-Saxon history. He and his descendants gradually built up the strongest kingdom England had yet known, in the process weathering storms which brought its rivals to the dust.

# Chapter VII

# A SPIRITUAL EMPIRE

The self-exiled Wilfrid's brief sojourn in Frisia ushered in what has been rightly called the heroic age of the Anglo-Saxon church. Though opposed in matters of observance to the disciples of Iona and Lindisfarne, as a Northumbrian Wilfrid was afire with that same missionary fervour which had led so many Irishmen like Columbanus to spend their lives preaching the gospel in foreign lands. Before the eighth century began Irish influence dominated at least fifty centres from Brittany to Salzburg and from the Belgian coast to Lombardy.

The Anglo-Saxons, mindful always of the Germanic homelands from which their forefathers had come to Britain, felt bound by strong ties of blood to attempt the conversion of their still heathen kinsmen. Their endeavours in this field may appear more relevant to continental than to English history, but they relied so much on the encouragement of their fellow-countrymen at home, and their characteristic devotion to the papacy had such far-reaching effects, that to ignore their achievement would be like writing a history of eighteenth-century England without any reference to Clive's exploits in India and their results.

It needed more than a visit of a few months to wean the Frisians from a heathenism rendered all the more obstinate by their hostility to the military power of the neighbouring Christian Franks. Their conversion was presently undertaken by Willibrord, a Northumbrian educated first in Wilfrid's monastery at Ripon and later in Ireland. In 690 Willibrord and eleven companions landed at the mouth of the Rhine. Soon after they had begun their work Willibrord went to Rome to seek the approval of Pope Sergius.

In his absence a fellow-countryman named Swithbert was chosen to assist him, and received episcopal consecration in England from Wilfrid. Willibrord, on his return from Rome, concentrated at first on the part of Frisia south and west of the Yssel which had been conquered by the Franks. He enlisted the support of the Frankish ruler, Pippin, who hoped that the establishment of Christianity would strengthen his hold on the conquered territory. Accordingly he sent Willibrord back to Rome with an embassy which asked the pope to consecrate him bishop of the Frisians. In November 695 Sergius did so and also gave him the pallium, the symbol of metropolitan jurisdiction. As archbishop, Willibrord fixed his see at Utrecht and for the next forty years worked from that base, building churches, founding monasteries, and training priests. He died in 739 in a monastery of his own foundation at Echternach on the Moselle.

Roman Christianity had begun as a religion of the urban proletariat; only after much blood had been shed did it become the religion of the emperors. In England it began as the religion of the kings and was more or less willingly accepted by their subjects. Remembering Gregory the Great and convert kings like Ethelbert and Edwin, the Anglo-Saxon missionaries on the continent founded their success on the combined support of the Frankish rulers and the papacy. These twin factors operated conspicuously in the career of Willibrord and in that of an even greater missionary whose point of departure was not Northumbria but Wessex.

Tradition fixes the birthplace of St Boniface at Crediton. His father must have belonged to the first generation of Anglo-Saxon settlers in Devon. The boy, under his baptismal name Wynfrith, was placed in a monastery at Exeter, but soon went on to the Hampshire monastery of Nursling, then in great repute for the ability, learning, and holiness of its abbot. As a monk at Nursling Wynfrith pursued an extensive range of studies – he wrote a Latin grammar and a book on prosody – and after a time became head of the monastic school. He would no doubt have risen to high rank in the English church, but he resolved to devote his life to the conversion of the heathen in Germany. In 716 he sailed to the coast of Frisia. He found that the heathen king had lately recovered the country south of the Yssel from the Franks, destroyed the Christian churches, and rebuilt the heathen shrines. Perceiving that he could do no good there for the present, he returned to Nursling with a clearer understanding of the difficulties but more determined than ever to overcome them. Taking with him a letter of recommendation from the bishop of Winchester, he set out for Rome to place himself at the disposal of Gregory II. The pope received him very cordially, gave him a general commission to labour among the heathen of central Europe, and conferred on him the name Boniface by which he has been known ever since.

A journey of preliminary inspection through Lombardy, Bavaria, Thuringia, and Franconia convinced Boniface that heathenism was still very much alive in Thuringia and that the Bavarian church founded by Irish missionaries was badly demoralized. But hearing that death had removed the most inveterate enemy of Christianity in Friesland, he felt it his duty to help Willibrord restore the ruined church in that country. He spent three years there, after which he set up his base of operations in Hesse, near the frontier of the Saxons, and laboured so successfully that Gregory II summoned him to Rome and consecrated him bishop of the Germans. Boniface for his part bound himself by a solemn oath of fealty to the pope and his successors.

The pope also gave him letters of recommendation to the great Frankish ruler, Charles Martel. That man of iron allowed him to return to Hesse. Here the intrepid Devonian struck a decisive blow against heathenism. With his own hands, in the presence of a huge crowd, he hewed down the oak of Geismar sacred to Thor, and used its timber to build a chapel which he dedicated to St Peter.

In Thuringia as in Hesse the energy and enthusiasm of Boniface was supported by repeated letters from Rome and seconded by numerous Englishmen from the monasteries of Kent and Wessex who joined his mission and carried the faith into the country districts far and wide. By ten years of continuous toil in these two provinces Boniface built up a church on the approved Roman model: an achievement recognized in 732, when Gregory III gave him an archbishop's pallium, with authority to ordain other bishops. He availed himself of this permission to found episcopal sees at Würzburg, Buraburg, Erfurt, and Eichstadt, at each of which an Englishman was appointed first bishop. Not until 747 did he fix his own see at Mainz.

In 738 Boniface, now sixty years of age, visited Rome for the third time. Gregory appointed him papal vicar and legate for all Germany, with a mandate to complete the reorganization of the church in south Germany. This brought about the foundation of bishoprics at Salzburg, Freising, Regensburg, and Passau, and the decadent church of Bavaria was brought to comply with Roman standards of organization, discipline, and faith.

On the death of Charles Martel his son Carloman promised to help Boniface reform the church in the eastern half of the Frankish kingdom, and his brother Pippin followed his example in the western half. For the best part of a century the rulers of the Franks had paid no more than lip-service to the papacy. They filled vacant bishoprics with nominees of their own, often in reward for political services, and the bishops spent much of their time in war or hunting. The office of metropolitan fell into abeyance. Learning decayed, and monasteries grew lax in their observance. This was the situation with which Boniface dealt, first in synods of the east and west Frankish clergy, then in a general synod of the whole Frankish church over which he presided as papal legate. By its decrees he enforced the authority of bishops over the lower clergy, put down idolatrous practices, and breathed new life into the organization of the church. His idea was that in Gaul and Germany, as in England, bishops should keep the clergy of their dioceses in order, and dioceses with fixed boundaries should be grouped into provinces under metropolitans deriving their authority from Rome, the only power which in the last resort could preserve ecclesiastical unity and support them against aggression by kings and nobles.

In 747 a synod of the Frankish church sent to Rome a document signed by all the bishops present, declaring "that we will maintain catholic faith and unity and subjection to the Roman church till the end of our lives; that we will be subjects of St Peter and his vicar; that we will hold a synod every year; that the metropolitans will ask for their pallia from that see; and that in all things we desire to follow the precepts of St Peter according to the canons, so that we may be counted among the flock entrusted to him."

This impressive declaration bears the imprint of Boniface's thinking in every line.

Four years later, Carloman having retired into a monastery, Pippin, with the approval of Pope Zachary, deposed the last of the Merovingian kings and was himself anointed king of the Franks by Boniface as papal legate. Carolingian policy and Anglo-Saxon devotion to the see of Rome met here on common ground, with decisive political and ecclesiastical consequences for the future of western Christendom.

Throughout these years devout men and women at home in England followed Boniface's activities with prayer, letters, and material help. In return he kept in constant touch with them by letters in which he comes very much alive. He consulted the leaders of the English church on knotty points of canon law, and he did not spare rebuke when he felt rebuke was deserved. The public and private conduct of King Ethelbald of Mercia drew from him a scathing denunciation. In 747 he urged the archbishop of Canterbury to restrain certain bishops who drank too much and encouraged what he described as this peculiarly English vice in others. Not that he demanded total abstinence; Boniface was too good a Christian to be an enemy of wine. He sent two casks of it to Egbert of York "for a merry day with the brethren."

For the diffusion of learning in his monasteries Boniface urgently needed books, and for a supply of books he turned to England. He wrote to his old bishop, Daniel of Winchester, who had gone blind and therefore had no further use for a copy of the six Prophetic Books which Boniface remembered to have seen clearly written by his old master Wynbert, abbot of Nursling. "I cannot procure in this country such a book of the Prophets as I need, and with my failing sight I cannot well read script which is small and filled with abbreviations." He wrote more than once to Archbishop Egbert of York and to the abbot of Monkwearmouth asking for copies of Bede's commentaries on the books of scripture. Eadburh, abbess of Minster in Thanet, sent him a manuscript of St Peter's epistles which she had written in letters of gold.

Boniface wrote Latin easily and well. The Englishwomen who wrote to him apologized for their Latin style, which however reflects no small credit on the minsters in which they had been trained. More than one abbess wrote to tell him of her troubles and ask for spiritual guidance. Through such relationships Boniface attracted women to his mission. One of them, Thecla, became abbess of Kitzingen. Another, Leofgyth or Leoba, a relative of Boniface on his mother's side, readily obeyed Boniface's call to Germany. He placed her in charge of a double monastery at Tauberbischofsheim in Baden. Besides being learned in biblical and patristic lore, she was a woman who combined remarkable practical qualities with a particularly charming disposition. The affection she inspired in the old saint shines through their correspondence. On the eve of his last mission Boniface begged her to remain in Germany after his death and hoped that the two of them might be laid to rest in the same grave.

He knew of other Englishwomen who could not be accounted saints. The custom of pilgrimage had its dangers for them. When they took the path to Rome, leaving their cold and misty island for the genial climate of Italy, the sunshine, wine, and Latin gallantry had the same effect on them as it does on some of their countrywomen today. So many succumbed that according to Boniface "there are very few cities in Lombardy where an English adulteress or prostitute is not to be found, a scandal and disgrace to the whole English church."

Of the men who accompanied or followed Boniface across the sea and helped him in his work, many are not known even as names, but Burghard, bishop of Würzburg, Hwita, bishop of Buraburg, Willibald, bishop of Eichstadt, Eoba, bishop of Utrecht, and Lul, who succeeded Boniface at Mainz, were all his fellow-countrymen.

To Boniface the reform of the Frankish church was a duty he could not shirk, but it was also an interruption of his real work. He was now more than seventy years old, but zeal for the conversion of the heathen still burned within him. In 753, with a company of priests, monks, and deacons, he passed into Frisia beyond the Yssel, where Frankish arms could not protect him. Thousands were baptized, but on 4 June 754, when he was about to confirm a number of new Christians at Dokkum near Leuwarden, a savage throng of heathen fell upon his encampment. He forbade resistance, and was butchered along with fifty-three of his companions.

The corpse of the aged martyr was retrieved and entombed at Fulda in Hesse, a Benedictine abbey of his own foundation. In 755 a general synod of the English church decreed that his feast-day should be celebrated annually. At the present time the bishops of all Germany gather once a year around his tomb at Fulda, in fitting homage to the apostle of whom it has been truly said that no other Englishman has ever made so indelible a mark on the history of Europe.

Foreseeing his death, Boniface sent a message to the Frankish king, thanking him for all his acts of kindness and begging that Lul, formerly his archdeacon, now his auxiliary bishop, might succeed him as head of the mission. He hoped that, God willing, the priests would have in Lul a master, the monks a teacher of the rule, and the Christian people a faithful preacher and shepherd.

Lul was educated at Malmesbury (*Mealdumesburg*) in the tradition of the Irish scholar Maildubh after whom the place is named, and of his pupil Aldhelm, who became abbot of the monastery and first bishop of Sherborne. As a man of letters and a copious writer of prose and verse, Aldhelm represents the learning of his age in its most advanced form, and transmitted it to the Anglo-Saxon missionaries on the continent. He dedicated a prose work in praise of virginity to one of Boniface's correspondents, Hildelith, abbess of Barking. Master of a deplorably inflated style and a vocabulary distinguished by the use of latinized Greek words, he exercised a powerful and almost wholly baneful influence on contemporary and later writers. Even Boniface in his early letters was not above turning an occasional phrase in Aldhelm's manner. Lul, a man of scholarly tastes and an eager collector of books for German monasteries, admired Aldhelm and sent to England for copies of his works. But he also appreciated the far superior genius of Bede. He sent the abbot of Monkwearmouth a robe of pure silk in which to enwrap Bede's relics, and asked for some of his books. In reply the abbot sent him Bede's prose and verse lives of St Cuthbert and apologized for not sending more on the ground that the winter had been so cold and stormy that the scribe was unable to write. He added that he would be obliged if Lul would send him a glass-maker, "for we are ignorant and destitute of that art," and a harpist, "for I have a harp and no one to play it."

Meanwhile Lul acquired Bede's *Ecclesiastical History*, which naturally whetted his appetite for books.

Lul duly became bishop of Mainz but did not receive the pallium until 781, and he never enjoyed the primatial standing of his great predecessor. He founded a monastery at Bleidenstadt near Wiesbaden, and another at Hersfeld of which the first abbot had an Anglo-Saxon name. Throughout his episcopate of forty years he remained in frequent correspondence with English churchmen. Milred, bishop of Worcester, apologized for not send-ing him a liturgical book on purple-dyed parchment because he had lent it to another bishop. Cynewulf, king of Wessex, and Alhred of Northumbria commended themselves to his prayers. He received letters from the abbots of Glastonbury, Monkwear-mouth, and Ripon, the bishop of Winchester, and the archbishops of Canterbury and York. Through him the English church main-tained for a generation after Boniface its active interest in the conversion of the Germans.

The conquests of Charlemagne, son of Pippin III, facilitated the work on which Boniface had set his heart but had been unable to complete. After struggle and bloodshed extending over more than thirty years Charlemagne incorporated the heathen Saxons into his empire, which now extended from Hungary to the north of Spain and from Holstein to southern Italy. Within its borders there was no place for heathenism. In 767 the Anglo-Saxon Aluberht was consecrated at York as bishop of the Old Saxons. From England too came Leofwine, who worked in the eastern Netherlands and was afterwards revered as a saint at Deventer, his last resting-place. The Northumbrian Willehad carried the gospel to the Danish border. In 780 Charlemagne sent him to convert the Saxons between the Elbe and the Weser. Two years later his mission was interrupted by a Saxon insurrection which drove him out and killed many of his associates. In 785 he was able to resume his work and restore his ruined churches. Finally in 787 Charlemagne caused him to be consecrated bishop of the Frisians and Saxons. He died in 789, a week after dedicating his cathedral at Bremen, being the first bishop of that great see and the last Anglo-Saxon evangelist of heroic stature.

Thus in the course of the eighth century, thanks largely to

English initiative, Europe from the Channel to the Alps had become a Christian land served by an educated clergy and effectively organized under bishops and metropolitans who acknowledged the more than nominal supremacy of the Roman see. England had repaid its debt to Gregory the Great with interest.

In or about 789 three ships' crews from Norway landed on the isle of Portland. The king's reeve of Dorchester, believing them to be traders, rode up with a few attendants to demand payment of toll. They slew him for his pains. Englishmen looked back to this incident as the first visitation of Norse pirates, a presage of the long series of disasters that lay ahead, threatening the very existence of the church in England and overwhelming most of its kingdoms. The time for missionary effort on the continent had passed.

Chapter VIII

# ALFRED'S ENGLAND

An incursion into Wiltshire led by the Mercian ealdorman of the Hwicce and defeated by the men of Wiltshire under their own ealdorman was the only untoward event which marred the accession of Egbert to the kingship of the West Saxons (802). He spent the first decade of his reign consolidating his power in Wessex and increasing it in the south-west. In 815 he invaded Cornwall and harried it from one end to the other. Ten years later he repulsed a Cornish raid into west Devon. Finally in 838 the Britons made common cause with an army of Danish marauders, but Egbert met them at Hingston Down on the heights to the west of the lower Tamar and routed the confederate host. These victories left the king of Wessex in a position of undisputed mastery over the whole of Cornwall. Kings of the native line continued to maintain a shadowy existence in the far west: the Welsh annals record the death of one of them in 875; but Egbert compelled the Cornish bishop to acknowledge the archbishop of Canterbury as his canonical superior, and enriched his own dynasty by annexing large domains in Cornwall, of which he gave a tenth to the bishop of Sherborne, with a mandate to show the Cornish church the error of its ways.

## Egbert's Achievement

Meanwhile the king of Mercia did not stand idly by while his southern neighbour went from strength to strength. In 825 he invaded Wiltshire, but was heavily defeated at Wroughton, three miles south of Swindon. Immediately after this battle the men of

Kent, Surrey, Sussex, and Essex submitted to Egbert, and East Anglia sought his protection. In 829 he conquered Mercia itself, and led his army to the Northumbrian border, where at Dore, near Sheffield, he exacted Northumbrian recognition of his overlordship. His meteoric rise to power seemed to the West Saxons to justify the addition of Egbert's name to the list of *bretwaldas*.

But Mercia was not finished yet. In 830 Wiglaf, the king of Mercia whom Egbert had driven out, regained the throne of a diminished but still powerful realm, to which Berkshire, at some point, was annexed. In 836 he is found presiding over an assembly at Croft in Leicestershire which was attended by the archbishop of Canterbury and three other southern bishops. But two years later Egbert and his son Ethelwulf entered into a concordat which bound the archbishop to the West Saxon dynasty in a pact of perpetual friendship.

Under Egbert and his immediate successors the head of the West Saxon royal house ruled directly in Wessex while his eldest son governed the eastern provinces for him with the title of king of Kent. Thus, in the course of a reign which lasted thirty-seven years and seven months, Egbert made himself and his successors masters of all southern England, from Thanet to Land's End. He disposed of a formidable military power, and knew how to profit by the resentment which the Mercian hegemony had aroused in the lesser kingdoms.

## The Vikings

Four years before Egbert's death Scandinavian pirates ravaged Sheppey. Thenceforth on both sides of the Channel men lived in dread of these raiders. It has already been mentioned that in the previous reign three ships' crews from Norway had descended on the coast of Dorset. The Norwegians, poor and politically disunited, were naturally tempted to seek fortune overseas. They took to the western seaboard, and established colonies in Shetland, Orkney, Caithness, Sutherland, and Ireland, where they founded a Norse kingdom of Dublin. The Danes more easily found their way to the mouth of the Rhine, and thence down the Channel to the coasts of Britain and Gaul.

Viking, the name given generally to these dangerous visitors from Scandinavia, is a word of uncertain meaning, and we can only surmise that the pressure of growing population in their homelands drove them to embark on piratical adventures abroad. It was rarely possible to intercept them at sea. In any case, their improvements in the technique of ship-building and the use of sail with oars gave them an advantage in naval warfare. On land, armed with shirts of mail, helmets, battle-axes, and long kite-shaped shields, they proved ferocious warriors, all the more terrible because as heathens they showed no respect for persons or things held sacred by their Christian victims. Landing at some point of their own choosing on an undefended coast, they plundered churches and minsters and ravaged freely until the local militia mustered and led by its ealdorman came up with them and either put them to flight or was itself routed. In 836 King Egbert in person took the field against the crews of thirty-five ships at Carhampton, between Watchet and Minehead, and a murderous battle followed, which however failed to dislodge the Danes. During the next three decades Viking descents occurred almost annually on the south and east coasts. They were not always victorious, but whichever side defeated the other a heavy price was paid in bloodshed. Twice during this period a Danish host wintered in England: in Thanet in 851 and in Sheppey four years later.

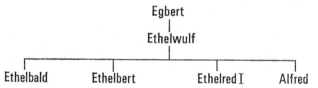

## The Reign of Ethelwulf

Ethelwulf, who succeeded Egbert in 839, was not a man to be trifled with, any more than his father. The annexation of Kent, Sussex, and Surrey was never challenged in his time, and he himself recovered Berkshire from the Mercian kings. In 851 he defeated the crews of 350 Viking ships, inflicting, says the chronicler, "the greatest slaughter on a heathen army that we ever heard of until this present day." Two years later he went to the assistance of the king of Mercia in a victorious campaign against the Welsh. For the remainder of his reign Wessex, except for one incursion, appears to have been unmolested by the Vikings. Ethelwulf's prowess in battle had taught them to be wary, and he may –though this is only conjecture – have allowed them to winter on the Kentish coast on the understanding that they would ward off others of their kind.

Recent study of Ethelwulf's charters has brought to light important details of his domestic policy. By an act of state carried out at Dorchester on 26 December 846 and embodied in a formal diploma Ethelwulf caused twenty hides of land in the South Hams of Devon to be assigned to himself in hereditary ownership. The boundary takes in an area nine miles wide, comprising some 65,000 acres of potentially very fertile land, at that time sparsely occupied by a population of Cornish-speaking Britons. The subsequent history of the area shows that Ethelwulf's primary motive was not to enrich himself, for only two estates, West Alvington and Chillington, linked by the bridge which has given its name to the later market town of Kingsbridge, were permanently annexed to the royal domain. From the rest of this large area the king meant to carve out new estates ripe for development and grant them as booklands to favoured thegns. In this process the initial assessment of twenty hides would gradually be increased to keep pace with the expansion of settlement and agriculture.

Until that time the royal prerogative of creating bookland had been exercised mainly for the endowment of the church. Few thegns, and those only of the highest rank, had received 'books', charters granting them land in perpetual inheritance. The great majority of their class held what was known as folkland, that is, land under customary law which the king might turn into either bookland or loanland. Loanland was a precarious tenure in the sense clearly expressed in a passage which Alfred the Great inserted into his translation of St Augustine's *Soliloquies*. "Every man," says Alfred, "when he has built himself a house on land lent to him by his lord, with his help, likes to stay in it sometimes, and to go hunting and fowling and fishing, and to support himself in every way on that loanland, both by sea and by land, until the time when through his lord's favour he may acquire bookland and a perpetual inheritance." In other words, the thegn, though he has the full beneficial enjoyment of the estate so long as he lives, cannot alienate it or leave it to his children without the king's permission, and if he dies without issue it will revert to the king. Only a 'book', a royal charter, can give him full power to sell, exchange, or bequeath it as he may think fit.

Many and various were the burdens incumbent on even privileged landholders. These burdens may be classified under three main headings: purveyance, public labour, and justiciary duties. Purveyance might be exacted in many forms. An example has been quoted earlier from Ine's laws of the food-rent due from ten hides of land. If the king, or a prince of the royal house, or an ealdorman, or an ambassador came upon the estate in the course of his travels, he was entitled to demand food, drink, and lodging. He might also requisition additional post-horses. To this list of uninvited but expensive guests one charter adds bishops. The king might quarter his horses, hawks, and falcons wherever he pleased. Cartage, and work on royal buildings, fell into the category of public labour. So did the obligation which it is convenient to epitomize in these pages as the three common dues: the construction and repair of bridges, the construction and repair of fortifications, and the duty of sending a certain number of armed men when the king or the ealdorman called out the host. So far as can be seen, Ethelwulf was the first king of Wessex to demand the universal enforcement of these three common dues.

Finally, every occupant of land was expected to help in the pursuit and arrest of thieves. There were other 'penal cases', or *witeraeden* as they were called in the mother tongue, arising from offences committed within the estate. Here, too, the responsibility for bringing the offender to justice rested squarely upon the landholder and his men. Justice would normally be done at the nearest *cyninges tun* – we shall hardly be coining a word if we call it a kingston – one of those estates which the king owned in every shire. The kingston, managed for him by a reeve, was a fundamental unit in the Old English organization of justice and finance. To it the tillers of the soil would deliver the produce which made up the monarch's food-rent.

In 844, the fifth year of his reign, Ethelwulf, while reserving the inevitable three common dues, granted to all holders of bookland, both churchmen and laymen, a reduced assessment of a tenth in respect of all other public charges. In calculating the incidence of such charges every ten hides were in future to be reckoned as nine. This is known as Ethelwulf's First Decimation. There is reason to think that it remained a dead letter.

In 853 Ethelwulf sent his youngest son, Alfred, then little more than four years old, to Rome with an imposing retinue. The Anglo-Saxon Chronicle and Alfred's contemporary biographer Asser both state that during this visit the pope, Leo IV, not only confirmed but also consecrated – Asser says more explicitly anointed – the child as a king and adopted him as his spiritual son. A precedent had been set in 781 when two infant sons of Charlemagne received kingly anointing and were similarly adopted by Adrian I. Of more immediate practical consequence was the family compact by which Ethelwulf bound his four sons. The details are complex and ambiguous, but the brothers apparently agreed that whichever of them lived the longest should succeed to the undivided inheritance, thus excluding from the kingship any children the others might leave. In the event only one of Ethelwulf's grandsons lived to dispute this arrangement, which ensured that the estate of the royal house should not be dissipated by division among coheirs, and that future kings of Wessex should dispose of ample resources in land and money, enabling them to reward their trusty thegns and to surround the monarchy with unprecedented splendour.

Early in 855 Ethelwulf travelled to Rome in great state. Before leaving, he enacted a Second Decimation. His charter on this occasion is obscurely worded and survives only in copies written after the Norman Conquest, but it seems that his intention was to bestow a tenth of his now vast domains on ecclesiastical foundations, and at the same time to transform the tenure of the lay thegns already settled on the lands affected by his gift from loanland into bookland. The charter was really an enabling act, meant to be put into operation by separate charters in favour of particular beneficiaries; and one or two of these have survived in authentic texts.

Ethelwulf reached Rome by June 855, and stayed there for twelve months. He was now a widower. On the way home he married Judith, daughter of Charles the Bald, king of the West Franks. For the short remainder of his reign he contented himself with the government of the eastern provinces, allowing his eldest son, Ethelbald, to rule in Wessex proper. Ethelwulf died in 858, leaving a will that prescribed yet a Third Decimation. He bade his successors provide from every tenth hide of his domain, so long as the land should be occupied and under cultivation, food, drink, and lodging for one poor man. He also charged them with an annual payment of 300 mancuses to the Roman see. Historians have only lately begun to accord Ethelwulf the distinguished place to which he is entitled in the long record of the West Saxon monarchy.

## Sons of Ethelwulf

King Ethelbald survived his father only two and a half years (858–60). The next brother, Ethelbert, reigned from 860 to 865, and the third, Ethelred I, from 865 to 871. Ethelred's accession coincided with a decisive change in the character of the Viking menace. No longer content with sporadic raids, the Danes were now prepared to stay year after year in England, striking at every weak point with the object of seizing land on which to settle. In 865 a great host landed in East Anglia, and within a year received the submission of that kingdom. Then they proceeded to Northumbria, captured York, and set up a vassal king of the region beyond the Tyne. Next they invaded Mercia, and from a base in Nottingham compelled King Burgred to buy peace. Towards the end of 869 they returned to East Anglia and defeated an army led by the young King Edmund, whom they took prisoner and killed. Revered as a martyr for his death at heathen hands, Edmund has given his name to Bury St Edmunds, where a great abbey was later founded in his honour.

The Danes were now in a position to strike at Wessex. Entrenching themselves at Reading, they attacked King Ethelred and his brother Alfred. The West Saxons gained a memorable victory at Ashdown, but in a series of general engagements which followed neither side gained a decisive victory. In April 871

Ethelred died, leaving Alfred, now about twenty-three years old and already an experienced warrior, to reign over a kingdom fighting for its life. By the end of his first year as king he had given the Danes enough trouble to make them leave him alone for the time being, at a price. Then they again turned their attention to Mercia. After a reign of twenty-two years King Burgred abandoned his throne and withdrew to spend the rest of his life in Rome. In his place the Danes appointed one of his thegns, Ceolwulf II, who gave them hostages and swore to hold himself in readiness to serve them whenever required.

Thus within less than a decade every English kingdom but Wessex had lost its independence. Mobility, speed, and a united command made the Danish onslaught nearly irresistible. Their fleets could move faster than any army on land, and when they disembarked they seized horses and rode in any direction they chose, looting and burning monasteries, and withdrawing as quickly when threatened by superior forces. Great sums had to be paid in order to buy them off. A charter dated 872 shows the bishop of Worcester mortgaging land to raise money for this purpose; it refers to the immense tribute taken by the heathen when they occupied London, and a Wessex charter, undated but not earlier than 879, speaks of "the magnitude of the tribute which our whole people used to pay the heathen." No Anglo-Saxon kingdom but one could organize defences on the necessary scale, and even Wessex found the burden all but intolerable.

## The Scandinavian Settlement

Three annals in the Anglo-Saxon Chronicle record all too concisely the main events in the Scandinavian settlement of England.

"876. Halfdene shared out the land of the Northumbrians, and they began to plough and support themselves." The area thus occupied by Halfdene and his men was approximately that of modern Yorkshire. The other half of the Viking host, led by a king named Guthrum, went on to attack Mercia and Wessex.

"877. The Danish army went away into Mercia, and shared out some of it, and gave some to Ceolwulf." They annexed what are now the shires of Leicester, Nottingham, Derby, and Lincoln, leaving Ceolwulf II to reign as their vassal over the western half of Mercia.

"880. The army went from Cirencester into East Anglia and settled there and shared out the land."

Behind this withdrawal to East Anglia lay a dramatic turn of fortune. King Alfred faced an enemy diminished in numbers but still formidable, and there were those among his subjects who would have preferred submission to a continuance of the struggle. Long afterwards men told picturesque tales of the straits to which Alfred was reduced, and indeed, with the enemy encamped at Chippenham, in control of west Wiltshire and north Somerset, the position looked threatening enough. But Alfred had already proved that Guthrum and his men were not invincible, and he now took the initiative. From a fortified retreat at Athelney in the almost impenetrable marshes of Somerset he constantly harassed the enemy. Meanwhile he kept in touch with his ealdormen, only one of whom is known to have deserted, and through the ealdormen with his loyal thegns. After seven weeks of guerrilla warfare, a carefully prepared plan of campaign brought the combined forces of Somerset, Wiltshire, and Hampshire west of Southampton Water to a rendezvous on the borders of their shires. There Alfred met them, and in the simple but deeply expressive words of the Chronicle, "they were glad to see him." All the hopes of Christian England were concentrated on this one man, the only member of an Old English dynasty who had kept his throne amid the wreckage of the other kingdoms. Two days later Alfred brought the Danes to bay at Edington, fifteen miles south of Chippenham, and inflicted on them a resounding defeat.

"The high tide!" King Alfred cried,
"The high tide – and the turn."

Guthrum and the remnant of his army fled back to Chippenham, where they held out for another fortnight while Alfred seized all the horses, cattle, and men who could not find refuge in the camp. In the end, hunger and terror reduced the Danes to the point of total surrender. They gave Alfred as many hostages as he demanded, and swore to leave his kingdom.

*Alfred Victorious*

It is one thing to triumph on the battlefield, another to be wisely magnanimous in making peace. Three weeks after receiving their submission Alfred met Guthrum and thirty of his most important followers at Aller, where he feasted them royally. There had been hard fighting, but there should be no hard feelings. In dictating terms of peace he required only that before leaving Wessex they should receive baptism. Neither Alfred nor his ancestors had ever reigned in East Anglia, and he was content that they should keep what they had gained there provided that as Christians they did not obstruct the church in its efforts to win over the rest of the Danish population. In the autumn of this memorable year 878 the Danes moved to Cirencester, in English Mercia, and twelve months later they proceeded to the systematic occupation of East Anglia.

Several times during the campaign the Danes, avoiding battle in the open, had sheltered in fortified strongholds, as at Wareham, Exeter, and Gloucester. At Reading they had entrenched themselves behind an earthwork which they built between the Kennet and the Thames. Their example was not lost on Alfred. He devised a far-reaching plan of national defence which was carried through to completion by his immediate successors. A document which dates from within twenty years of his death gives a list of twenty-nine *burhs*, boroughs or fortified strongholds, distributed over England south of the Thames, from Pilton and Lydford in the west to Hastings and Southwark in the east. To the name of each *burh* is appended a statement of the number of hides required for its maintenance and defence, calculated at the rate of 16 hides for an acre's breadth or 22 yards of wall. "If every hide is represented by one man, then every pole of wall ($5\frac{1}{2}$ yards) can be manned by four men." The still existing ramparts at Wareham and the medieval wall at Winchester strikingly confirm these measurements. Any visitor to Wallingford, Cricklade, or Wareham will be impressed by the scale on which they were laid out. The *burhs* were meant to be permanently garrisoned and to provide secure refuges for the rural population and their livestock in time of peril, but some at least appear to have been designed as fortified towns, with a rectilinear street plan, to be organized as trading centres. By contrast, some *burhs* were very small forts; some were natural promontories with an earthwork built across the neck; and others again were Roman towns with their ancient walls repaired. The construction of so many new fortifications implies a large expenditure of man-power. Alfred's biographer speaks of them as often tardily begun and still more tardily completed, and the Chronicle records that in 892 Viking raiders took by storm a half completed fortress near the Kentish coast, occupied only by a few rustics who had been detailed to build it.

The Chronicle states that Alfred designed an entirely new type of warship, swifter, steadier, and higher than the enemy's. We can only guess at the organization by which his navy was maintained. We do know that he engaged competent Frisian sailors, and that in at least two naval engagements he routed Viking crews.

Guthrum was perhaps unable to keep all his Danes under control; at all events, in 885 the Danes in East Anglia broke the peace. Alfred reacted strongly, and in the following year took London by storm. London had long been a Mercian town, and Alfred refrained from annexing it to his own kingdom. Ceolwulf II, the last English king of Mercia, being now presumably dead, the part of Mercia not under Danish rule was governed by an ealdorman named Ethelred. Alfred entrusted the government of London to him and gave him his daughter Æthelflaed in marriage. Thus far Mercian independence was respected, but Ethelred never assumed the kingly title, and was content to reign as Alfred's viceroy. The war had raised the West Saxon king to a position of leadership recognized by all the English in the island. A silver penny bearing Alfred's name gives him the title REX ANGLOR(UM) which only the great Offa among earlier kings had ventured to assume.

After the campaign of 886 a formal treaty between Alfred and Guthrum defined the boundary of Danish East Anglia as running from the mouth of the Thames, then up the River Lea to its source, thence in a straight line to Bedford, and then up the Ouse to Watling Street. This gave Guthrum and his men the modern shires of Huntingdon, Cambridge, Norfolk, Suffolk, and Essex, the north-eastern portions of those of Hertford, Bedford, and

Buckingham, and all but the north-west quarter of Northampton-shire. A clause in the treaty binds both parties on oath not to let either slaves or freemen pass over to the other side without per-mission. Another clause appoints the same *wergeld* for the Danish freedman as for the English *ceorl*: 200 shillings in each case. This was natural enough: we shall see that for Alfred and his public a typical *ceorl* was a half-free husbandman, on a par with the Roman *libertinus*. The treaty refers to him as a *ceorl* settled on *gafol-land*: in other words, a half-free *gebur* who pays rent. If this implies that there were some English husbandmen not paying rent, they are most likely to have been still lower in the social scale: cottagers, perhaps, with little more than a garden plot or an acre or two in the fields, and owing service but little or no rent. Concerning the upper classes, the treaty simply provides that the same value, namely eight half-marks of pure gold, shall be placed on the life of a man who is slain, whether he is an Englishman or a Dane.

In the east midlands the Danes grouped themselves round five principal strongholds, the boroughs of Lincoln, Stamford, Nottingham, Leicester, and Derby. The old kingdom of Deira was ruled by a line of Danish kings, with their capital at York, but north of the Tyne an English ruler, Eadwulf, maintained an in-dependent earldom at Bamburgh and kept in touch with Alfred.

## Alfred's Educational Policy

The years of peace between 887 and 893 enabled Alfred to give more time to raising the intellectual standard of his subjects. He complained that when he came to the throne not a priest south of the Thames, to the best of his recollection, could translate a Latin letter into English. The decay of scholarship was hastened by the destruction of the monasteries, but even before the Danish ravages monastic life, under the system of proprietary churches, had lost much of its appeal. Some monasteries remained standing, and even kept their libraries and muniments intact, but their estates had reverted to the king, and their so-called abbots were merely priests or even laymen who administered the property by royal favour. At Glastonbury, which like other decayed monasteries was in the king's hand, a company of learned Irishmen, very probably encouraged by Alfred, opened a school for the sons of the nobility which later numbered Dunstan, the future archbishop, among its pupils. Alfred's own household was a school of liberal education for boys of noble birth and even for some commoners. Conscious of deficiencies in his own education, he desired that all the free-born youth of England should learn at least to read English; those destined for the priesthood might then go on to master Latin.

Having formulated this enlightened plan, Alfred set to work to have selected passages of Latin read to him and translated into English. He determined to provide English translations of those books which he deemed most necessary for all men to know. These were the *Dialogues* of Gregory the Great on the lives of the early saints; the same pope's handbook for bishops, entitled *Pastoral Care*; the history of the world from the creation to A.D. 407 written in Latin by the Spaniard Orosius; Bede's *Ecclesiastical History of the English People*; the *Consolation of Philosophy* in which Boethius had shown that men need not be slaves to fate; and the Christian meditations or *Soliloquies* of St Augustine.

Scholars are not agreed how much of this literary work is Alfred's own. His hand is certainly not visible in the translation of Bede's *History*, which is a fairly straightforward rendering of the Latin text. Werferth, bishop of Worcester, translated Pope Gregory's *Dialogues* for him. In the preface to *Pastoral Care* he acknowledges the help of Plegmund, whom he appointed to the see of Canterbury; Asser, a Welshman whom he made bishop of Sherborne; Grimbald, a monk from St Omer; and another monk named John, a native of continental Saxony whom Alfred placed in charge of a monastery he founded at Athelney. But the conception of the whole plan was his, and it laid the foundation of English prose literature. However much his assistants contributed, Alfred freely inserted notes and thoughts prompted by his own experience; and here the king, speaking with his own voice, unmistakably reveals himself as the master-mind. In the same preface he tells how he organized the multiplication of copies, intending to send one to every bishop in his kingdom.

It seems likely that the same method of publication was employed to circulate the Anglo-Saxon Chronicle, first put together in Alfred's time, probably at his direct instigation. Seven manuscripts of this work are extant, which fall into four groups, all virtually identical down to 891, after which they begin to diverge as further material was added from different sources of information. The Chronicle is nothing like a complete or unbiased account of early English history. It ignores or glosses over West Saxon reverses, exalts Alfred's ancestors, the fighting kings of Wessex, provides his father Ethelwulf with a grandiose pedigree tracing his descent back to Adam, and denies the status of *bretwalda* to any Mercian king. It must have helped considerably to put heart into Alfred's subjects when the fortunes of Wessex were at their darkest, and to convince them that in the long run their royal house would emerge victorious.

### Alfred's Laws

After making a careful study of the laws promulgated by Ethelbert of Kent, Ine of Wessex, and Offa of Mercia, Alfred drew up a code with a preamble stating that he has reproduced what seemed to him the best enactments of these earlier kings and has added a few of his own. The oldest manuscript, written, it is thought, about 925, includes the laws of Ine as an appendix; it looks as if Alfred meant them to remain in force. He does not reproduce the scale of *wergelds*, ranging from 50 to 600 shillings, which Ine had appointed as compensation for murdered Britons of various grades. The only *wergelds* specified by Alfred are 200, 600, and 1,200 shillings, and we are not told in so many words to what classes these belong, but fines equivalent to a fortieth of the *wergeld* are prescribed for breaking into a man's premises, and the detailed tariff shows that the 1,200-shilling man was a noble inferior in status to a bishop or an ealdorman, and the 200-shilling man a *ceorl* or husbandman. Under Ine 600 shillings had been the *wergeld* of a Briton with five hides of land, and we cannot be sure that it was anything else in Alfred's time.

The laws add little to our knowledge of the lowest class. It appears that the ordinary husbandman might employ a slave-woman as his domestic servant. Slaves and unfree labourers are placed on a level where holidays are concerned; they are not granted the full thirty-seven days in a year allowed to all freemen, but the four Ember Wednesdays are reserved for slaves who may wish to sell anything they have received in alms or earned by working in their free time.

## The "Ceorl"

All tillers of the soil other than slaves are comprehended under the generic word *ceorl*, husbandman, whatever their legal or economic status. For Alfred the typical *ceorl*, though not a slave, had still some way to go before he could be accounted fully free. The Alfredian translation of Orosius equates him with the Latin *libertinus*, or freedman, needing a further act of emancipation before he could enjoy the full and undisputed status of a freeman.

The laws imply that both husbandmen and some men of noble birth live under lordship. A man may not fight against his lord, even to defend a kinsman, but he may defend his lord from attack without incurring the reprisal of a blood-feud. He may leave one lord and seek another, but if so he must do it with the cognizance of the ealdorman. It is highly improbable that this freedom to change lords was enjoyed by any but men of high standing: it could hardly extend to the rustic whose master was empowered by the still unrepealed law of Ine to seize him and fine him heavily if he took himself off without permission.

## The "Ceorls" of Hurstbourne

The chequered history of an estate in Hampshire tells us something of what subjection to a landlord meant in practice. In the last quarter of the eighth century an ealdorman named Hemele gave Hurstbourne Priors to the church of Abingdon. Presently King Egbert, by an exchange of land with Abingdon, acquired Hurstbourne and left it to his son Ethelwulf. Ethelwulf in turn bequeathed it by will to Alfred for his lifetime with remainder to the church of Winchester. When Alfred succeeded to the kingdom another exchange was effected; the Winchester clergy gave up 100 hides at Cholsey to the king in return for Chisledon and Hurstbourne, which by this time was assessed at 60 hides. But presently, finding themselves unable to pay the heavy sum required to buy peace from the Vikings, they asked Alfred to pay it for them and to take back Chisledon and Hurstbourne: which he did. While Hurstbourne was in Alfred's hands he detached a portion of the estate and entrusted it as a *sundorfeoh*, a separate holding, to a certain Ecgulf, a thegn, perhaps, or a royal reeve. This *sundorfeoh*, assessed at ten hides, lay at Stoke, four miles north-west of Hurstbourne itself, the assessment of which was thus reduced to fifty hides. When the time came for Alfred to make his will, he left both Hurstbourne and the *sundorfeoh* to the church of Winchester in accordance with his father's injunction. Less than twelve months after his death his son and successor, Edward the Elder, executed two charters, one for Hurstbourne and one for Stoke, assigning both to Winchester and thus restoring the integrity of the original sixty-hide estate.

Such frequent changes of ownership are apt to unsettle people's minds. Now that Winchester had regained possession, it was important that the economy of the demesne should not be injured by subtraction of dues or clandestine withdrawals of man-power. The Stoke charter therefore provides expressly that the land shall come to the minster with all the men who were there both at Stoke and at Hurstbourne when the great Alfred went the way of all flesh; and to close any possible loophole the obligations of these men are recorded in detail. The custumal included in the Stoke charter is the earliest surviving statement of the dues which English kings and churchmen claimed from the tillers of the soil. A document of such importance for social history must be given in full.

"Here are written the dues which the husbandmen (*ceorlas*) ought to render at Hurstbourne. First, from each hide (*hiwisce*) they should pay 40 pence at the autumnal equinox, and 6 church-measures of ale, and 3 sesters of wheat for bread; and they should plough 3 acres in their own time and sow them with their own seed and bring it to the barn in their own time; and give 3 pounds of barley as rent; and mow half an acre of meadow as rent in their own time, and make it into a rick; and supply 4 fothers of split wood as rent, made into a stack in their own time; and supply 16 poles of fencing as rent, likewise in their own time; and at Easter they should give two ewes with two lambs, reckoning two young sheep to one full-grown; and they should wash the sheep and shear them in their own time; and work as they are bidden every week but three – one at midwinter, the second at Easter, the third on the Rogation Days."

It is obvious that the *ceorls* of Hurstbourne were closely involved in an agricultural routine organized in relation to their lord's demesne. The number of holidays allowed to them is appreciably fewer than the thirty-seven days which Alfred's law provided for every free man. These husbandmen, ancestors of the *villani* and *bordarii* whom the emissaries of the Norman conqueror will find at Hurstbourne, may well be descended from slaves or *coliberti*. Nor can it be assumed that each of them occupies a hide of land. The word *hiwisc* can mean household as well as hide. If it means hide in this context, "forty pence from each hide" is only another way of saying "tenpence from each yardland," which is exactly what we shall find the eleventh-century *Rectitudines* demanding from the half-free *gebur*.

## The Place-Name Charlton

The ten hides which Alfred detached from Hurstbourne to form a separate holding for Ecgulf did not last long as a *sundorfeoh*, and therefore left no trace in local nomenclature, but often enough the village thus detached took its name from the new owner; thus the place in Rutland granted by King Edward to a thegn called Æthelstan became *Æthelstanestun*, now Ayston. Once begun, the process of erosion may be carried very far indeed. Provision has to be made for the king's younger sons; great noblemen demand favours; old companions in arms expect their reward; and there are churches to be endowed. In the end nothing may be left of the original estate except the king's *tun* itself and one neighbouring village which is not granted away because the rents and services of its inhabitants are vital to the economy of the capital manor. This village, geographically distinct from the king's *tun* but close to it, and tenurially distinct from the alienated *tuns* which now pay dues to other lords, becomes known as Charlton, *Ceorlatun*, because it is where the king's own husbandmen live, tilling the soil partly on their own account, but partly also, and perhaps chiefly, for the king. Where conditions are similar the name and the thing may equally well occur on private estates. Thus the episcopal manor of Cropthorne (Worcs) has its Charlton about a mile away. The Charltons are not confined to any one part of England, and the place-name illustrates a well-marked phase of social development. It denoted a village on an estate which included more than one unit of settlement. It was not the principal unit, being situated a mile or more away from the seat of lordship, but it was subject to the same lord, and the dues and services of its husbandmen were indispensable to the economy of the estate as a whole.

## Labour Services

It is important, in reading the Hurstbourne and later custumals, to bear in mind that the enumeration of labour services must always be understood as a formal statement of total liability. If every husbandman at Hurstbourne really spent an unlimited time each week at work on his lord's demesne, he could scarcely have wrung a livelihood from his own holding, even with the help of such able-bodied men and women as could be mustered from his own household. But there can never have been a time when the available services did not outrun the demand. Every well-organized estate would aim at providing a margin over current needs. These husbandmen do week-work "as they are bidden," a pregnant phrase which may mean only that they do it if required, but it can also mean that they must undertake any task of husbandry which may be demanded of them at the discretion of the lord's reeve or bailiff. The essence of serfdom was not labour service but subjection to the will of the lord. It will be noticed that apart from renders in kind, of ale, barley, wheat, hay, timber, and sheep, each quarter-hide pays tenpence a year. This is the only rent paid in cash, but we cannot be sure that some small additional payment was not required in lieu of service if the labour was not needed in a particular year. Such temporary commutation, or "sale of works" as it is called in later manorial accounts, may well be as old as the system of labour services itself.

Alfred's laws provide only occasional glimpses of husbandry in practice. A reference to the theft of bees implies the private ownership of bee-hives. Trees may be either felled or burnt; the case is envisaged of accidental manslaughter caused by a falling tree when a band of men are at work in a privately owned wood. Here we may picture a landlord employing servile dependants to clear part of his woodland, perhaps with the intention of settling them as *coliberti* on the soil thus cleared.

## Church Dues

When he had satisfied the claims of the lord of the soil, the husbandman had still to meet those of the church. Bishops and minsters owned considerable tracts of land. Even a parish church would own a yardland or two of glebe, making the priest a partner in the husbandry of his flock. But the income from land was supplemented by regular payments of tithe and church-scot. All Christians were expected to set aside, as a matter of religious duty, a tenth of their income not only for the maintenance of the clergy, but also, and even primarily, for the relief of pilgrims and the poor. To Archbishop Theodore tithe was part of the revenue of the church as a whole rather than a means of supporting the parish priest. He expressly decreed that the poor must suffer no wrong in the customary payment of tribute to the church. In 786 a council presided over by papal legates enjoined the payment of tithe on all men, preferably in the form of private almsgiving. Not until the tenth century would the obligation be enforced by secular law.

In this respect tithe differed from church-scot. This too was a payment in kind, usually of grain or poultry, the amount being calculated in proportion to the payer's holding. The laws of Ine decree that it shall be paid at Martinmas (11 November), and that the defaulter shall pay twelve times the amount due, besides a fine of sixty shillings to the king. The amount varied from place to place, but every tiller of the soil other than a slave was bound to pay it.

These were local payments. By his testament King Ethelwulf bade his successors pay 300 mancuses a year to Rome, two-thirds of the sum to provide oil for lighting the basilicas of St Peter and St Paul, and one-third as a personal offering to the pope. This bequest was certainly carried out, for the Chronicle records that in 887 the ealdorman of Wiltshire "took to Rome the alms of King Alfred and the West Saxons." The wording of the annal implies that the people were associated with their ruler in this liability, and in fact several later kings issued laws enforcing payment of "Rome-scot" or Peter's Pence upon their subjects.

Unlike the regular payments which have been described, soul-scot arose as a voluntary offering, made by a dead man's heirs. It consisted of a portion of his goods offered to the parish priest. The amount varied in proportion to the wealth of the deceased, and its purpose was to secure prayers for his soul.

Altogether the demands of church and state bore heavily upon the tillers of the soil. We must not draw too dark a picture, nor minimize the rough sense of equity with which the demands would be enforced – if indeed they were enforced at all, for English monarchs had not yet learnt to refrain from enacting regulations that were as likely as not to remain dead letters. King Ine might threaten the defaulter who failed to pay his church-scot with a swingeing twelvefold penalty, but the priest knew as well as his flock if a succession of bad harvests had left the barns empty. The poets lauded generosity as the prime virtue of a nobleman, and public opinion required him to protect those on whose labours he depended for support. Moreover, at a time when man-power was not over-abundant, it was not in a landlord's interest to drive his tenants away or to let them die of hunger. Even so, for the Anglo-Saxon husbandman life must often have been a grim struggle, and at best his toil would leave him only a meagre margin over current needs.

## Bookland

In the passage already cited Alfred speaks of the man who dwells on land lent to him by his lord. The context shows that the lord in this case is the king, for it is the same lord who will eventually give him the 'book' that transforms loan tenure into a heritable possession, and only the king can grant such a book. In the early days of book-right, when it was still equated with church-right, the lay recipient could found a minster and bequeath it to his descendants, who if male would have to take holy orders or if female take the veil. But any testator who made a will in these terms inevitably faced the likelihood that a time would come when these conditions could not be fulfilled: the founder's kin would die out, or refuse to give up the lay state. To provide for such contingencies, and to prevent the estate from being secularized, he often arranged that the ultimate heir should be the local bishop. In course of time many properties by this means went to swell the episcopal endowments, and, not surprisingly, the appetite of laymen for unshackled freedom of testamentary disposition became too strong to resist.

One of Alfred's laws forbids the holder of inherited bookland to alienate it if his forbears have entailed it in the family. In general, however, the recipient of a book could give, sell, or bequeath the land to whomsoever he pleased. This freedom was the essence of book-right, but it was not the only power book-right conferred. If the king or other previous owner had reserved part of the land for exploitation as his demesne, that demesne passed to the book-holder as his *inland* or home-farm, to be cultivated for him by his servile dependants. This is clearly what happened when the king of Sussex endowed Wilfrid with Selsey and fifteen other villages. Bede says he gave Wilfrid the lands, the men, and "omnes facultates," that is, all the powers inherent in book-right. These powers Wilfrid used to set free 250 male and female slaves, some at least of whom must have been previously employed on the royal *inland*: what other reason could there be for their existence? Book-right, therefore, included the power to manumit slaves, as well as the direct ownership of such land as had been reserved for seignorial demesne.

Bede's language, however, implies that the slaves were only one element in the population of the sixteen villages. There must also have been free and half-free husbandmen, who had formerly helped to support the king and would thenceforth support the bishop and his clergy. Wilfrid and his companions who had accompanied him into exile were not going to farm the land themselves, any more than the king had done. In giving him book-right, the king had not only empowered him to free slaves: he had also invested him with what has been conveniently termed a "superiority" over the other tillers of the soil. Their numbers were henceforth swollen by the former slaves, who by Wilfrid's action probably became *coliberti*, half-free husbandmen still bound to give both rent and service to their lord.

Something has already been said of the rights which kings reserved to themselves when granting land by charter to a subject. Of the rights they made over to a beneficiary the most ancient and universal was the *tributum*, rent in money or in kind. Thus in the seventh century when the king of Kent granted Islingham to the bishop of Rochester, he gave it "with all the *tributum* which was paid thence to the king." This might be a substantial food-rent: Alfred's law refers to minsters which are entitled to receive the king's food-rent. From their estate at Tichborne, for example, the clergy of Winchester expected to receive each year 12 sesters of beer, 12 of Welsh ale, 20 vessels of clear ale, 200 large loaves, 100 small loaves, 2 oxen – one salt and one fresh – 6 wethers, 4 swine, 4 flitches of bacon, and 20 cheeses.

## Justiciary Rights

There can be little doubt that book-right, once fully developed, conferred on its holder not only heritable tenure and economic benefits, but also justiciary powers. We must ask how these were fitted into the prevailing system of law-enforcement. Normally the king did not do justice in person, but particularly serious and difficult cases might be referred to him for decision: we hear of one instance when litigants who appealed to King Alfred found him washing his hands in his room at Wardour and had to wait for his pronouncement until he had finished. Alfred's code speaks of folk-moots held under the presidency of ealdormen and royal reeves, and two centuries earlier King Ine had contemplated the possibility that a nobleman might intercede with the king or the ealdorman on behalf of his dependant. The ealdorman governed a shire; therefore in the public moot over which he presided we

138

catch a glimpse of the shire-court, in which the landed gentry of the shire gave judgement and the ealdorman passed sentence. At a lower level offenders would be haled before a royal reeve. Two Mercian landbooks of the early ninth century stipulate that if a malefactor is thrice caught red-handed he must be handed over to a kingston, a "regalem vicum." In the kingston, a royal estate provided with a jail and managed by the king's reeve, we find the precursor of the hundred-court, and we can understand why Domesday Book will speak of such ancient royal manors as Bensington, Headington, and Bampton as possessing "soke" or jurisdiction over two or more hundreds. But if the evil-doer is to be taken to a kingston only at the third offence, the implication is that up to that point his own lord will have dealt with him. We have seen that already in Ine's reign the state was imposing upon each lord a general responsibility for the behaviour of his men. Alfred, in the introduction to his laws, declares that from the time of the conversion to Christianity secular lords have been allowed to take from first offenders the fine prescribed for almost every misdeed.

It was in full accordance with these ideas that in 801 a *gesith* named Pilheard paid 200 shillings to the king of Mercia and undertook to pay 30 shillings a year thereafter to have his Middlesex estate freed from most of the usual public burdens, including penalties imposed in folk-moots ("popularia concilia"). This does not mean that transgressors were to go unpunished. No lord would wish his territory to be a sanctuary for murderers and thieves. It means that when wrong is done Pilheard himself will do justice on the offender. It may be added that since he is a layman the estate is not to be exempt from the three common dues, but the charter provides that when military service is required, only one man shall be sent from every six hides. And in case of theft, nothing more than the simple value of the stolen property need be paid to the owner; if a fine is imposed on the thief, the fine will go into Pilheard's pocket.

As Pilheard already holds the land with its earlier charter and has to pay the king in order to enjoy the profits of justice, it is clear that the fiscal aspect of seignorial jurisdiction is not yet automatically inherent in book-right. Some thirty years earlier an under-king of the Hwicce had granted a small estate at Aston in Stoke Prior (Worcs) to a thegn with the same clause providing that no fine should be paid to outsiders: compensation to an outside owner of stolen property would be paid at the boundary of the estate. Here, although the grantee is a layman, book-right is still thought of as church-right, and in fact the recipient receives another charter four years later on the same terms but limiting his tenure of Aston to three lives, with remainder to the church of Worcester. During the first half of the ninth century a number of charters confer the profits of justice on high-ranking churchmen, but by now the concept of book-right as church-right is obsolescent, and in 842 Ethelwulf of Wessex grants lands in Somerset to a lay magnate subject to the three common dues but free of all other secular burdens, including penal causes and the arrest of thieves. Seven years later the king of Mercia, having obtained from the church of Worcester a lease of some of its land, proceeds to assign it to one of his thegns, free of all secular dues except the obligation to have claims by outsiders dealt with on the boundary of the estate.

By the end of the ninth century clauses with this tenor have disappeared from the landbooks. We must suppose that freedom from outside interference in dealing with offenders, and the concomitant right to take the profits of justice, are henceforth covered by the normal exemption from all public burdens but the inevitable three. What the charters of the period do not tell us in so many words is whether the owner of bookland was entitled to hold a court of his own. We shall have to wait until the middle of the tenth century for an explicit mention of the right to hold a private court. But from the earliest time it must have been convenient, if not necessary, to hold periodical assemblies under the presidency of the lord or his reeve in order to settle disputes between the lord's tenants and to regulate the husbandry of the demesne. Such an assembly could deal, at least as a court of first instance, with the offences of delinquent serfs, and it could easily attract within its orbit any free husbandmen whose original dues to the king had been made over to the landlord by including their farmsteads within the area of his bookland. The details of the process remain hidden from us; it is at any rate clear that by Alfred's time the state has given many landlords a vested interest in the misdeeds of their tenants. It has done so because this is the easiest way to extend local government and to provide increased facilities for law-enforcement. The process would in time lead naturally to the creation of private 'hall-moots' side by side with the public moots of shire and hundred.

## Bookland or Manor

The Anglo-Saxon name for a chartered estate was *boc-land*. In the shires which made up Alfred's kingdom it occurs frequently on modern maps as the place-name Buckland. More than a century after the Norman Conquest the men of Devon, that conservative shire, would still speak of "jurors from four neighbouring booklands." This was long after the Normans had introduced their own word *manerium*, our manor. Some historians, having convinced themselves that what they call manorialism did not make its appearance until towards the end of the Anglo-Saxon period, have been shy of calling the ninth-century bookland a manor. Yet the mosaic of evidence pieced together in these pages has shown men called lords reserving part of their estate for exploitation as a private demesne. It has shown the demesne being cultivated for them by slaves and also by half-free husbandmen who owe labour services like those due to their lord from the husbandmen of Stoke and Hurstbourne. So far the bookland figures as an economic unit organized to yield a livelihood for the lord and his tenants. But it is also a unit of local government, with a part of its own to play in policing the land. Held responsible from the first for the good behaviour of his men, the lord has begun to take their fines and will soon hold a court, if he has not already begun to do so, in which the fines will be imposed. This dual function, economic and judiciary, is characteristic of the manor properly so called. The institution will become more widespread and more highly organized as time goes on, but already in the ninth century it is firmly established over a vast area of continental Europe. And it is only pedantry that can inhibit us from speaking of the manor as already rooted in the soil of Alfred's England.

141

## A Great King

There is a wistful note in the translation of the *Soliloquies*. Alfred speaks of men living pleasantly and at ease summer and winter, "as I have not yet done." War broke out again in 892, when a Viking fleet sailed from Boulogne and landed in two detachments, one on the southern and the other on the northern shores of Kent. Although supported by the Danes of York in alliance with the North Welsh, they were unable to make any deep impression on Wessex. During the next four years they made periodical incursions into West Mercia from bases in the Danish east, and their marauding bands harried the south coast. But whenever they ventured into the open they were heavily defeated. There was never any danger now that the English defences would collapse, and Alfred slowly, not least by diplomatic moves, isolated the forces allied against him. The Danes, however, could not be dislodged from the eastern half of the island, and Alfred did not try to do so. He was content to hold his own as king of Wessex and overlord of English Mercia, recognized as leader both by the Welsh princes and by the English of the far north. The second half of the ninth century had established an uneasy balance of political and military power between the two halves of the island, and this was still the situation on 26 October 899 when King Alfred died, the greatest man who had ruled in western Europe since the death of Charlemagne.

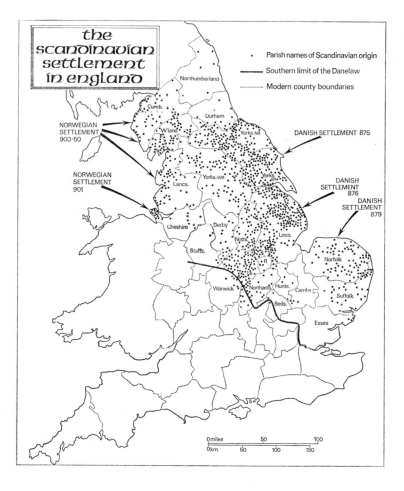

**the scandinavian settlement in england**

• Parish names of Scandinavian origin
—— Southern limit of the Danelaw
----- Modern county boundaries

Northumberland

Cumb.

NORWEGIAN SETTLEMENT 900-50

Durham

W'land

Yorks. NR

DANISH SETTLEMENT 875

NORWEGIAN SETTLEMENT 901

Lancs.

Yorks. WR

Yorks. ER

DANISH SETTLEMENT 876

DANISH SETTLEMENT 879

Cheshire

Derby

Notts.

Lincs.

Staffs.

R.

Norfolk

Warwick

Northants.

Hunts.

Cambs.

Suffolk

Beds.

Essex

0 miles        50              100
0 km      50        100        150

143

# Chapter IX

# ENGLISHMEN AND DANES

Ethelred I had left a son named Ethelwold who, on Alfred's death, attempted to seize the throne. The magnates of Wessex would have none of him; they were all for Alfred's son Edward the Elder, but the pretender managed to secure recognition from the northern Danes and during the next three years gave Edward much trouble. In 901 he collected a fleet overseas and established himself in Essex. A year later he led the army of East Anglia in a great raid over English Mercia and the north of Wessex. In reprisal Edward ravaged the East Anglian fenland. At the close of this expedition the Kentish contingent of his army disregarded Edward's order to retire and were overwhelmed by the Danes, but the battle cost Ethelwold his life.

## Norse Immigration

In this period bands of Scandinavians, mainly Norwegians, but with some admixture of Danes and Irish, were crossing from Ireland and settling in the north-west. In the peninsula of Wirral the place-name Thingwall, five miles south-west of Birkenhead, denotes the meeting-place of their *thing*, or public assembly. Another Thingwall, north of the Mersey, shows that the Norsemen spread into south Lancashire, where Old Norse place-names occur chiefly along the coast in a region which may have been only sparsely inhabited before the Scandinavian influx. Compared with the Danish occupation of eastern England, the Norse migration is barely noticed in written sources. Only the modern analysis of place-names has provided clear evidence that the invaders from

144

the north spread far and wide over Lancashire north of the Ribble, over Cumberland and Westmorland, and across the Pennines into Yorkshire.

The possibility that they might make common cause with the independent Danish forces in eastern England naturally alarmed the government of English Mercia. The ealdorman Ethelred, as loyal to King Edward as he had been to Edward's father, was now a sick man, and responsibility devolved upon his wife, Alfred's daughter Æthelflaed. In 907 she repaired the walls of Chester and placed a garrison there to control disaffection in Wirral. Three years later the Northumbrian Danes raided over the whole of Mercia, and were on their way home when King Edward, commanding the levies of Mercia as well as Wessex, overtook them at Tettenhall near Wednesfield in Staffordshire and inflicted on them a crushing defeat. It was a blow from which their kingdom never fully recovered.

## The Lady of the Mercians

In 911 Ethelred of Mercia died, and Æthelflaed acquiesced when Edward annexed London and Oxford to his own kingdom. The doughty princess, half Mercian by descent on her mother's side, was known as the Lady of the Mercians. For the rest of her life she collaborated loyally and effectively with her brother in a campaign to subdue the independent Danish armies in England.

The key to their strategy was the extension of the system devised by Alfred, of building fortresses, 'boroughs', to protect English territory from Danish inroads and to serve as bases for operations against the enemy. By the end of 911 Edward had established an outpost against the Danes of Bedford and Cambridge by building a fortress on the north bank of the Lea at Hertford. In the following year he built one at Witham to preclude any western advance by the Danish army of Colchester, and he completed the defences of Hertford by a second fortress on the other side of the Lea. Meanwhile Æthelflaed fortified *Sceargeat*, a place as yet unidentified, and Bridgenorth on the Severn, a favourite crossing-place of Danish war-bands. In 913 she built fortresses at Tamworth to protect the Mercian border from attack by the

Danes of Leicester, and at Stafford to bar entry into the valley of the Trent. Next year she repaired a prehistoric camp at Eddisbury from which a garrison could intercept raiders landing from the Mersey. She also fortified Warwick, while Edward had boroughs constructed on both sides of the Ouse at Buckingham and received the submission of Bedford. In 915 Æthelflaed secured her frontier with mid-Wales by a fort at Chirbury and guarded the head of the Mersey with one at Runcorn. By 916 a line of fortresses from Essex to the Mersey, eleven of them built or repaired by Æthelflaed, sixteen by Edward, menaced the Danes, who hurled themselves against them in vain. The last known Danish king of East Anglia perished in battle. Within a year the army of Northampton surrendered, Huntingdon was occupied, the armies of Cambridge and East Anglia submitted to Edward, and Derby, the first of the five principal Danish boroughs, was taken by Æthelflaed. There remained Leicester, Nottingham, Stamford, and Lincoln. In 918 Edward advanced to Stamford and overawed the Danes there into submission, while Æthelflaed made her entry unopposed into Leicester. Before the end of the year Nottingham had surrendered and all England south of the Humber acknowledged Edward as its master.

### Edward the Elder in Mercia

Throughout this masterly campaign, brilliantly conceived and prosecuted with unwavering determination, the Lady of the Mercians acted in perfect accord with her brother. Both of them displayed generalship of the highest order. By contrast, the lack of cohesion between the various Danish armies weakened their resistance to the victorious pair. But Æthelflaed did not live to see the final triumph. She died on 12 June 918, leaving one child, a daughter Ælfwynn. To forestall any separatist tendency, Edward promptly occupied Tamworth, received the submission of the Mercians, and took command of their levies. Then he completed Æthelflaed's defences of her northern frontier by building a new fortress at Thelwall, and repairing the Roman fortifications of Manchester, meanwhile allowing Ælfwynn to exercise nominal authority in her mother's place. But the arrangement lasted less than a twelvemonth. In the winter of 919 Edward deported his niece into Wessex, where she presumably ended her days in a convent. This masterful act may or may not have been welcome to the Mercians, but it swept away the last vestige of their independence.

In remodelling the administration of his enlarged kingdom Edward showed an equally ruthless disregard of local traditions. Here again the boroughs constituted the focal points. The borough, with its garrison, mint, and trading population, drew its resources from a surrounding district assessed at so many hides. Edward divided his kingdom into a number of such districts, which were not at first called shires but came to be known as such early in the next century by analogy with the older shires of Wessex. Each of the new Mercian shires took its name from a town. As Hampshire and Wiltshire were the districts administered from Southampton and Wilton, so Gloucestershire and Herefordshire were the districts administered from Gloucester and Hereford. Their military origin stands out clearly in the annal for 914 which tells how a strong force of Viking raiders in the Severn estuary was routed by "the men from Hereford and Gloucester and from the nearest boroughs." The boundaries of the newly created shires boldly overrode those of ancient kingdoms. The former kingdom of the West Angles was divided into Herefordshire and Shropshire; that of the Hwicce into Gloucestershire and Worcestershire, except the most easterly portion which was annexed to Warwickshire. In the east midlands the districts which had been occupied by the Danish armies of Bedford, Huntingdon, Cambridge, Northampton, Nottingham, and Leicester fell more easily into the system. The governing principle seems to have been that each new shire should contain as nearly as possible either 1,200 hides or twice that number.

## New Dioceses

In the sphere of ecclesiastical reorganization Edward's decisions were less far-reaching and permanent in their effects. In 909 he divided the two bishoprics of Wessex. Winchester kept Surrey and Hampshire but lost Berkshire and Wiltshire to a new diocese with its cathedral at Ramsbury. Somerset, Devon, and Cornwall were taken from Sherborne and assigned to two new sees, Wells for Somerset and Crediton for Devon and Cornwall. Two years later, when Edward annexed London, he appears to have charged its bishop with episcopal responsibility for the whole of East Anglia, the old bishoprics of Dunwich and Elmham having collapsed under Danish occupation. Those of Lindsey and Leicester had also come to an end, and Dorchester-on-Thames became the episcopal headquarters of the whole region between the middle Thames and the Humber. In the north a thread of continuity had been maintained by an impoverished archbishop of York and by a bishop who had wandered from Lindisfarne to one refuge after another, taking his clergy and the relics of St Cuthbert with him, until he found it possible to settle at Chester-le-Street.

Edward the Elder was an educated man; his father had seen to that. Society, as classified by King Alfred, consisted of three orders: men of prayer, fighting men, and toilers; but Edward, preoccupied with his great campaign for the reconquest of East Anglia and Mercia, had good reason to put warriors first. It was probably with the idea of making provision for some of his thegns that he extorted from the bishop of Winchester a life-lease of Beddington, a large episcopal manor in Surrey. The bishop told him that he had found the manor stripped bare by the Vikings, but had now got it back into working order, and he besought the king almost tearfully to refrain from making further demands on the estates of his church. This did not deter Edward from pressing the next bishop for a similar lease of Downton in Wiltshire. In fact, nearly all his dealings with churchmen bespeak a ruler with a predominantly secular outlook. His charters show him effecting certain exchanges, apparently with the object of securing in his own hands vantage-points on the great estuaries of the southern coast. Thus, he obtained Plympton, on the shore of Plymouth Sound, from the bishop of Sherborne in exchange for lands in Somerset, and Portchester, commanding Portsmouth harbour, from the bishop of Winchester in exchange for the inland manor of Bishops Waltham. He did indeed carry out his father's injunction to found a new minster at Winchester side by side with the old, and an uncertain tradition credits him with the foundation of a nunnery at Romsey, but this completes the tale of his bene-factions to the church.

## Edward and the Scots

In his last years Edward turned his attention to the politics of north Britain. The Picts had been subject to a line of kings who succeeded one another by right of maternal descent. In the middle of the ninth century this right had apparently devolved upon Kenneth MacAlpin, king of the Scottish Dalriada, who succeeded in making good his claim to Pictland and combined both realms in a united kingdom of Alba, comprising most of Scotland north of the Forth. His successors fixed the seat of their monarchy at Scone, near Perth, where the ancient stone, called the Stone of Destiny, on which his successors were enthroned, remained until 1296, when Edward I removed it to its present home in West-minster Abbey. In the south-west the British kingdom of Strath-clyde extended from the Clyde into a Cumberland now heavily infiltrated by Norsemen from Ireland. North of the Tees and west of the Pennines the surviving fragments of the old Northum-brian kingdom were governed by virtually independent ealdor-men, the most prominent being Eadwulf, who from Bamburgh ruled the country between the Tees and the Firth of Forth. But at some date between 912 and 915 a formidable Viking named Racgnald descended upon the coast of Northumbria, won a great battle at Corbridge, and divided a large territory between his followers. In 919 he captured York and established himself there as king.

In 920 King Edward moved from Nottingham to Bakewell in the Peak of Derbyshire and planted a fort and garrison there, near a junction of valleys which offered alternative routes towards the north and north-west. Thereupon the kings of York, Strathclyde, and Alba, and the ealdorman of Bamburgh, with all their subjects, English, Danes, Britons, Scots, and Norsemen, promised to respect his territory, and to help him against his foes; in the words of the Chronicle, they "chose him as father and lord." It was the climax of his reign. The Welsh princes had recognized his over-lordship two years before.

Edward's north-west frontier remained insecure, and he had just suppressed a movement of disaffection at Chester when he fell ill and died at Farndon on the Dee (17 July 924). As a boy he had seen his ancestral kingdom fighting for its life; at the end of his reign he was indisputably the most powerful ruler in all Britain. His energy, his strategic sense, and his patient concentration of purpose had brought him to this point, and in the process had given a new meaning to the name of England. His achievement prepared the way for the establishment of a new Anglo-Danish state under the kings of Wessex.

*Accession of Athelstan*

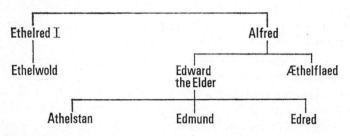

Edward had taken the precaution of having his son Athelstan brought up by the Lady of the Mercians. Athelstan was therefore well known to the Mercian nobility, who willingly accepted him as their king. There are hints that the magnates of Wessex were not so instantly amenable, but the only certain fact is that his general recognition was deferred until 4 September 925, when he was hallowed at Kingston, on the Surrey bank of the Thames but close to London and territory on the other bank which had been Mercian until his father annexed it. For the fifteen years of his reign he basked in the sunshine of his father's achievement.

The new power and splendour of the English monarchy made a great impression on Athelstan's contemporaries at home and abroad; but the Chronicle, which for the three previous reigns has the value of a detailed contemporary record, suddenly fails with his accession. It devotes a line or two to one of his warlike expeditions, and includes the text of a spirited poem about the great battle of *Brunanburh*; for the rest we depend upon foreign sources and fragments of a tenth-century panegyric on the king from which William of Malmesbury, writing early in the twelfth century, drew some important details.

## Scots and Welsh

Within six months of his consecration at Kingston Athelstan gave one of his sisters in marriage to Sihtric, the successor of Raegnald as king of York. But Sihtric died in 927, leaving by his first wife a son named Olaf, who claimed the kingdom and was supported by his uncle Guthfrith, king of the Irish Norsemen. Athelstan replied by an invasion of Northumbria and succeeded in expelling his enemies. At Eamont, near Penrith, on the frontier between his dominions and Strathclyde, Constantine of Alba, Owen of Strathclyde, and Eadwulf of Bamburgh formally acknowledged his supremacy and undertook to suppress heathen worship among their Norse subjects. Guthfrith, however, managed to collect a war-band in Scotland and laid siege to York, but was compelled to withdraw and return to Ireland, while Athelstan took possession of the city, destroyed its Danish fortifications, and distributed the treasures that he found there.

Next he dealt masterfully with the Welsh princes. Summoning them to a meeting at Hereford, he secured from them an undertaking to pay a large annual tribute in gold, silver, oxen, hounds, and hawks, and a recognition of the River Wye as the boundary between English and South-Welsh territory. That his overlordship was more than nominal is shown by the number of his charters witnessed at various dates by the kings of Dyfed, Gwynedd, Morgannwg, Gwent, and Brecon while visiting his court.

## Athelstan in the South-West

Immediately after the meeting at Hereford Athelstan turned his attention to the south-west. He held several councils in Devon, notably at Exeter in 928 and at Lifton in 931. The name of a Cornish king, Ricatus, has been found on a cross near Penzance which is unlikely to be earlier than the beginning of the tenth century, but it seems certain that the native dynasty came to an

151

end about this time, and that its extinction gave the signal for measures designed by Athelstan and his council to bring Cornwall more closely into line with the political and ecclesiastical system of Wessex. The six tribal divisions of Cornwall were reorganized as hundreds on the English model, and Wessex law was brought into operation over the whole peninsula. This transformation provoked disaffection serious enough to call for a show of force. Athelstan removed the Britons who still inhabited Exeter and various pockets in Devon, resettled them on the Cornish side of the Tamar, and made that river the boundary between Cornwall and Devon. He also repaired the Roman walls of Exeter. These moves were balanced by conciliatory gestures towards the Cornish church. Without removing Cornwall from the diocese of Crediton he gave the bishop an auxiliary with a British name whom he established at St Germans, assigning three of the Crediton manors in Cornwall for his maintenance.

## The Victory of "Brunanburh"

Meanwhile the northern kings were becoming restive. In 934 some unspecified provocation led Athelstan to assemble massive forces and ravage Alba by land and sea. Three years later Olaf, son and successor at Dublin of the Guthfrith who had been driven from Northumbria in 927, naturally ambitious of recovering what his family had lost overseas, brought a large fleet from Ireland and joined the kings of Alba and Strathclyde in a concerted invasion of England. The allies penetrated far into the country before Athelstan and his brother Edmund overtook them. A murderous battle followed by a long pursuit shattered the invading forces, leaving five kings and seven earls dead upon the field, besides a son of the king of Alba. The site of the victory, *Brunanburh*, celebrated in a famous poem, is identified with great probability as Bromborough on the Mersey shore of Wirral in Cheshire. The Scottish kings escaped with difficulty, and Olaf took only a broken remnant of his army back to Dublin.

Athelstan's prestige was such that foreign potentates eagerly sought his alliance. He gave one sister in marriage to the duke of the Franks, another to the king of Burgundy, and a third, Edith, to Otto the future emperor. In 936 he helped his godson Alan to recover part of his inheritance in Brittany which had been seized by Norse invaders. Harold Fairhair, king of Norway, sent his youngest son to be brought up at Athelstan's court.

In his loftily worded charters Athelstan used various titles to express his overlordship. He styled himself "king of all Britain," and sometimes "*basileus*" – the Byzantine word for emperor – "of the English and of all the nations round about." Between 928 and 934 a number of his land-grants exempt the beneficiaries from all secular charges, including, if they mean what they say, even the three common dues – an eloquent indication that he believed his kingdom to be impregnable. Six codes of law issued by Athelstan have been preserved, as well as a brief ordinance concerning the maintenance of paupers and the release of penal slaves. The first code deals with tithes, the second and fourth mainly with the administration of justice, while the third, in the form of a letter to the king from the magnates of Kent, largely repeats the provisions of the others. The fifth begins by stating that the decrees already promulgated have not been well observed, and appoints more stringent penalties. The sixth is a memorandum explaining how the property-owners of London have organized themselves into a guild for the maintenance of the public peace: a striking proof that the means of law-enforcement available to the central government were not so plentiful that it could dispense with the support of voluntary private action.

## Boroughs and Ports

The law frowned on transactions not conducted under the eye of responsible officials who would see to it that tolls were duly paid. It demanded regular markets, and the best place for a regular market was a town. The policy of Alfred the Great, continued by Edward the Elder and the Lady of the Mercians, of covering England with a strategic network of *burhs*, gave a new impetus to the growth of urban life and institutions.

At a time when the military significance of the *burh* was uppermost in the public mind, legislators employed another word, *port*, borrowed from the administrative terminology of the Carolingian state, to denote not a sea-port but a market centre, whether inland or on the coast. Edward the Elder prohibited all buying and selling except in *ports*. Athelstan, re-enacting this law, first limited its application to goods worth more than twenty pence, and finally repealed it altogether. At the same time he took steps to bring the coinage under control, for without a steady supply of money trade would languish and die. He decreed that there should be one coinage throughout his realm, and that no man should coin money except in a *port*. He went on to give a list of mints, with the number of recognized moneyers in each: eight in London, six in Winchester, and so on for twelve other named towns; finally, one moneyer in each of the other boroughs.

Not every *port* was a *burh*, but the words were beginning to be interchangeable, and would remain so for centuries. The officer who collects the tolls and rents for the lord of a *port* and by his presence authenticates commercial transactions is styled the port-reeve. A road leading to a town is called a Portway or Port-street. Oxford still has its Port Meadow. The Anglo-Saxons spoke of portmen where the Normans would speak of burgesses.

Athelstan, a connoisseur and avid collector of sacred relics, and a generous donor of books to the churches, maintained a splendid court and held great councils attended by Welsh princes, Danish earls, and magnates from every part of England. After a reign of fifteen years he died in 939, and was succeeded by his eighteen-year-old half-brother Edmund.

## Accession of Edmund

When the news reached Dublin Olaf Guthfrithson immediately mounted a second invasion and gained the support of Wulfstan, archbishop of York. Before the end of the year he occupied York, and early in the next year he raided far and wide over the midlands. King Edmund brought an army to face him at Leicester, but the archbishops of Canterbury and York arranged a treaty which gave Olaf what are now the shires of Leicester, Derby, Nottingham, and Lincoln. For the moment it looked as if the work of Edward the Elder was undone by this ignominious surrender. In 941 Olaf invaded Northumbria, but he died before the year was out, and his kingdom passed to a weaker cousin, Olaf Sihtricson. Meanwhile Edmund bided his time, knowing that the Danish population had no love for their Norse masters. In 944 he led his army northward, expelled the Norse king, and was welcomed as a deliverer by the Danes of the Five Boroughs. Olaf had been supported by Dunmail, king of Strathclyde, whom Edmund punished by ravaging his territory. The king of Alba, Malcolm I, saw chances of profit in his neighbour's misfortune. He entered into an alliance with Edmund, the terms of which put him in possession of Strathclyde, but within a few years Dunmail regained his throne. For the short remainder of his life Edmund ruled a reunited England. He had shown himself forceful enough to regain Athelstan's predominance, and prudent enough to set a limit to his kingdom in the north.

His reign also marks the early dawn of a monastic revival which was destined to change the face of religion in England. Monasticism had already drawn the breath of new life with the foundation of Cluny in 910 and the reformation under Cluniac influence of the ancient house at Fleury on the Loire. Foreign visitors to Athelstan's court brought news of the movement to England, and one or two bishops took vows of celibacy and had themselves tonsured as monks, but these were acts of personal devotion; there was still no organized monastic life. At Glastonbury a lady named Æthelflaed, closely related to the royal house, installed a number of priests, not monks, in the derelict abbey and maintained them at her own expense. Dunstan, who as a boy had been a pupil in the Irish school there, became her right-hand man and eventually her executor. Under the influence of his kinsman Ælfheah, bishop of Winchester, he gave up thoughts of marriage and determined to become a monk. On the death of Athelstan he divided his time between Glastonbury and the court of King Edmund. One day the king had a narrow escape from death while hunting a stag on the cliffs of Cheddar. He sent for Dunstan, took him to Glastonbury, and installed him in the abbot's chair, promising to endow the abbey as a regular monastery. With this backing Dunstan gathered disciples round him and reintroduced the Rule of St Benedict; but the movement had scarcely begun to affect other houses when, in 946, his royal patron was stabbed to death at Pucklechurch in Gloucestershire by an outlaw who had returned from banishment.

## Edred Succeeds Edmund

Edmund left two sons, Edwy and Edgar, both under age. Consequently his brother Edred, though physically far from robust, shouldered the responsibilities of kingship. At Tanshelf near Pontefract he received the submission of the archbishop of York and the other northern magnates. But the archbishop soon found himself between two fires. Eric Bloodaxe, son of Harold Fairhair, king of Norway, exiled from his native country, gathered a Viking fleet and descended on Northumbria, where the Norsemen hailed him as the restorer of their independence. Edred replied by invading their country. In the process of ravaging, his army burned down St Wilfrid's ancient minster at Ripon, and though its rearguard was overwhelmed at a crossing of the Aire, he was able to cow the Northumbrians into submission by threatening that if they did not abandon Eric he would utterly destroy them. During the next six years northern politics were confused by the reappearance of Olaf Sihtricson, who had been ruling in Dublin since his expulsion by Edmund. He had some success, but Eric returned and drove him out in 952. For two more years Eric maintained himself at York, without the support of the archbishop who had been arrested and deported by King Edred. In the end Oswulf, who ruled what remained of English territory beyond the Tees with the title of high-reeve, defeated and killed Eric, and was rewarded by the king with an earldom comprising all southern Northumbria. The last independent Scandinavian power in England thus collapsed, leaving Edred, during the last year of his life (955), unchallenged in his monarchy. In his reign of nine and a half years he had recovered all his father's gains and finally checkmated the union of Dublin and York in a single Viking state.

He and his successors often used imperial titles in their charters. On occasion they explicitly named the Northumbrians as a people subject to them, but their authority in the north remained little more than nominal, depending on the loyalty of magnates like Oswulf. In the east midlands and East Anglia a now firmly rooted Danish population kept its own distinctive usages which the kings were careful to respect, and the confederation of the Five Boroughs remained in being as a largely autonomous unit of government.

## The Scandinavian Impact

It is arguable that the invaders who took part in the great land-divisions were numbered in hundreds rather than thousands, but later they must undoubtedly have been reinforced by waves of immigrants arriving from their homeland. At the close of the ninth century England north of the Thames was still a half empty land. There was room to spare for vigorous, land-hungry immigrants. When studied in detail, the evidence of archaeology, place-names, and personal names shows that the strangers made full use of their opportunities, founding scores of new villages and settling down in more or less peaceful co-existence with their English neighbours. Their language could be understood by any Englishman who would take a little trouble. Indeed, they contributed greatly to the enrichment of the native tongue. Many of our commonest words, such as *anger, fellow, husband, root, skill, skin, sky,* and *wing,* are borrowed from the Scandinavian. It has been remarked that in any conversation on the thousand nothings of everyday life or on the five or six things of paramount importance to high and low alike such borrowings are bound to occur. An Englishman cannot *thrive* or be *ill* or *die* without involving the use of Scandinavian words.

The two commonest Scandinavian elements in place-names are *-by* and *-thorp. -by* is believed to have originated in Sweden and to have meant at first a secondary settlement formed by colonization from a parent village. As population grew, *-by* came to mean simply 'village'. In Denmark it had already acquired that sense in the early Viking age. In England it could be applied to older English settlements taken over by the Danes, as when *North-worthig* became Derby, *Streonaeshalch* became first Prestby, then Whitby, and Badbury (Northamptonshire) became Badby. In Scandinavia *-by* is most often combined with elements relating to natural features or to the parent village. The English picture is different: here approximately two-thirds of the -*bys* are combined with personal names, in many cases probably the name of the first Danish occupant.

The greatest concentration of -*by* names in the north-east midlands is found on the Lincolnshire wolds. The older English villages are situated near the coast, on the light soil of the chalky boulder clay, easily cleared and cultivated. With one exception, all the settlements with Danish names lie to the west, on a belt of glacial gravel, where the soil is less fertile, much of it rough pasture and heathland. The Danes clearly liked the slopes of river valleys. Where these had already been occupied, they settled along the banks of tributaries and minor streams. The pattern is repeated in south-east Kesteven, Nottinghamshire, and Leicestershire. In Leicestershire Danish colonists spread out, not along the Soar, which had already been substantially settled by the English, but on less attractive sites along the Wreak and its tributaries. They seem in general to have preferred sandy and gravelly soils, which perhaps resembled those of their homeland.

*Thorp*, used either alone or in combination, denotes an outlying, dependent settlement colonized from an older and larger one. Thus Barkby (Leicestershire) has its Barkby Thorpe, Ewerby (Lincolnshire) its Ewerby Thorpe, and Ixworth (Suffolk) its Ixworth Thorpe. In compounds, personal names form a high proportion of first elements, high enough to suggest that many of them were new settlements made by individual pioneers. Some *thorpes* may have come into being when the original settler died and his land was divided among his heirs.

The application of a Scandinavian element to an older English village stands out very clearly in the common place-name Charlton. A glance at the map will show that in regions exposed to Danish or Norse influence the Scandinavian *karl* has been substituted for the Old English *ceorl* and the name is transformed into Carlton. A corresponding sound-change alters church to kirk.

As with place-names, so with personal names. These too bear witness to Anglo-Scandinavian interpenetration. As late as the twelfth century large numbers of countrymen in East Anglia bore Scandinavian names. So did those of the Lincolnshire fens and the Yorkshire wolds. Feminine names like Thora, Tola, and Gunhild survived for centuries, and have been taken by some scholars to suggest that the armies sent for their womenkind when they turned from war to agriculture. But we ought not to overlook the influence of fashion. It was not unusual for English families to mingle Scandinavian names with those of native origin. Oda, archbishop of Canterbury, a Dane by birth, had a nephew named Oswald. The records of Ely tell of a priest named Athelstan, of whose two brothers one bore the Scandinavian name of Bondo, the other the Old English Ælfstan. Stigand, the future archbishop, whose name was Danish, had a brother called Æthelmær. The example of these bilingual mixtures is very likely to have been followed in the humbler ranks of society. Personal names, therefore, cannot be accepted as proof of ancestry or national origin, any more than a Danish or Norse village name, taken by itself, proves that the village was founded by Scandinavian immigrants.

Nevertheless, when all due qualifications have been made, we are left with massive evidence that the invasion opened a new chapter in English social history. In all likelihood the topmost layer of society was at first the one most adversely affected. When the Viking Raegnald descended on Northumbria and won the battle of Corbridge, he seized the estates of St Cuthbert's old bishopric. He gave all the lands between Billingham and Castle Eden (Durham) – approximately eleven miles in a straight line – to one "mighty warrior," and a slightly larger share between Castle Eden and the River Wear to another. School Aycliffe in Heighington (Durham) is believed to derive the first part of its name from Scula, the warrior who received the southern portion. This method of sharing the spoils is very likely to have been employed in the three great land-divisions recorded in the Chronicle. The leader of a victorious expedition would assume control of a large region – in the case of East Anglia a whole kingdom – and assign handsome shares to his chief lieutenants, who in turn would deal out smaller portions to the rank and file. But the Viking chieftain who stepped into the place of an English landowning churchman or layman would need the services of the native tenants to make the most of his acquisition. There can have been no extermination of the English peasantry in the heart of the Danelaw. Even where the Scandinavian settlement was most intense, and Scandinavian place-names are most numerous, much of the older Anglian nomenclature survived.

In East Anglia the Norfolk Broadland shows a heavy concentration of villages with names of the purest Scandinavian type, as well as a large number of Scandinavian field-names. Except at Caister and Yarmouth there is no archaeological evidence of older settlement. With its great extent of marsh, the region can hardly have attracted the earliest settlers. All its -*by* names except Stokesby are compounded with Scandinavian personal names. It looks, therefore, as if these villages were appropriated and colonized by Danish owners after whom they were named; but the Danes may well have employed English freedmen and slaves to do the work.

## Scandinavian Society

The social system with which they had been familiar at home resembled at several points the one they found in England. In Scandinavia as in England the lowest rank was filled by slaves. The Frostathing Law of mid-tenth-century Norway takes three slaves to be the proper complement of a farm stocked with twelve cows and two horses; a lordly estate might well require thirty or more. The Old English word for slave, *theow*, has left no representative in our vocabulary, but we still speak of thralls and thraldom. Here and there the Scandinavian *thraell* is to be found in place-names; *Threlfall* (Lancashire) denotes a clearing in which the trees have been felled by slaves. All over England the temptation for a slave to desert his old master and take service with a new one in the hope of better conditions must have been strong indeed, and the Scandinavian invasion offered him many chances. In an attempt to block the process, a clause in the treaty between Alfred and Guthrum binds both parties on oath not to let either slaves or freemen pass over to the other side without permission.

Between slaves and freemen stood an intermediate class in process of emancipation. The process was a lengthy one, for the *leysing*, or freedman, remained subject in many respects to his former master and could not bring legal proceedings against him. Generations might come and go before his posterity attained full freedom. The Scandinavian *leysing*, as might be expected, has left more visible traces of his presence than the thrall. It is not certain whether Lazenby, near Kirkoswald (Cumberland), Lazenby near Wilton (Lincolnshire), and another Lazenby in the North Riding, represent settlements founded by individuals or by groups of freedmen planted there by their lords. If the latter, they would correspond in some sort to the English Charltons. It may be significant that Lazenby in the North Riding stands as close to the obviously Danish village of Danby Wiske as any Charlton to its capital manor; and the form Laysingthorpe (a lost place in the east of Lindsey, formerly too the name of a place in the West Riding which has changed to Lazencroft) supports the idea of a dependent settlement. But the Scandinavian *leysing* was more numerous than can be gathered from surviving place-names. A note in the sacrist's register of Bury St Edmunds records a bequest to the abbey on the eve of the Norman Conquest of Wereham (Norfolk) with its *leysings* and slaves. They were evidently a ubiquitous and important class.

The Yorkshire place-names Dringhoe and Dringhouses attest the former presence of the Scandinavian *dreng*, who has been described as a petty squire burdened with agricultural and personal services of a rather humble kind. In many respects the *dreng* resembled the Anglo-Saxon *geneat*. He received a holding from the king or other magnate, and was expected to attend his lord in hunting, ride on his errands, and send reapers to cut his crops. He is perhaps best described as a yeoman farmer.

The Danish aristocracy comprised a first rank of men distinguished by the title of *jarl* or earl, equivalent to the Anglo-Saxon ealdorman, and a second rank of *holds*. Two *jarls* and five *holds* are named in the Chronicle as having fallen in the battle against Edward the Elder in 910. The district of Holderness in the East Riding is believed to derive the first part of its name from a noble of the second class, and if the derivation is correct it shows how large an allotment might fall to a *hold* who survived to reap the fruit of victory.

Between the *hold* and the *leysing* stood the free Danish farmer, the *bondi*, owner of land and stock on almost every scale from a small-holder to a rich franklin. A society in which men of this class flourished must have been accustomed to a looser system of lordship than prevailed in England. In law and politics the *bondi* enjoyed an appreciably higher status than his English counterpart. He could pronounce verdicts in the courts and speak his mind on even the weightiest matters of state in the general assembly. Not for centuries, if indeed at any time in the past, had Wessex or Mercia known anything like him. A fictitious resemblance to him colours much that the older historians have written about the English *ceorl*.

The Danes had ideas of their own on currency, law, and administration, so much so that men could speak of the area governed by those ideas as the Danelaw. Already in Alfred's treaty with Guthrum we encounter the mark, a novel unit of reckoning which denotes eight 'ores' of sixteen silver pence each. The Danes produced a long-lasting and highly individual body of customary law, with distinctive forms of procedure. In the reign of Ethelred II we begin to hear of an institution unknown to Old English law, the sworn jury, consisting of twelve leading thegns in each district. Domesday Book will record the presence of twelve "judges" at Chester and twelve "lawmen" at Lincoln and Stamford, personages whose specialized knowledge gave them a leading part in the framing of judgements. Later still a kind of public prosecutor called a sacrabar, the Old Norse *sakarábeiri*, will appear spasmodically in legal records.

Under Scandinavian direction Yorkshire and Lindsey were each divided into three Ridings. This too is a disguised Norse word meaning a third part. The Ridings and the territory of the Five Boroughs were divided into wapentakes, the Old Norse *vápnatak*, or "weapon-taking." The extension of the term to cover both the local assembly and the district from which its members came is peculiar to the Danish colonies in England.

Land transactions in the Danelaw were authenticated not so much by charters and leases as by the testimony of the wapentake. When an English ealdorman purchased an estate from one Frena at a meeting of the army of Northampton, "the whole host was security on his behalf" that the vendor's title was sound. The comparative ease with which land could be bought and sold encouraged the multiplication of freeholds, and helped to undermine in the Scandinavian east of England the manorial structure which remained intact in areas under the direct control of the English crown.

The Scandinavian wapentake has its counterpart in the English hundred. As late as the eleventh century the same district could be described indifferently as a hundred or a wapentake, the choice being determined in the end by the relative strength of the Danish and English strains in the local population. The archaic system under which a district was appended for administrative and judiciary purposes to a kingston was being transformed into the hundredal system. An area comprising in theory one hundred hides, though in practice it might be a good deal less, now constituted the regular unit of judicial, fiscal, and military organization. It may well be that the military aspect predominated at first. In Scandinavia the "weapon-taking" seems to have been purely symbolic, a brandishing of spears or battle-axes to signify approval of a decision proposed to the assembly, but when the armies of the Five Boroughs responded to a call to arms their weapon-taking would be more literal than symbolic. And the hundred, like the wapentake, had its military function. The Anglo-Saxon Chronicle, recording the incursion of the Hwicce into Wiltshire in its annal for 802, merely states that the Hwicce were defeated by the men of Wiltshire under the command of Weohstan, their own ealdorman; but the chronicler Æthelweard, writing two centuries after the event, and using the language of his own time, says that Weohstan met the invaders "with the hundreds of Wiltshire."

## Units of Assessment

The subdivision of the shires into districts called hundreds or wapentakes, each consisting of so many hides, compels us to ask: What was now the hide? And the answer to this question will reveal that under Scandinavian influence the unit of assessment has assumed an entirely new complexion.

It will be remembered that the hide, when first encountered, appeared as a unit imposed in round numbers upon a whole people for the purpose of levying tribute to the paramount king. Local rulers imposed it on the lands within their jurisdiction as a convenient method of apportioning the renders payable in money or in kind to themselves or their beneficiaries. Hence an estate is granted as a land of so many hides. Behind this assessment lay a rough estimate of total resources, actual or potential, rather than an exact calculation of arable or pastoral capacity, either of which might predominate in a given case. But the Scandinavian settlement produced an all-important modification. The Danes, in particular, put arable cultivation in the forefront of their husbandry, and treated all other branches as appendant to it. All their calculations revolved consistently around the ox-drawn plough.

An estate at Wittering (Northamptonshire) is described in a tenth-century document as consisting of one hide less an oxgang. About 1030 another document refers to oxgangs and ploughlands in Yorkshire. Both terms are rooted in the conception of an eight-ox team and the amount of land it can plough in the course of the agricultural year. Divided by eight, the amount becomes an oxgang. It may be doubted whether the Danes had used these measurements in their homeland, but in the duchy of Normandy, founded by their kinsmen in 911, grants of land were frequently expressed in terms of the ploughland, latinized as *terra aratri* or *terra caruce*, the later *carucata*. The Normans were also acquainted with the oxgang or *bovata*.

The ploughland, *terra unius aratri*, in English *sulung*, and its fraction the *jugum* or yoke of two oxen, will be recalled as having been the usual terms of assessment in early Kent. Outside Kent it seems to have been unknown. The Tribal Hidage assesses the whole of England in hides. Bede and other writers of his age refer to hides in Northumberland and Yorkshire, and successive charters from the seventh to the ninth century apply the term to estates in Lincolnshire. It was not immediately ousted in the Danelaw. In one of the texts already cited hides, ploughlands, and oxgangs figure side by side. But in the shires where Danish influence had predominated – those of Lincoln, York, Derby, Nottingham, and Leicester – and occasionally in other shires, the carucate rather than the hide will be the normal Domesday unit of assessment.

This emphasis on the plough and its work reflected the realities of agrarian life in a country where more and more land had been deforested or drained and brought under tillage. The Old English word for plough, *sulh*, has left no descendant in our vocabulary. *Ploh* is found only with the meaning of "a measure of land"; our modern "plough" is more nearly affiliated to the Danish name of the implement itself.

It made little difference in practice whether local usage dictated that the land should be assessed in hides or carucates, for both were now, theoretically at least, on the same level. The hide could still be divided into four yardlands of 30 acres more or less, but its fractions could also be expressed in oxgangs. The ideal extent of an oxgang was 15 acres, and eight oxgangs made a hide. Both the hide and the carucate therefore end by being held to consist of 120 arable acres, the average stint of an eight-ox team. In an agricultural routine which begins in October, continues until Christmas, is resumed on Plough Monday, and carried on until the fallow receives a light stirring between May and July, there will be time enough, even allowing for Sundays and spells of bad weather, for 120 acres to be ploughed. So a mid-tenth-century will refers to "a hide of 120 acres," and in the last quarter of that century, when a dispute arises over the purchase of three hides in the Cambridgeshire village of Chippenham, a party of men go round the land and measure it, expecting to find 360 acres, but find only 226, or 2 hides less 14 acres.

The change from a system based on arbitrary assessment imposed from above, and bearing only a distant relationship to the facts of husbandry, to one based on arable acreage measurable on the ground, was nothing short of a revolution in the life of rural England. It provided the working countryman with an intelligible framework for the apportionment of the services he owed to his lord and the adjustment of rights he enjoyed in common with his neighbours. Naturally it could not and did not supersede at a stroke the older conception of the hide as an assessment of pasture and woodland as well as arable. In 1086 the Domesday commissioners will find that at Abbots Langley (Hertfordshire) one hide consists of "wood and field," and at Chedworth (Gloucestershire) "wood, field, and meadow" together account for 15 hides. They will also find that "in this hide there are only 64 acres when it is ploughed" at Hambrook (Gloucestershire), a cryptic statement which may perhaps be explained by the proximity of Hambrook to the Kingswood ironfield. In the ninth century the Kentish *sulung* had been equated with two hides, but charters of Edmund and Edred show that in the interest of uniformity it had been reduced by their time to one hide, varying, as it appears from the Kentish Domesday, between 180 and 200 acres. All sorts of local variations, a small acre here, a larger there, will help to complicate the system, even within the Scandinavian third of England. In Lincolnshire the average oxgang comprised not 15 but 20 acres. But when money was needed for the defence of the realm, a uniform assessment provided a rational basis for taxation, and the monarchy, whether under a Danish, an English, or a Norman king, would struggle against all odds to impose it. Hence the Conqueror will instruct his commissioners to find out not only the existing assessment of each manor but how many ploughs are in fact at work there; and more than a century later Richard I will levy a "carucage" of two shillings on each ploughland of 120 acres.

# Chapter X

# MONKS ASCENDANT

To a society in which so much depended on the personal character of the monarch it boded ill that after the death of Edred the
next four kings all ascended the throne as minors. Their youth and
inexperience exposed the country to all the pernicious rivalry of
faction. In early Wessex the ealdorman had been the governor of
a shire and leader of its militia in time of war, but during the tenth
century the practice grew up of placing two or more shires under
one ealdorman: thus Athelstan, nicknamed the Half-King because
of his great power, governed the whole of East Anglia, where he
was succeeded by his eldest son Ethelwold, while Ælfhere held a
similar position in Mercia. They and their peers were closely
connected by descent or marriage with the royal house, and
though they owed their appointment to the king, who could at a
pinch revoke it, in practice these over-mighty subjects were well
on the way to transforming their spheres of office into hereditary
principalities.

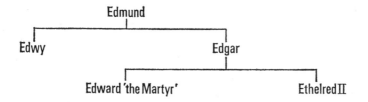

*An Ill-Starred Reign*

As King Edred left no issue, the next in line were the two sons
of Edmund, namely, Edwy (Eadwig) and Edgar, the elder of

whom cannot have been much more than fifteen years old. Nearly sixty charters issued by Edwy in the first twelvemonth of his reign are extant. No other single year can show such a prodigality of land-grants, and their profusion suggests a degree of irresponsibility in the king who made them. So does his betrothal to a lady within the prohibited degrees of kinship; the union was annulled by the church. He despoiled his grandmother Eadgifu, widow of Edward the Elder, of all her possessions, and he quarrelled with Dunstan, who had been in high favour during the two previous reigns but was now driven into exile. Barely two years after his accession Edwy's authority was repudiated by all England north of the Thames, and his brother Edgar was recognized as king everywhere but in Wessex, where Edwy continued to reign for the short remainder of his life. He died, conveniently, on 1 October 959, and Edgar at once became king of all England.

## Edgar and the Monastic Revival

Edgar had been brought up under the care of Dunstan's contemporary and fellow-monk Ethelwold, a forceful character whom Edred had appointed abbot of Abingdon. In leaving Glastonbury for the decayed minster by the Thames, Ethelwold took with him three priests from the Somerset house, one from Winchester, and one from London. These formed the nucleus of a genuinely monastic community, governed by the Rule of St Benedict as practised at Fleury. Its influence on the young Edgar, and through him on the political and ecclesiastical life of the country, was profound. Edgar, a boy-king in 957, was under the control of advisers who did not wait for his brother's death to recall Dunstan from the reformed monastery at Ghent where he had spent his exile, and to appoint him bishop of Worcester. In 959 Edgar removed him to London, and in the following year made him archbishop of Canterbury. Dunstan persuaded him to appoint Oswald, another disciple of Fleury, bishop of Worcester (961), and Ethelwold bishop of Winchester (963). For the whole of the reign this trio of monastic prelates dominated the English church, with the enthusiastic support of the devout and zealous young king.

Ethelwold, in particular, was an austere monk, intent on converting the sluggish minsters and derelict abbeys into power-houses of an exalted spirituality, and he shrank from no measure that seemed likely to further this design. The first requirement was that monasteries should be endowed with land enough to support the monks in a complex and expensive way of life which demanded fine churches, communal living-quarters, and all the costly apparatus of vestments, precious vessels, and music needed for solemn liturgical celebration. The lands of Abingdon, which consisted of only forty hides when Ethelwold took charge, were enlarged to six hundred hides and more; and the records of Ely show him indefatigably acquiring properties for that house by purchase, exchange, or royal gift. He displayed equal zeal for the endowment of Peterborough and Thorney.

Under his aegis and that of his colleagues in the episcopal triumvirate, the fashion for Benedictine monasticism spread rapidly. It made little or no impression on the west midlands and the north, but south of the Humber more than thirty monasteries of men and at least half a dozen convents of women were founded or revived. The accumulation of so much landed wealth in monastic hands was not accomplished without friction. Flaws could be found in title-deeds, and sometimes vendors complained of being subjected to undue pressure. The movement bore with especial severity upon the married priests and canons in posses-sion. At Winchester the cathedral, or Old Minster as it was called, seems at this time to have borne some resemblance to Trollope's Barchester before the Proudies, with a staff of easy-going, well-born canons of the same stamp as the Hon. and Rev. Dr Vesey Stanhope, who lived with their wives and children in houses of their own, spent no more than a decent minimum of time in church, and held each his portion of the endowments as a separate prebend. Few passages in Old English history are more vivid than the scene in the cathedral on 20 February 964, when Ethelwold, with a high-ranking lay representative of King Edgar at his side, confronted the shrinking canons with the choice between turning themselves into Benedictine monks or vacating their prebends. All of them left under protest, and monks from Abingdon were installed in their place. Ethelwold's biographer denounces the canons as a lazy, luxurious, and immoral lot, and later writers of the monastic party vie with one another in heaping scurrilous abuse upon them; yet it is noticeable that the moment of Ethelwold's irruption found them not wallowing in low debauchery but peacefully finishing their mass in choir. Similar expulsions followed at the New Minster, Chertsey, and Milton. The scheme of 'reform', pursued relentlessly all over southern England, upset numerous vested interests and could never have been carried through without the help of the royal power.

In one of its most invidious aspects, the Benedictine revival, which some historians have gone so far as to call "the tenth-century reformation," involved the repudiation of measures by which the churches had been deprived of lands once legally theirs. An account of the movement which is generally held to have been composed by Ethelwold himself deplores the threefold losses occasioned by kings who gave away church land to laymen, churchmen who give it to their kinsmen, and lay magnates who confiscate it on the ground that the occupant has committed some offence incurring forfeiture. All three dangers can be illustrated from the history of the Winchester endowments. In 955 King Edred had given a four-life lease of Highclere to the married bishop Ælfsige, who left the estate by will to his own kindred; and King Edwy gave him a similar lease of Taunton, which, however, the bishop surrendered into the king's hand when he came to make his will. Again, some time before 879 Bishop Tunbeorht gave a lease of Alresford to a layman for his lifetime only. When the lease ran out, the son of the original lessee, named Alfred, obtained a renewal from Bishop Denewulf, to whom he was related. Presently Alfred was found to have deserted his wife and to be living in open adultery, whereupon his possessions were declared forfeit, and Denewulf had to pay the king 120 mancuses of gold in order to recover the land. But this was not the end of the affair. The immoral Alfred left a son named Ælfric, who contrived in the first year of Edwy's reign to procure from that ill-advised young monarch an unconditional grant of the estate to him and his heirs. Not until Ethelwold had taken charge, with the strong arm of Edgar to assist him, was this grant annulled and Alresford returned to its rightful owners.

## Churchmen with Secular Power

One way of fortifying the churches against such detrimental occurrences was to give the bishops and abbots full secular jurisdiction over their lands. By doing so, the king could provide himself with a useful counterpoise to the formidably powerful lay magnates by whom the country was largely dominated. The problem had already arisen on the continent. In Germany and Italy Edgar's contemporary and uncle by marriage, the emperor Otto, had solved it by granting secular power to bishops and abbots. In England Edgar did the same by giving them large powers over the hundreds in which their estates lay. The most conspicuous beneficiaries of this policy were the two arch-promoters of the monastic revival, Ethelwold of Winchester and Oswald of Worcester. Ethelwold received the lordship of the hundreds of Chilcomb in Hampshire, Downton in Wiltshire, and Taunton in Somerset. According to a statement later made by Edgar's widow concerning the large manor of Taunton, the king "commanded every one of his thegns who held land on the estate that they should hold it conformably with the bishop's will, or else give it up." All the inhabitants, including those of the highest rank, became as fully subject to the bishop's lordship as the inhabitants of royal manors were to the king's. Amercements and forfeitures, all the profits of justice, henceforth went to the bishop. He also took the market tolls and burgage rents from Taunton itself, the earliest known example in England of a mediatized or seignorial borough: a borough, that is to say, which belonged not as most of them did to the king, but to a private lord.

Similarly in Worcestershire Bishop Oswald acquired full secular jurisdiction over the triple hundred of Oswaldslow, to the complete exclusion of the ealdorman of Mercia and his deputies. The king thus alienated his royal rights on a grand scale in favour of these and other churchmen on whom he could rely, and they responded by habitually magnifying his royal dignity to the highest possible pitch.

How Ethelwold turned his newly acquired powers to account may be seen in the case of Ruishton, an estate near Taunton which his predecessor had acquired in Alfred's reign. When

Edgar turned all his tenants in the hundred of Taunton into tenants of the bishop, a certain Leofric, at that time holding Ruishton, surrendered the title-deed to Ethelwold, who was then prevailed upon by the queen and Leofric's sister to grant him a lease of the property, but only for his lifetime and that of his wife.

## Oswald's Leases

Thanks to the exceptionally careful preservation of the Worcester records it is possible to see how Bishop Oswald used his viceregal powers over the three hundred hides of Oswaldslow. The texts of seventy-two leases granted by him between 920 and 980 are extant. Fifty-six of them deal with properties of less than five hides, and only five with lands of higher assessment. Eight of the recipients are churchmen, four are the bishop's kinsmen, one is a "matron," and two are artificers, but the great majority are thegns, *ministri*, occasionally styled *milites*, *cnihtas*, or *fideles*, the last probably implying men who had taken an oath of fealty to the bishop. They must have been petty thegns indeed, unless they possessed other lands of their own, as presumably did the king's thegn to whom Oswald granted three hides. Nineteen leases impose the three common dues; thirteen require the payment of church-scot; thirty state no conditions at all.

Strictly speaking, land held on lease should have been described as loan-land, but Oswald did his best to give his leases the form and semblance of royal charters creating bookland. In three cases, indeed, he states that the recipient of his "book" already holds the land as loan-land. He even goes so far as to speak of perpetual inheritance, but the inheritance is not really meant to be perpetual; it is limited to a term of lives, normally three lives, after which the land must revert to the church of Worcester. It becomes clear on closer study that the main object of these so-called "books" is to put on record the reversionary title of the bishop and his church, a very necessary precaution, for experience showed that it would be anything but a matter of course to regain possession of an estate held on lease by one family over three lifetimes.

The terms on which Oswald granted his leases, then, are not

fully revealed in these texts. For fuller information we turn to the solemn letter by which Oswald informs King Edgar how he has been granting to his faithful men for the term of three lives the lands committed to his charge. He does so to the end that "succeeding bishops may know what to exact from these men according to the covenant they have made with me." The men must "fulfil the whole law of riding which belongs to riding-men." They must pay church-scot, toll, and pannage; lend their horses and ride on errands themselves; be ready to build bridges and to burn lime for church-building; erect a hedge for the bishop's hunt and lend their own hunting-spears if required. In consideration of the fief ("beneficium") which they hold on loan, they must swear to obey with all humility and subjection the bishop as their lord and *archiductor*, their commander-in-chief. When the term of the lease expires, the bishop shall be free to keep the lands for his own use or to let them out for a further term, always provided that these services are duly rendered in accordance with the quantity of the land.

Historians preoccupied with the abstraction they call feudalism have argued at length about Oswald's famous letter. Some find and others fail to find in those riding tenants the precursors of the Norman knights. The bishop's leases, it is true, contain no specific demand for service of a military character, but we must not ignore the significance of the fact that Oswald styles himself *archiductor*. This undoubtedly means that in time of war the bishop would either command the levies in person, as a later bishop, Ealdred, did in 1049, when he took the field against the Welsh, or delegate the work to a lay captain, such as that Edric who in the Confessor's reign led the bishop's "army" into battle, and was also helmsman of the bishop's warship. It is true that the English *cniht* of the tenth century differs in many respects from the knight of the twelfth, but the transition from the one to the other is one of military tactics, equipment, and organization, rather than of simple tenure.

## The "Regularis Concordia"

After a few years the leaders of the monastic revival met at Winchester to agree on a code of uniform practice. The document they produced, known as the *Regularis Concordia*, drew much inspiration through Dunstan and Ethelwold from Ghent and Fleury. Under this programme the monks were to rise in summer at 1.30 a.m., in winter an hour later. Every morning some two hours were set aside for manual, artistic, or intellectual work, but most of the day was to be spent in the round of liturgical offices, interspersed with frequent prayers for the king and the royal family, which in the English curriculum took a far more prominent place than anywhere else in Europe. In winter the monks would eat one meal a day at 18 o'clock; in summer one at noon, another at 15.30. Bed-time was 18.30 in winter, 20.15 in summer.

Altogether the *Regularis Concordia*, while providing the inmates of a monastery with more peace and even comfort than they might have enjoyed in the world outside their gates, made few concessions to human weakness, and it is not surprising that in 1014 Ethelred II found it necessary to exhort monks and abbots to observe the rule more strictly than they had been in the habit of doing. The *Concordia* also provided that where a monastic community served a cathedral church it should elect the bishop. There was no parallel to this on the continent, and as it impinged upon the royal power of appointment it was to become a fruitful source of trouble in later centuries.

Edgar's impetuosity in pushing on the monastic revival in Wessex was ill-advised. Not that his more educated subjects disliked the monks as such; it mattered little to them if numbers of men chose to remain unmarried, to abstain from eating meat, and to spend most of their waking hours in singing psalms; but the thegns who had held land directly from the king and now found themselves at the mercy of a bishop or abbot, the influential canons who had been dispossessed, and the ealdormen who saw their jurisdiction eroded by the growing secular power of the churches, naturally resented these moves, and it is not unlikely that Edgar, had his reign been prolonged, would have had to contend with serious resistance.

### An Anointed King

For the moment he had it all his own way. He asserted his power in the north by procuring the retirement of the elected archbishop of York and appointing Oswald to hold the see in plurality with Worcester. Then he sent Oswald to Rome. One object of Oswald's mission was to obtain the pallium for himself, but it is reasonable to surmise that he took the opportunity to broach the subject of the king's anointing. He could count on the support of the emperor Otto, who was in Rome at the time and consistently upheld his kinsman's interests. Anointing was a papal privilege, not granted to every king: the kings of Scotland had to wait for it until 1331. Those of Mercia and Northumbria had apparently enjoyed it in the past, and Athelstan had succeeded as the heir of Mercia, but Edgar's reign had begun in rebellion against his brother, and above all there was no precedent for anointing a king of all England. The pope evidently gave his consent, for on Whit Sunday 973, the year after Oswald's visit to Rome and the sixteenth of Edgar's kingship, both archbishops assisted in the anointing of Edgar, which took place in a splendid ceremony at Bath.

## Edgar's Policy

Immediately after his consecration Edgar summoned a meeting of all the kings in Britain and took care to impress his power and new-found dignity upon them by a naval demonstration in the estuary of the Dee. At Chester Kenneth of Alba, Donald of Strathclyde, Maccus of the Isles, Iago of Gwynedd, and at least two other princes acknowledged his supremacy and promised to serve him by sea and by land. According to a late but credible tradition, Edgar ceded to Kenneth, in return for homage, Lothian, which at that time included all the territory between the Firth and the Tweed. This formal recognition of the Tweed as the northern boundary of England did not establish a secure permanent frontier, but it set a definite limit to English ambitions in the north.

Even within his own borders Edgar limited his responsibilities by conceding autonomy to his Danish subjects. "It is my will," he declared, "that secular rights shall be in force among the Danes according to as good laws as they can best decide on. Among the English, however, that is to be in force which I and my councillors have added to the decrees of my ancestors." He almost apologizes for enacting regulations against cattle-thieving which were to hold good everywhere; then he repeats that he has ever allowed the Danes to make their own laws and will allow it all his life "because of the loyalty they have always shown him." Thus in the most explicit fashion he recognizes that English law is one thing, Danish quite another; and within a generation the shires of Danish England were known collectively as the Danelaw.

It is on record that in 969 Edgar ordered the ravaging of Thanet to punish the inhabitants for having robbed some merchants coming from York. He certainly showed himself solicitous for the welfare of traders; indeed, to one xenophobic chronicler he appeared altogether too partial to foreigners and their evil customs.

Perhaps the greatest achievement of Edgar's reign was the reform of the currency. An entirely new penny, of uniform type throughout the kingdom, superseded all previous issues. The obverse design never varied; the reverse carried the names of the moneyer and mint. Nearly thirty mints are known to have been in operation, many of them newly opened, so that few traders needed to travel more than fifteen or twenty miles to exchange old coins for new. The dies were recalled at regular intervals, every two, three, or six years, and the government issued dies of new design in their place. Perhaps no country in western Europe at the time could boast of a more efficiently managed currency.

Edgar is also believed to have introduced ship-sokes, a system under which hundreds were organized in groups of three to provide the crew of a warship. Mention has already been made of the triple hundred of Oswaldslow in Worcestershire and of the helmsman who commanded the bishop's warship. As lord of the ship-soke the bishop was empowered to ensure that military and naval service was duly rendered from his triple hundred. If one man served from every five hides, they would man a ship of sixty oars. The king is credited with having organized efficient naval patrols around the shores of Britain. It is not easy to determine how far the country owed its immunity from foreign attack during Edgar's reign to prudent measures by his government, and how far to the capital of prestige and power he inherited from his father and uncle.

## A Disputed Succession

Two years after his coronation, on 8 July 975, Edgar died suddenly, being only thirty-two years old. All the resentments provoked by his favour to the monasteries at once exploded in civil strife. Two rival factions crystallized among the magnates, each with its own candidate for the throne. The writers of the monastic party on whom we mainly depend for our knowledge of events at this period gloss over the irregularities of Edgar's private life. Three women in turn had shared his bed. The first, Wulfthryth, bore him an only daughter, Edith, who became a nun at Wilton. By the second, Æthelflaed, nicknamed the White Duck, he was the father of a boy Edward. To both these ladies he seems to have been betrothed but not married. But in 964 he married with full benefit of clergy the beautiful and high-born Ælfthryth, widow of Ethelwold, the son and successor of the Half-King as ealdorman of East Anglia. Ælfthryth was the first consort since Judith to be styled not merely "the Lady" but queen, *regina*, in Wessex, and she was entrusted with a general oversight and protection of all the nunneries in the kingdom. She bore Edgar two sons, Edmund and Ethelred, of whom the first predeceased his father. The succession thus lay between Edward, then still in his teens, and his half-brother Ethelred.

Edward was an ill-conditioned boy whose violence of speech and behaviour had made him generally objectionable, and his origin was not above reproach. Lay, and at that time some clerical, opinion was prepared to recognize the legitimacy of a child born after betrothal but before wedlock, but it is noteworthy that in the New Minster charter of 966 the attestation of the infant prince Edmund appears immediately after that of Archbishop Dunstan, coupled with an emphatic reference to his legitimacy; then follows that of Edward, with a bare statement that he is the son of the king; then Ælfthryth is named, with a pointed reference to her status as the king's lawful consort. But Edward was the elder of the late king's surviving sons, and though there is no contemporary evidence of his consecration he was evidently accepted by the church.

His brief reign was marked by a disastrous failure of the harvest, by the unexplained exile of Oslac, ealdorman of Deira, and by an abrupt reversal of Edgar's ecclesiastical policy. There is no doubt that the monks had become intensely unpopular. Whenever one of them showed himself in public the vulgar greeted him with catcalls or worse. Ælfhere, the powerful ealdorman of Mercia, took the lead in reinstating the clergy who had been dispossessed, and all the work of the monastic revival would have been undone had not Æthelwine, ealdorman of East Anglia and patron of Oswald's new foundation at Ramsey, stood out as a champion of the monks. Behind the disturbances lay a more or less open struggle for power between rival magnates.

## Accession of Ethelred II

On 18 March 978 Edward paid a surprise visit to the dowager queen Ælfthryth and her surviving son at Corfe in Dorset. He was met in the courtyard by the household thegns, and what happened next was never clearly known. An affray of some sort took place, in the course of which Edward received a wound, leapt from his horse, and fell dead. His body was carried to Wareham and buried without any mark of honour. No one was punished for the violence, which may have been unpremeditated, brought on by his own behaviour. Certainly his own kinsmen did nothing to avenge it. Within a month his step-brother Ethelred was anointed and crowned at Kingston-on-Thames by the two archbishops amid general rejoicing.

A year later Ælfhere of Mercia removed Edward's body from Wareham to Shaftesbury. But before long the misfortunes of the succeeding reign brought about a revulsion of popular feeling. Virtues of all kinds were attributed to the deceased; his remains were believed to work miracles; and he was acclaimed a saint and martyr, a victim to the supposed machinations of a wicked step-mother. Thirty years later Ethelred's advisers caused the festival of St Edward the Martyr to be celebrated in all the churches of England: as curious a cult as any in the history of canonization.

During his first years as king, Ethelred II, a boy aged between ten and twelve at the time of his accession, was naturally much under the influence of Archbishop Dunstan, the queen mother, and her brother Ordulf, the founder of Tavistock Abbey. Anti-monastic activity ceased; the monks whom Ælfhere had expelled returned to Winchcombe, Pershore, and Evesham; new abbeys were founded at Cranborne and Cerne in Dorset, at Eynsham in Oxfordshire, and at Burton-on-Trent, and the bishop of Sher-borne turned his cathedral clergy into a Benedictine community. Disciples of Dunstan, Oswald, and Ethelwold became bishops in their turn; indeed, for the remainder of our period the great majority of candidates for episcopal office were trained as monks.

*Fruits of the Monastic Revival*

That monastic life need not be a materially unproductive pursuit now appeared from its varied fruits. The multiplication of scriptoria meant the multiplication of books. Archbishop Oswald gave a three-life lease of Bredicot near Worcester to a priest named Godinge on condition that he should produce the manuscripts required by the cathedral monastery. From a series of meagre annals the Chronicle, especially in its continuation at Abingdon, became again a detailed record of events, reported, however, not from the centre as in Alfred's time, but as observed and not always fully understood by the inmates of the cloister. Ethelwold's pupil Ælfric, monk of Cerne and subsequently abbot of Eynsham, became the outstanding literary figure of the time. He was not an original thinker, but his two sets of sermons, intended for delivery by parish priests, his Lives of the Saints, and his translations from scripture, all in English, gave a great impetus to the literary use of the mother tongue. At Ramsey a study of the ecclesiastical calendar, around which clustered a considerable body of mathe-matical, astronomical, and medical learning, was propagated by Abbo, a monk who came over from Fleury at Oswald's invitation, and by his pupil Byrtferth, whose handbook of chronology was written in Latin for the monks and in English for the unlearned clerks of the neighbourhood.

Under Ethelwold Winchester developed a school of magnificent formal penmanship, which has had a notable influence in the modern revival of calligraphy. Masterpieces of illumination pro-duced in the Winchester and other scriptoria excelled in delicate colouring and their blend of naturalistic with stylized ornament. Plainer manuscripts were often adorned with outline drawings of figure subjects, rapidly executed and admirably expressive.

Dunstan and Ethelwold, both skilled craftsmen in gold and other precious metals, were followed by monks who carried the decorative arts to a high pitch of excellence, and by choir-masters who developed Gregorian chant into the thing of beauty which it has remained to this day. Elaborate additional modulations prolonged the most important parts of the chant, and a system of polyphony, in which the trebles of the boy choristers mingled in combination or contrast with the voices of the monks, provided a rich musical feast. Great use was made of organs; one of these instruments at Winchester contained 400 pipes and could produce a thunderous volume of sound.

Ethelwold was a great builder. The new monastic churches appeared magnificent to contemporaries, though small compared with the Norman structures which presently took their place. Altogether the monastic revival, whatever reserves may be felt about its political aspect, did much for English civilization. It bore notable fruit in art and letters, and left its mark on the ecclesiastical life of the country for half a millennium to come.

Ethelred II inherited a rich and, in appearance, powerful kingdom. Something, however, has already been said about its weaknesses. An unstable northern frontier; a Danish population in East Anglia and the east midlands prepared to give their allegiance only to a king who left them very much to their own devices; and the rivalry of powerful ealdormen: these factors did not make for consolidation. As soon as public affairs took a downward turn, people began to murmur that they were bound to do so under a king who, though blameless himself, had come to the throne in mysterious and possibly criminal circumstances. Moreover Archbishop Dunstan died in 988; Ælfthryth the queen-mother spent her last years at Wherwell, a convent of her own foundation, and died in 1002; her brother Ordulf died about eight years later. Thereafter Ethelred had no advisers he could wholly trust. He was neither a fool nor a weakling. But a ruler of men, whatever his character and the quality of his advisers, needs luck, and we shall see that Ethelred had no luck whatever.

Chapter XI

# THE REIGNS OF ETHELRED
# AND CNUT

At the time of Ethelred's accession Harold, nicknamed Blue-tooth, reigned over the united kingdoms of Denmark and Norway. His attempts to establish Christianity by dictatorial methods aroused strong resentment among his Danish subjects. This, and something more than a suspicion of English weakness, impelled a number of them to take ship and raid the undefended English coastline. Small companies landed without warning in Hampshire, Thanet, and Cheshire in 980, in Devon and Cornwall in 981, and in Dorset in 982, seizing as much plunder as lay to hand and departing before they met with any but local resistance. During the next six years their homeland was rent by faction, and they left England alone until Swein, son of Harold Blue-tooth, put himself at the head of the malcontents and drove his father from the kingdom. Then in 988 another raiding party landed at Watchet and did much damage before they were routed by the thegns of Devon.

They and their fellows could rely upon the sympathy of their kinsmen in Normandy to provide a safe refuge for their ships in Norman ports. The friction this naturally engendered between the governments of England and Normandy became serious enough to engage the attention of Pope John XV. Thanks to his mediation a treaty was arranged between Ethelred II and Duke Richard I, binding each of the parties not to entertain the other's enemies. It was the first move in an Anglo-Norman relationship destined to have far-reaching consequences for both countries.

## The Battle of Maldon

In the summer of 991 Olaf Tryggvason, a descendant of the old Norwegian royal line, led a fleet of ninety-three ships to Folkestone. They harried the coasts of Kent and East Anglia, and spent the next four months extorting large sums from the people of the eastern and southern coasts. One incident in the campaign, not in itself particularly important, inspired a famous poem commemorating a battle at Maldon where Byrhtnoth, the white-haired ealdorman of Essex, defying the invaders, fought until they cut him down. Seeing him dead, a number of his followers took to flight, but there were some who refused to outlive their lord. "Thoughts must be the braver, heart more valiant, courage the greater as our strength grows less," cried one of them. "I will not leave the field, but mean to lie by the side of my lord, by the man I held so dear." And with desperate courage they fought on until the last was killed.

## Viking Inroads

In the following year Ethelred ordered his navy to assemble at London, hoping to intercept the raiders at sea, but the Danes eluded the ships from the southern ports and routed those from East Anglia and London. It was next the turn of Northumbria and Lindsey. Then in 994 Olaf Tryggvason and Swein of Denmark, with a fleet of ninety-four ships, laid siege to London, unsuccessfully, but raided far and wide over southern England. It was afterwards alleged that some Englishmen of standing were prepared to welcome Swein in Essex: an early manifestation, perhaps, of the treason against which Ethelred II had to contend for much of his reign.

Either in 991 or 994 – it is uncertain which – Sigeric, archbishop of Canterbury, Aelfric, ealdorman of Hampshire, and Æthelweard, ealdorman of the south-western shires, negotiated a formal treaty between the king and Olaf Tryggvason. In return for provisions and a large subsidy Olaf undertook to keep the peace and join with the English in attacking any other raiders who should visit the English coast. Olaf and his army spent the winter of 994 at Southampton. Already a baptized Christian, he was confirmed in Ethelred's presence at Andover, with the king for sponsor. He then sailed away, promising never to return as an enemy of England; and he kept his promise. The treaty cost England 20,000 pounds in gold and silver.

## Danegeld

It seems likely that Ethelred's advisers calculated – rightly, as the event proved – that this costly arrangement would drive a wedge between Olaf and Swein. But it set a disastrous precedent, for it showed the Danes how easily tribute could be extorted as the price of peace. At intervals over the next ten years they collected huge sums in Danegeld, only to grant an ephemeral truce, which they often violated, for there was no concerted plan of campaign and no strong central direction to keep the various ships' companies under control. The Danegeld rose to 24,000 pounds in 1002 and 30,000 (or 36,000, for the various recensions of the Chronicle differ in their statements here) in 1007. We do not know in detail how the money was raised, but may guess that what the royal treasury could not provide was made up by an impost levied on the shires of Wessex and English Mercia. The Vikings carried much of it back to their homelands; large hoards of silver pennies from English mints have been unearthed in Scandinavian soil. But a surviving charter which shows King Ethelred selling an estate in Oxfordshire to a Dane named Toti suggests that some of the raiders invested their share of the spoil in English land.

As a rule they took care to avoid pitched battles. Ethelred could have mustered a larger force than theirs, and did so more than once, but either through miscalculation or the selfish folly of magnates playing for their own hand he could not prevent the Vikings from burning towns, ravaging the countryside, and escaping with their booty. "When they were in the east," says one chronicler, "the English army was kept in the west, and when they were in the south, our army was in the north." Ethelred summoned his council to devise new measures of defence, "but if anything was then decided, it did not last even a month. Finally there was no leader who would collect an army, but each fled as best he could, and in the end no shire would even help the next."

In 1000, during a temporary respite from the Vikings, Ethelred led his army to the north in a punitive expedition against the Britons of Strathclyde, who had perhaps been trying to play off the Norse colonies in Galloway and Cumberland, their neighbours on the west, against the English of Bernicia on the east. The king's first wife is said to have been a daughter of Thored, the Viking earl of Bernicia, and he gave one of his daughters in marriage to Uhtred, whom in 1006 he appointed earl of all Northumbria. Another daughter married Ulfcetel, the Danish earl of East Anglia. These marriages look like a politic attempt to make royal influence felt in regions where it had previously counted for little.

On no better evidence than an interpolated charter and a patently absurd entry in the Chronicle, it has been freely stated that Ethelred ordered all the Danes in England to be killed on St Brice's day (13 November) 1002. Since perhaps as many as a third of his subjects were Danes, it is clear that no such order can have been given, much less carried out, and in fact the names of only two victims, Pallig and his wife Gunnhild, are on record. Pallig, a Danish captain who had pledged loyalty to Ethelred in return for large gifts of money and land, collected some ships and joined a Viking force to ravage, burn, and slay along the southern coast. Not surprisingly, Ethelred's council advised him to make an example of such traitors. In English eyes the sanctity of the pledged word, especially when given on oath, counted as inviolable; to the Danes it was merely a convenient way of disarming their victims. An enemy who accepted terms of truce and broke his word forfeited the lives of the hostages he had given, and Pallig's wife had offered herself as a voluntary hostage. The so-called "massacre of St Brice's day," therefore, in all probability should be understood as an execution, accordant with the accepted usage of the time, of some known traitors and a not large number of Danish hostages. Unfortunately Gunnhild was a sister of Swein, and her death added the motive of personal revenge to the Danish king's hostility.

*The Norman Marriage*

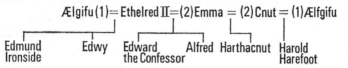

In the same year Ethelred took as his second wife Emma, sister of Richard II, duke of Normandy. It was a political marriage, and although Emma bore three children to Ethelred, one of whom was later to become king of England, there appears to have been little sympathy between the royal pair.

Natural as well as man-made disasters added to the miseries of the time. In 1005 the harvest failed and a cruel famine afflicted the people. Nine years later a great tide flooded widely over the country, destroying villages and drowning many of the inhabitants.

Surrounded at a time of crisis by self-seeking magnates, unwise counsellors, and a demoralized people, King Ethelred did not give up the struggle. There may well have been moments when only the memory of his great ancestors encouraged him to battle on. In an effort to make better provision for the defence of central England by placing the shire-levies under a single command, he revived the great ealdormanry of Mercia, which had been in abeyance ever since 985. The post was entrusted to a thegn of obscure antecedents named Eadric Streona, a shifty but plausible character, all too ready to betray his king and fellow-countrymen for his own advantage. It was the most unfortunate appointment Ethelred ever made. Nor was his next important measure attended with much better success. In 1008 he ordered a new fleet of warships to be constructed. The whole country was divided into ship-sokes, or triple hundreds, each of which was required to furnish a ship of sixty oars. To arm the crews, every eight hides throughout the kingdom had to provide a helmet and corselet. The country responded to this call, and by the following year the largest royal navy England had ever possessed assembled at Sandwich. But before the Danes appeared a charge of treason was brought against one of its commanders, a Sussex thegn named Wulfnoth. The accused made off with a detachment of twenty ships and took to piracy along the south coast. His accuser followed in pursuit with eighty ships, but a great storm arose in the Channel and wrecked them all. At the news of this disaster Ethelred and the survivors of his fleet withdrew to London.

At the beginning of August the enemy appeared and anchored off Sandwich. They harried Kent, attacked London without success, made their way through the Chilterns, and burnt Oxford. In the following spring their fleet moved into East Anglian waters. They stormed Ipswich and spent three months ravaging the country. Thetford, Cambridge, and Northampton were burnt down before they returned to their ships at Christmas. A chronicler writing in 1011 estimated that in the sixteen months since their arrival they had ravaged the whole or part of fifteen shires besides East Anglia. The country was utterly exhausted, and it was not until the middle of April 1012 that the Danes could be paid the sum of 48,000 pounds which they exacted as the price of their departure.

### Murder of the Archbishop

In the meantime they had taken Canterbury and seized the archbishop, Ælfheah, for whom they demanded a separate ransom. The archbishop refused to let his tenants be mulcted on his account, and in a drunken assembly at Greenwich he was done to death, although one of the chief commanders of the Viking fleet, Thorkell the Tall, did his best to save him. Ever afterwards great veneration surrounded the memory of Saint Alphege the Martyr, as the murdered archbishop was called – incidentally with a far better claim to be so regarded than Ethelred's half-brother "Saint Edward the Martyr," whose feast-day the council four years earlier had ordered to be celebrated throughout England. Before the end of the year Thorkell the Tall, disgusted perhaps by the barbarous act, changed sides and took forty-five warships with him into the service of King Ethelred.

### Swein as King

By this time Swein was determined on the conquest of all England. Secure at home in Denmark, aware that the backbone of English resistance was already broken, and counting on a welcome from the inhabitants of the Danelaw, he set sail in the summer of 1013. After touching at Sandwich, he sailed northward to the Humber and disembarked at Gainsborough in Lindsey, twenty miles from the mouth of the Trent. Northumbria, Lindsey, and the whole of Danish England at once accepted him as king. After taking hostages and demanding horses and provisions for his army, he turned southward, everywhere harrying the countryside into submission. Oxford and Winchester surrendered as soon as he appeared, but an attack on London failed. King Ethelred with his household troops was there, supported by Thorkell with the crews of his ships. Turning away from London, Swein marched through Wallingford to Bath, where he received the submission of the western thegns. Then he returned to his fleet at Gainsborough. Ethelred meanwhile sent Queen Emma and her sons to safety in Normandy. By this time the whole of England had recognized Swein as king, and the citizens of London, despairing of further resistance, gave in. Ethelred withdrew to the Isle of Wight, escorted by Thorkell, and after Christmas followed his wife and sons to Normandy.

## Restoration of Ethelred

Swein's triumph did not outlast the winter. He died suddenly at Gainsborough on 3 February 1014, leaving Cnut, his younger son, in charge of his fleet and with the men of Lindsey prepared to join him in ravaging the country. But meanwhile the leading English magnates, ecclesiastical and lay, sent a deputation to Normandy inviting Ethelred II to return. They assured him that no one was dearer to them than their natural lord, but they asked that his rule should be less arbitrary than it had been of late. Ethelred in reply asked for pledges of their unanimous loyalty, and promised that if these were forthcoming he would be a gracious lord to them all. Both parties being satisfied by these exchanges, the king returned to England and was joyfully welcomed by his people. In April he put himself at the head of his army and drove Cnut into ignominious retreat. Before sailing for Denmark, Cnut cut off the hands, ears, and noses of the hostages who had been given to his father and put them ashore at Sandwich.

In the same year, 1014, the archbishop of York, Wulfstan, published a celebrated jeremiad. He painted a lurid picture of the chaos into which a great part of England had been plunged by the Danish conquest. Widows, he said, were wrongfully forced into marriage; poor men were cruelly defrauded and sold out of the country into the power of foreigners; the rights of freemen were withdrawn and those of slaves restricted. "Often a slave binds very fast a thegn who previously was his master, and makes him into a slave." At the same time, "free men are not allowed to keep their independence, nor go where they wish; and slaves are not allowed to keep what they have gained by toil in their own free time."

When all due allowance has been made for what a great French historian calls "the natural pessimism of sacred oratory," it is entirely credible that so massive an intrusion of foreigners should have gravely disturbed the social fabric. Many an English thegn, and perhaps his son too if of age to bear arms, must have perished in battle, leaving no one to inherit his land. In a region where the English king's writ did not run there was nothing to prevent a Dane from stepping into the dead thegn's place. In these conditions numbers of countrymen would seize the opportunity to emancipate themselves, by purchase or mere usurpation, from the demands of lordship, especially on those great discontinuous estates which had wielded authority over villages miles away from the capital manor. The degree of emancipation would vary from village to village, and even between one tiller of the soil and his neighbour, with results that were still being felt when the Normans came and did their best to reimpose seignorial control.

For all the monotonous tale of disaster, England in the first half of the eleventh century had great reserves of strength and recuperative power. Towns might go up in smoke, but their wooden houses were quickly rebuilt. Five or ten miles from the track of a hostile army countrymen could pursue the routine of husbandry unshaken by more than a brief alarm. If money was drained away in tribute, some of it was spent in England by the recipients, and there were still treasures of gold and silver in the churches and noble houses that could be melted down in emergencies. London remained a city of rich merchants. The administrative system never collapsed.

## Treason of Edmund Ironside

The restoration of Ethelred II was marred by an outbreak of dissension in the royal family. In the course of a great council held at Oxford in 1015 two of the richest landlords in the Danelaw, Sigeferth and Morcar, were put to death, having apparently been impeached for treason, by Eadric Streona. The king confiscated their estates and ordered the arrest of Sigeferth's widow. But Edmund, later to be nicknamed the Ironside, son of Ethelred either by his first wife or by an unknown mistress, carried off the widow and married her in defiance of his father. He then went north and took possession of the dead men's property. Before the end of August he was recognized as lord by the confederation of the Five Boroughs.

At this juncture Cnut brought a fleet down the Channel and landed in Wessex. While his men harried Dorset, Somerset, and Wiltshire, Edmund and Eadric Streona, uneasy allies, were raising troops, but they failed to agree on a plan of action and separated without fighting the Danes. The slippery ealdorman of Mercia then determined to throw in his lot with Cnut. He knew that King Ethelred was now a sick man, worn out at last by the strain of that catastrophic time and by the rebellion of his disobedient son, with all the confusion and discredit Edmund's completely selfish behaviour brought upon the English cause.

The Ironside was determined not to give up the struggle, but the army refused to fight unless they were led by King Ethelred in person. Edmund, however, did enlist the help of his brother-in-law Uhtred, earl of Northumbria, and spent the early months of 1016 ravaging the west midlands while Cnut harried the eastern shires. In April Edmund went to London, where Ethelred now lay on his deathbed. Father and son may be supposed to have been reconciled before death at last released Ethelred from a life which had brought little joy to him and less to his subjects.

## Character of Ethelred's Reign

As a lawgiver Ethelred had carried on the tradition of his predecessors. In ten codes issued at intervals during his reign he reaffirmed existing legislation and added new enactments of his own. His third code, issued from Wantage, perhaps in 997, was mainly concerned with the Danelaw. While extending certain English institutions into the area, it recognized the validity of the Danish customary law followed in the courts of boroughs and wapentakes and in the general assembly of the Five Boroughs, the most authoritative in this hierarchy of local courts. One article bids the reeve and the twelve leading thegns in each wapentake swear to accuse no innocent man nor conceal any guilty one. This is the earliest reference in English law to the sworn jury of presentment, ancestor of the grand jury which survived in England until 1933 and is still empanelled in the United States of America.

Another article in the Wantage code lays it down that no one is to have any jurisdiction over a king's thegn except the king himself. Ethelred appears in his later years to have construed this as authorizing him to dispense with legal process in dealing with the lives and property of such men as Sigeferth, Morcar, and Wulfgeat, this last a favourite reeve whose property Ethelred confiscated "because of his unjust judgements." In all probability it was these arbitrary stretches of the royal prerogative which his subjects asked him to renounce when they negotiated his return from Normandy.

His fifth code, issued in 1008, mentions that he has reformed judicial procedure in Northumbria, particularly the abuse by which a man was allowed no defence against a charge of murder if it was made on oath on the day of the victim's death. The code devotes much attention to the status and obligations of the clergy, among whom it distinguishes three groups: the celibate monks, the married canons of the unreformed minsters, and the parish priests. It enjoins celibacy on them all. In this particular Ethelred's legislation had no more effect than that of his predecessors.

In the year of his restoration, 1014, he declared that "a Christian king is Christ's deputy in a Christian people." His later codes, inspired and possibly drafted by Archbishop Wulfstan, are little more than sermons calling upon an ungodly people to mend its ways.

Throughout the reign the administrative system built up by his predecessors did not break down, but responded effectively to the heavy demands made upon it. When the ealdormen became earls governing large provinces, every shire needed an officer of subordinate rank to represent the king. There had always been local reeves who managed the domains of the crown, collected the king's dues, and presided over the public courts, but under Ethelred II the shire-reeve, or sheriff, first comes plainly into view as the chief executive agent in local government, responsible to the king who appointed him for the conduct of public business in the shire. The earls, while keeping in touch with at least the greater landowners within their jurisdiction, and retaining the presidency of the shire-court, became more and more political figures preoccupied with issues that affected the nation as a whole, leaving the daily routine of administration to the sheriff.

The king conveyed his orders to these officers by means of sealed writs. Formal diplomas, landbooks, charters, continued to be drawn up in the writing office which served as the king's chancery. They were written in stately, not to say pompous, Latin, and either the originals or copies were folded several times, endorsed for easy reference, and filed in the king's treasury. By contrast, the writs by which the king signified his commands were written in English and were relatively terse. They were authenticated by the royal seal. A grant of fiscal exemption or justiciary rights would be notified by this means. When the Danes extorted enormous sums, the king could set in motion the machinery of local collection by sending down a writ addressed to the earl, the sheriff, and the thegns of a shire, who knew exactly the number of hides for which they were accountable, ordering them to raise their quota. Copies of two writs issued by Ethelred II have been preserved, and from his day to the present the sovereign's writ under seal has remained in use as a most efficient executive instrument.

Our knowledge of the reign is derived mostly from contemporary annalists who were heavily biased against the government and not particularly well informed. They freely imputed motives on mere guesswork. It is, however, clear that Ethelred's path was beset with pitfalls created by untrustworthy magnates and by his unhappy choice of advisers. His name means 'noble counsel', but before the thirteenth century some reader of the Chronicle coined for him the nickname *Unraed*, 'no-counsel'. In the sixteenth century this was mistranslated as 'unready', and it is as Ethelred the Unready that he still figures in modern schoolbooks.

## The Ironside's Bid for the Crown

After burying the king in St Paul's, the Londoners and those magnates who were in the city offered the crown to Edmund Ironside. But the most influential Englishmen were not minded to follow suit. A deputation of bishops, abbots, ealdormen, and thegns went to meet Cnut at Southampton and tendered their allegiance to him in return for a promise of good government. During the next seven months the country was rent by a titanic struggle between the Englishman and the Dane.

If energy and valour could have made good Edmund's claim, he had both in full measure. He betook himself at once to Wessex and raised an army which fought two bloody but indecisive battles against his rival's followers. He then attempted to relieve London from a blockade by Cnut, but the effort, which at first promised to be brilliantly successful, failed to dislodge the Danes. The city, however, still held out, and Cnut, after provisioning his army by a raid over East Anglia and Mercia, brought it into Kent. It was overtaken at Otford and defeated by Edmund. Immediately after the battle Eadric Streona parleyed with Edmund at Aylesford long enough to let the Danes escape by sea. Crossing the estuary of the Thames, they raided Essex and the adjoining Mercian shires. They were on their way back to their ships when Edmund caught up with them at *Assandun*. This has usually been identified with Ashingdon, but a stronger case has been made out for Ashdon in north Essex. The battle ended in disaster for Edmund. Believing or pretending to believe that he had been killed, Eadric Streona with his Mercian contingent fled from the field; the ealdormen of Hampshire, Lindsey, and East Anglia, the bishop of Dorchester, and the abbot of Ramsey all lost their lives; and Edmund barely escaped to Gloucestershire, with his rival in hot pursuit. But the Ironside was still considered formidable, and Eadric Streona saw possibilities of advantage in holding the balance between the rivals. A meeting took place by arrangement on an island in the Severn near Deerhurst, where agreement was reached on a partition which left Edmund in control of Wessex and gave the rest of England to the Dane. The large possibilities of trouble inherent in this division were forestalled by Edmund's death a few weeks later. No contemporary chronicle sheds any light on the circumstances of his end. After the Norman Conquest various conflicting tales were told, and we have to wait until nearly the end of the twelfth century for record of what looks like a trustworthy local tradition that Edmund received a fatal wound from an assassin at Minsterworth on the west bank of the Severn and was carried to Ross-on-Wye, where he died.

## Cnut Becomes King

He left two infant sons and a younger brother Edwy. The infants were sent to a safe refuge in Hungary, and Edwy was driven into exile. After wandering for a while on the continent, he crept back to England, a sick man, and died at Tavistock. Cnut, now master of England, divided the country into four earldoms, giving East Anglia to Thorkell the Tall, and leaving Eadric Streona in charge of Mercia. Eric of Norway, his father's choice, remained earl of Northumbria, and Cnut kept Wessex for himself. These arrangements were short-lived. Before the end of 1017 Eadric and four other Englishmen of the highest rank were put to death. Eadric's record laid him open to suspicion, but we hear of no specific charge and nothing of any trial. To forestall possible intervention from Normandy on behalf of the sons Emma had borne to Ethelred II, Cnut sent for the widow and married her, although during Ethelred's lifetime he had espoused a high-born Englishwoman, Ælfgifu of Northampton.

In the following year Cnut destroyed thirty Viking crews which ventured into English waters. He then dismissed all but forty of the ships which had brought him to England, first exacting 10,500 pounds from the Londoners and 72,000 pounds from the rest of England to pay the crews. Not long afterwards the leading Englishmen and Danes assembled at Oxford and agreed to live in peace together under the system of law which had prevailed in Edgar's reign.

## Character of Cnut's Reign

In 1019 Cnut went to Denmark to claim the throne of that country, left vacant by the death of his childless elder brother. His military prowess, and the money he had raised in England, assured the success of the expedition. In a letter to his English subjects he took credit for having thus prevented a renewal of Viking enterprise at their expense. The archbishop of Canterbury had secured Cnut's recognition as king of England by the pope, Benedict VIII, who sent letters and messages exhorting him to suppress injustice and to maintain the security of his people. The bloodthirsty young barbarian, who had been baptized in Germany, saw the necessity of a good understanding with the church, and willingly allowed his bishops to teach him how a Christian king was expected to behave.

In 1023 Cnut again visited Denmark and left Thorkell the Tall to govern there in his name. Three years later he led a combined Anglo-Danish naval armament against an alliance between the kings of Norway and Sweden. He managed to drive them apart, and engaged the Swedes in a battle which left neither side decisively victorious but removed the threat to Denmark. After the battle he travelled to Rome, where he attended the coronation of the Emperor Conrad II (26 March 1027). He was the first of his line to be admitted into the brotherhood of civilized kings. While in Rome he persuaded the emperor and the king of Burgundy to allow pilgrims and merchants exemption from tolls and unmolested passage through the Alpine passes. From John XIX he obtained a reduction of the fees exacted from English archbishops when they went to Rome for the pallium. On his way home he sent a long letter to England by the hands of Lyfing, abbot of Tavistock and bishop designate of Crediton. With obvious pride he related his honourable reception by the foreign princes and the success of his various negotiations. In the following year he attacked Norway and was accepted as its king. Leaving his former wife Ælfgifu of Northampton and her son Harold to rule that country for him, he returned triumphantly to England.

On his return he found it necessary to take measures for the security of the northern frontier. In 1016 or thereabouts Earl Uhtred of Northumbria had been worsted at Carham on the Tweed by a Scottish army under Malcolm II of Alba and Owen the Bald of Strathclyde. Owen may have been killed in this battle; he was certainly the last of his line. The ancient British kingdom of Strathclyde which for more than four centuries had held out manfully, with varying fortunes, against the Picts, the Scots, the English, and the Norsemen, fell to pieces. By a process of which the details are hidden from us the English gained possession of Cumberland, and Malcolm II obtained the territory north of the Solway for his grandson and successor Duncan I. The kingdoms of Alba and Strathclyde thus merged into a united kingdom of Scotland. Immediately after his return from Rome Cnut led his army to the north and by a display of overwhelming force compelled Malcolm to recognize him as overlord of Britain.

He could not have undertaken his frequent journeys abroad if he had felt his position in England to be insecure. He surrounded himself with a strong bodyguard of disciplined fighting-men called housecarls. They ranked as thegns, and were paid out of the proceeds of an annual levy called *heregeld*, or army-tax. Payment was strictly enforced; if an estate could not pay its quota within three days from the appointed date, any stranger who produced the money could displace the rightful owner and take possession. At that time perhaps more Danes than Englishmen had money waiting to be invested. Partly by this means, and partly by royal gift in reward for exceptional service – two of Cnut's housecarls are known to have received estates in Dorset – Danish landowners became familiar figures in the countryside, so that in 1042 an episcopal lease was attested by "all the thegns in Worcestershire, both English and Danish."

As well as the standing military force of housecarls, Cnut maintained a permanent fleet, reduced by the end of his reign from forty to sixteen warships. It has been estimated that the crews of this navy cost England between 3,000 and 4,000 pounds a year in wages. What with this and the *heregeld*, a heavy burden of annual taxation took the place of the occasional Danegelds levied under Ethelred II. Nevertheless England appreciated the internal peace and the security from foreign inroads which the country enjoyed under Cnut, and on the whole men afterwards looked back to his reign as a beneficent and prosperous time.

The earls appointed by Cnut in the early part of his reign nearly all bore Scandinavian names. Siward, a warlike Dane who married a grand-daughter of Earl Uhtred, kept Northumbria in some sort of order. But English as well as Danish witnesses attest Cnut's charters, and in his later years he relied chiefly on the advice of two Englishmen, Leofric of Mercia and Godwine of Wessex. A thegn of obscure antecedents, Godwine was created an earl in 1018 and married a Danish princess, Gytha. From then until his death in 1053 he played an active and sometimes dominant part in English politics.

Many of Cnut's laws merely repeat those enacted by his predecessors, including Ethelred II, and when they deal with religious or ecclesiastical subjects they frequently echo the homiletic style of Archbishop Wulfstan. In one matter he seems to have taken a step forward. The kings had long been insisting that all men should give sureties for keeping the peace, unless they were slaves or unfree dependants upon a lord who could be relied upon to keep them in order. Under Athelstan the citizens of London had organized themselves in tithings and hundreds, groups of ten and of a hundred households, with responsibility for the pursuit and arrest of thieves. Cnut perfected the system by requiring all free men over the age of twelve to be enrolled in a tithing or hundred. Over much of England the tithing took shape as a territorial division of a hundred rather than an association of ten households; but the system, later known as frank-pledge, continued for centuries to hold every member of a tithing answerable for the good conduct of each and all of his fellow members.

## Death of Cnut

After a reign of nineteen years Cnut died at Shaftesbury on 12 November 1035. The Norwegians had already regained their independence, but Cnut intended that Harthacnut, his only son by Emma, should inherit Denmark and England. Harthacnut, however, was in Denmark at the time of his father's death, and Norwegian hostility made it unsafe for him to leave. In his absence Harold Harefoot, son of Cnut by Ælfgifu of Northampton, was accepted in England, at first as regent, but in 1037 as king.

In the previous year Alfred, one of the two surviving sons of Ethelred and Emma, left his Norman exile and set sail for England, ostensibly to visit his mother at Winchester. It is said that he had refused an offer of troops from Baldwin V, count of Flanders, but the same authority says he brought with him 600 men, which seems a large escort if his errand was really peaceful. However that may have been, he was intercepted at Guildford by Earl Godwine, and his followers were blinded, mutilated, or sold into slavery. The prince himself was put on board ship, blinded, and taken to Ely, where he soon died of his injuries. The atrocity, which Alfred's brother Edward never forgot or forgave, cast a shadow over Godwine's reputation. He afterwards asserted on oath, an oath supported by magnates from all over England, that he had neither wished nor advised that Alfred should be blinded, and that he had acted only in obedience to Harold.

### Accession of Harthacnut

It seems probable that Harthacnut, from the moment when he came to terms with the Norwegians, intended to claim his inheritance in England. The premature death of Harold Harefoot (17 March 1040) prevented him from taking forcible vengeance on the usurper, but after landing shortly before midsummer he ordered Harold's corpse to be dug up and thrown into the Thames. The English appear to have been well disposed towards him, but soon changed their minds when he exacted 21,099 pounds to pay off the crews of the sixty-two ships he had brought to England. He kept thirty-two of them in his service, at a cost to the country of 11,048 pounds. This, at a time of general scarcity, when the price of corn rose to an unprecedented height, proved a crushing burden. Two of the king's housecarls, who had been sent to collect the tax in Worcester, were killed by the infuriated populace. Enraged by this act of rebellion, Harthacnut ordered his earls to assemble an army and ravage Worcestershire. The country people took to flight; the men of Worcester defended themselves successfully on an island in the Severn; and their city was burnt.

*End of the Danish Interlude*

What promised to be an intolerable tyranny came to an abrupt end on 8 June 1042. Harthacnut was attending the marriage-feast of one of his father's retainers when a sudden seizure carried him off. He was not yet twenty-five years old, and a presentiment may have warned him that he had not long to live, for in the previous year he had sent for his half-brother Edward, the only surviving son of Emma by Ethelred II, and welcomed him at his court.

The death of Harthacnut brought the Danish interlude to an end. Even before he was buried a strong movement in favour of the ancient dynasty caused Edward to be acclaimed as king, and on Easter day 1043 he was crowned at Winchester. Half Norman by birth, Edward had spent the whole of his youth and early manhood in Normandy. No one as yet thought of him as a saint, or styled him a Confessor, nor could any one then foresee that his accession would usher in a new phase of English history, marking the true beginning of the Anglo-Norman state.

Chapter XII

# THE LATER ANGLO-SAXON
# LANDSCAPE

More than half a millennium had elapsed between the first settlement of the Anglo-Saxons in Britain and the accession of Edward
the Confessor. In that long spell of time the face of the land had
changed beyond recognition. Despite warfare, civil strife, and
natural disasters, population had increased and the work of
developing the resources of the land to feed the growing number
of mouths had been pursued with vigour. Marshes were drained,
and the woodlands greatly reduced. Above all, there had been a
vast extension of the area under plough.

In the boundary surveys of tenth-century land-charters we
frequently come across terms which indicate that the small square
or nearly square fields of primitive agriculture, with their short
furrows, are now a thing of the past. We hear, for instance, of the
headland, a margin left at the top and bottom of the field so that
the plough-team may have room to turn. When the rest of the
field has been worked over, the headland in its turn is ploughed,
at right angles to the rest, and it is then sometimes called the fore-
earth. If the field is not perfectly rectangular, it may be necessary
to plough a 'gore' consisting of one or more 'gore-acres' taper-
ing at one end, so that the sides of the gore are not parallel like the
sides of the ordinary plough-strip. Gores and headlands are
familiar features of the open fields as delineated in the field-maps
of later centuries.

In the early Kentish charters the word for the plough is
*aratrum*; in the tenth-century Danelaw it is *caruca*. Strictly speaking, the *aratrum* was a light implement which made no very deep
incision and was chiefly suitable for ploughing well-drained soils,

in contrast with the heavy wheeled *caruca* which produced deep furrows and plough-strips about ten times as long as they were broad. But it would be rash to construe the charters as implying a real distinction between the types of plough in use at the time. And the old idea that the use of the *caruca* is related to the shape of the long-strip fields as cause and effect has been discarded in the light of evidence that in several parts of the world, and notably in Sweden, strip fields were produced by the *aratrum*, and the *caruca* properly so-called was unknown. It is now widely held that social and tenurial conditions exert as much influence on field-shape as any single technical factor.

## The Open Fields

The tantalizing reference in Ine's laws to arable share-land must be recalled here, a reference which provoked more curiosity than it satisfied. The term meets us again, a little more instructively, in the third quarter of the tenth century. At Ardington (Berks) the land is described as lying in common with other share-land, and the charter goes out of its way to explain what this means: it states that the open pasture is common, the meadow is common, and the arable is common. Where arable alone is in question, another way of expressing it is to declare that the land lies always acre between acre. In such cases a proportionate share in the common pastures and meadows is almost certainly taken for granted.

We may ask: why should any man share plough-land with others? The answer surely is that he can seldom afford not to do so. Capital resources in the form of oxen are scarce. We have already met in Ine's laws the husbandman who finds it necessary to hire oxen from his neighbour. The lord who sets up a group of slaves or freedmen on plots of their own is unlikely to provide them with more than two oxen apiece, and on heavy soil a stronger team may well be required. Men will huddle together on sites recommended by a natural water-supply, and will till the land lying as near to the settlement as possible. All their working hours will be taken up with tending their livestock and raising their none too abundant crops. They will have no time for walking to distant fields or for making and maintaining more hedges than are absolutely necessary.

## Intermixed Holdings

Although Ine's law proves that some form of arable share-land was known in seventh-century Wessex, it tells us nothing of its earlier history. Moreover, while the law makes it clear that two or more husbandmen might plough together in one field, the regulations about fencing suggest that each man's share lay undivided in one block. But now in the tenth century charters provide unquestionable evidence of intermixed acres: what a later age will call the "mingle-mangle" of the open fields. In 956 King Eadwig granted to his thegn Wulfric five hides at Charlton by Wantage (Berks). The charter states that the land is separated by no fixed bounds, for the acres adjoin other acres. A later grant of the same five hides declares that they are "in common land" and "are not demarcated on all sides by clear bounds because to left and right lie acres in combination one with another." Still more explicitly, three hides at Avon (Wilts) are described as consisting of "single acres dispersed in a mixture here and there in common land."

## Causes of Intermixture

It is natural to wonder how this intermixture had come about. We shall be well advised not to postulate a single governing factor, but to consider more than one possible explanation.

First, have we here an effect of partible inheritance? A man dies leaving what he has to leave to his three sons, A, B, and C, in equal shares. The most equitable way to apportion the arable will be to give A, B, and C three or four acres apiece, in that order, and then repeat the process until the whole is allotted.

We know too little about customs of inheritance in the humbler ranks of Anglo-Saxon society to speak with any assurance on the subject. We do know that landlords occasionally framed their leases on these lines. For example, Oswald, bishop of Worcester, granted a lease of one and a half hides at Alveston (Wark) with "every other acre in the divided hide at Upper Stratford"; and the same Oswald, leasing Moreton in Bredon (Worcs) to two brothers arranged that "the elder shall always have three acres and the younger the fourth, both central and outlying."

Oswald's language confronts us with a third possibility: that the intermixture of parcels may have been imposed on the tillers of the soil by the combined powers of church and state in order that dues and services might be justly and efficiently apportioned. This is the period when the king is beginning to take a hand in enforcing payment of tithe. King Edmund says that "every Christian man" who refuses to pay tithes must be excommunicated. King Edgar does not leave it to the church; he orders his reeves to accompany the bishop's reeve and the local priest and seize what is due from a recalcitrant payer; and Ethelred II, re-enacting this law, defines tithe as "the produce of every tenth acre as traversed by the plough." This method could be applied anywhere, even on demesne land, but it would obviously be the simplest and most effective way of collecting tithe-corn from a community of husbandmen whose arable lay in open fields.

## Scandinavian Influence

One of the most influential churchmen of the age, Oswald, two of whose leases have been cited, held the see of Worcester from 961 and with it that of York from 972 until his death in 992. Himself of Danish or partly Danish parentage, he was well placed for observing the usages of the Danelaw. His predecessor at York, the Danish-named Oscytel, had received a grant of 20 hides at Southwell (Notts) with jurisdiction over a number of other villages. One of these was Normanton, where the church was given "every third acre." In the same period we find a nobleman with a Scandinavian name selling "every eighth acre" at Brandon (Suffolk). Transactions in these terms could obviously generate an intermixture of arable parcels even if it was not already present.

In all these cases the grants are made either to thegns or to powerful churchmen. One of our greatest historians, Maitland, could not believe that the system was invented by such people. He granted that they might think fit to maintain it where they found it already established, but he held that it must have been originally the work of free and equal peasants who "could not be prevented from sacrificing every interest of their lords on the shrine of equality." Now, if we look in the England of the tenth century – not of the seventh, as Maitland did – for a class of men strongly imbued with the idea of equality, and free enough to act upon it, we have not far to seek. We have already met the *bondi*, the free Danish warrior-farmer who attended the wapentake and enjoyed an appreciably higher status than English countrymen of the same economic standing. The Norse word 'man's lot', applied to holdings of no great size, pretty clearly implies an allotment of standard shares. When a community of free and equal Danish farmers colonized virgin soil in England and founded a new -*by*, it might well occur to them to lay out their man's lots in regular sequence over the arable field or fields, with the strips of B, C, and D consistently lying between those of A. This would be the simplest method of allotting to each a fair share of good and bad soil alike, and confining no man to a part of the field which might often become water-logged. Documents from the thirteenth century onwards bear witness to the persistence of this remarkably regular pattern in the areas of Scandinavian settlement. The method could equally well be applied when an established English or Danish community, under pressure of growing population, took in land from the common pasture and put it under plough.

The Danish emphasis on arable husbandry, and its far-reaching effects on fiscal assessments, were noticed in an earlier chapter. It may now be suggested, very tentatively, that the effects were far-reaching enough to bring about a reorganization of the arable fields in many villages of older settlement. Dramatic changes are rare in agriculture, but there are indications that agrarian and fiscal concepts were being radically modified in the reign of Edred. In 949 Edred issued a charter from which we learn that the Kentish ploughland (*sulung*) was now equated with one hide, not with two as of old. Some historians have held that the open-field system goes back to the earliest days of Anglo-Saxon settlement. We cannot prove the contrary, but we have seen good reason for doubting that it is as old as that. It has certainly left no traces in charters earlier than the tenth century. Can it be mere coincidence that we begin to find clear documentary evidence of intermixed arable holdings shortly after the Scandinavian occupation?

## Geography of the Open Field

A number of charters indicate that open-field husbandry was very much at home in tenth-century Berkshire. Clear traces of the system are found also in Oxfordshire, Hertfordshire, and Wiltshire. But while the charters vouch for the existence in the Thames valley and the eastern counties of arable tilled in common and frequently speak of it as common land, they leave it uncertain whether the fields were grazed by the stock of all the commoners after harvest and in fallow seasons. Nor do they provide any clue to the rotation of crops. If we subscribe to the austere doctrine that these are essential features of the developed system, we may have to wait until the twelfth or thirteenth centuries for evidence to justify us in speaking of common fields thus strictly defined in any part of England. There is at any rate no difficulty in believing that the system took a long time to mature.

## Infield and Outfield

South-west England took a different course. Here the ploughland consisted of an area close to the farmstead or hamlet, called the infield or in-ground, which was permanently cultivated, while the outfield or out-ground was an area taken in from the common pasture, cropped for a year or two, and then allowed to revert to its former state, after which the process might be repeated on another part of the common. This intermittent cultivation of the outfield was particularly suitable for regions where great tracts of moor and heath provided a superabundance of rough pasture. It was practised in Cornwall and Scotland down to the eighteenth century, and traces of it have been found in Devon and elsewhere in the highland zone.

A solitary reference to outfield cultivation occurs in a charter dated 958 by which King Edwy granted two and a half hides and 25 acres at Ayshford and Boehill in east Devon to a certain Eadheah. The document includes a perambulation of the twin properties in the usual form. Then a laconic postscript adds: "there are many hills there that one may plough." This almost casual reference evidently takes for granted a well-established practice, and there are hints of it in documents from other parts of the country.

## The West Midlands

In the west midlands we might for a moment imagine ourselves back in open-field country. In 904 the bishop of Worcester granted a lease of Barbourne with 60 acres of arable to the north and 60 acres to the south. Barbourne, however, is a stream-name, so the bishop may have merely been giving a geographical description of a single holding. Another episcopal lease refers to 30 acres in the two fields of share-land outside the bounds of Cudley. Barbourne and Cudley are both in the suburbs of Worcester, and it sounds as if the pattern at Cudley was the classic pattern of the two-field system, with a rotation of crop and fallow alternating either between the two fields or within the area of each.

But we must beware of reading too much into the evidence. Rotation seems to be ruled out in places where we find patches of arable assigned more or less permanently to particular crops. The bounds of Himbleton (Worcs) run "along the hedge to the rye-growing croft, along the headland of the croft to the other headland, from that headland to the barley-growing croft." Elsewhere there is mention of beanland, barley-land, "the bishop's oat-land" and of a road to the flax-fields (*linaceran wege*) where there is now a farm called Linacres. In granting a lease of two hides at Wolverton (Worcs) Archbishop Oswald excepted 60 acres which he had attached as wheat-growing land to his manor of Kempsey. The archbishop was a business-like prelate who carried out far-reaching tenurial changes on his lands, and the Wolverton lease shows him in the act, here at least, of reorganizing the agricultural pattern. On the evidence of other leases it has already been suggested that his experience in the Danelaw may have prompted him in some cases to create mixed arable holdings on the lands of his west midland see.

## Regional Varieties

A charter for Bromley shows that in 987 Kent remained faithful to the custom of providing a manor with appurtenances in the shape of distant swine-pastures: Bromley had five such *denns* miles away in the Weald. No contemporary evidence informs us how the Kentish arable was managed.

For the rest of England the sources fail us. Thus the accidents of survival oblige us to make what we can of information from sources that are unevenly distributed and far from sufficiently detailed. The data which have been briefly examined in these pages point to four distinct varieties of practice. In the Thames valley and the eastern counties we find what has been called the midland system, based on farming by village communities who held their pasture and meadow in common and their arable in scattered strips. In Kent, and probably also in Sussex and parts of Hampshire, the economy is based largely on stock-raising, and therefore lays great stress on the use of distant forest pastures. In the south-west and possibly elsewhere the intermittent cultivation of the outfield supplements a more intensive crop-raising nearer home. Finally in the west midlands the arable appears to be so managed as to preclude crop-rotation, with no preponderance of tillage over pastoral husbandry; but the picture is indistinct, for here and there we find intrusions of the midland system. Later evidence will no doubt fill in these outlines, and may well multiply the number of regional variations.

## Livestock

The interest of kings and magnates in stock-raising has been mentioned in an earlier chapter. Occasionally the documents allow us glimpses of individual estates and their livestock. For example:

Beddington (Surr): 9 full-grown oxen, 114 full-grown pigs, 50 wethers, besides the sheep and pigs to which the herdsmen are entitled, 20 of which are full-grown; 110 full-grown sheep, 7 slave-men, 20 flitches of bacon.

Luddington (Wark): 12 slave-men, 2 teams of oxen, 100 sheep, 50 fothers of corn.

Norton (Worcs): 1 man, 6 oxen, 20 sheep, 20 acres of corn sown.

Egmere (Norf): 7 oxen, 8 cows, 4 grazing bullocks, 2 inferior horses, 115 sheep and lambs, 180 acres sown, 1 flitch of bacon, 1 pig, 24 cheeses.

If the horse was ever used for ploughing or harrowing, the fact is not mentioned in our sources. It is known, however, that Anglo-Saxon magnates maintained stud-farms. There was one at Ongar (Essex) belonging to a lord named Thurstan. Aelfhelm leaves half his stud at Troston (Suffolk) to his wife and half to his companions. The lady Wynflaed's will speaks of horses some of which are unbroken, others tame. The founder of Burton Abbey, Wulfric, gives the monastery 100 wild horses and 16 tame geldings, with other livestock. Another will speaks of a white horse and two stallions, one black, the other pied.

## Mills

One important feature of the agrarian landscape, the water-mill, found no place in our earlier survey. The laws of Ethelbert show that the kings of Kent employed slave-women to grind corn for them, and doubtless their subjects did the same. But when slaves grow scarce or costly, the expedient suggests itself of applying water-power instead of human muscles. The water-driven mill, no novelty in the Mediterranean world, took centuries to supersede the hand-quern in northern Europe. The capital outlay and the cost of repairs would be unprofitable unless there were a large enough quantity of grain to be ground. Only kings and magnates could face the expense, and only they could successfully assert a legal right to draw off the necessary water.

A village in Saxony on the River Unstrut, founded by Frankish warriors in 775, is significantly named Mühlhausen. The English equivalent of this name is *Mylentun*, borne by an estate at or near Otford which the archbishop of Canterbury purchased from King Ceolwulf in 822. But if a record from St Augustine's, Canterbury, can be trusted, the abbey had preceded the archbishop as a mill-owner. It possessed one at Chart, and in 762 made over half the miller's rent in order that the tenant might have pasture in the Weald for one herd of swine. A mill at Chart, perhaps the same one, is recorded in 814. From this time onwards mills appear fairly often among the appurtenances of Kentish estates. It is not surprising that the water-mill should make its earliest appearance in Kent, which from its proximity to the European mainland was naturally receptive of continental ideas, but once introduced it would not for long be confined to the south-east. In 956 the bounds of an estate in Tadmarton (Oxon) begin and end at "Edward's mill." About this time a mill-leat nearly three-quarters of a mile long, with a flat bottom over twenty feet wide and a depth at its maximum of about twelve feet, was dug across a loop of the Thames at Old Windsor to drive a large mill equipped with three water-wheels. Of windmills we shall hear nothing until the twelfth century is nearly over, but at the close of the Old English period water-mills in this country would be numbered in thousands.

## Salterns and Saltways

The sea and natural inland springs provided the Anglo-Saxons with that essential commodity, salt. All round the coast and in the estuaries lay salterns where sea-water was boiled to extract the salt by evaporation, consuming large quantities of fuel in the process. Inland the main sources of supply were the brine springs of Droitwich in Worcestershire and Nantwich in Cheshire. Early in his reign Ethelbald of Mercia gave the church of Worcester a plot of ground on the south bank of the River Salwarp for the construction of three salt-houses and six furnaces, in exchange for six other furnaces and two salt-houses on the north bank. He and his successors drew a steady revenue from the tolls they levied on the trade in salt.

From the main inland centres tracks called saltways radiated in all directions to be travelled by distributors of this essential commodity. Place-names and documentary references enable the routes of many saltways to be traced and mapped. They must have played nearly as important a part in the Anglo-Saxon road system as the prehistoric ridgeways. These, following high ground in order to avoid river-crossings, remained in use, as also did the great Roman roads. The Anglo-Saxons turned the Latin word *strata* into *straet*, our "street," to denote a paved road, usually but not invariably Roman. A road used primarily for military purposes or leading to a well-known battle site was called a *here-paeth*, or army path. *Weg*, the commonest of all words for a road, covered a wide variety of tracks, from a Roman road like the Fosse Way to the innumerable unnamed country lanes which figure in charter boundaries.

A charter by which King Ethelbald exempted two ships belonging to the bishop of Worcester from payment of tolls in the port of London is only one of many evidences for the regular use of water transport.

## Minsters

Churches, like mills, required an outlay of capital for their construction and, like mills again, were expected to provide an income for their founders. No account of Anglo-Saxon architecture will be given here, but the different grades of church must be briefly described. The cathedral, where the bishop had his seat, was called a minster, *monasterium*, because his clergy were monks or at least shared a communal life. From this central power-house priests went out to preach and offer mass at rural spots marked at first only by standing crosses. Presently noblemen built churches on their estates for the convenience of their tenants and for their own temporal profit. They appointed a priest and bargained with him for a share of the offerings and tithes. With the growth of population and settlement such churches multiplied, giving rise to conflicts of pecuniary interest. King Edgar laid down a rule that the old minsters should keep their tithes, but that a thegn who had a church and graveyard on his bookland might pay that church a third of his own tithe; if there was no graveyard he could pay the priest what he liked out of the nine remaining parts. Church-scot from all free hearths was still reserved to the old minster. The legislation of Ethelred II and his Danish successors classified churches as 'head minsters' or cathedrals, 'ordinary minsters', the original mother-churches of a district, lesser parochial churches possessing graveyards, and 'field churches' built for recently established communities and not yet possessing the graveyard which entitled them to the burial-fee called soul-scot. In forested regions these humble structures might be log-built and roofed with thatch, but where stone quarries abounded the builders naturally availed themselves of the more durable material. Most Anglo-Saxon churches were small; even the cathedral at North Elmham had a nave only 66 ft long. They tended to be rectangular in plan, with narrow nave facing a diminutive chancel, walls about 2½ ft thick, and windows set high in the walls. But in all except the smallest churches a western, or less commonly a central, bell-tower formed the most conspicuous external feature, sometimes rising to a considerable height. The fine tower at Earl's Barton (Northants), decorated with narrow bands of stonework which project an inch or so from the surface of the walls, is perhaps the best-known example.

## Boroughs and Ports

Where men congregated for worship they would remain to buy and sell. The dairy-woman with a cheese to spare, the farmer desirous of selling a sheep or cow, the reeve buying seed-corn for his master's land, would find an informal market ready-made outside the church on Sunday. Athelstan tried to prohibit Sunday trading, but later repealed the prohibition. Ethelred II made more persistent efforts in the same direction, as also did Cnut after him, seemingly to no avail. The law frowned on transactions not conducted under the eye of responsible officials who would see that tolls were paid. It demanded regular markets, and the best place for a regular market was in a town.

It is not now believed that urban life became totally extinct after the collapse of Roman administration. Canterbury, London, Dorchester-on-Thames, and York, to name no other Roman towns, have provided convincing archaeological evidence of continued habitation, and the establishment of bishoprics there after the conversion of the English must have strengthened their chances of survival. But in an earlier chapter we saw that the greatest impetus to the growth of urban life and institutions came from the policy of Alfred the Great and his successors in constructing a network of boroughs (*burhs*), primarily for strategic purposes. Excavations and topographical study of the sites at Lydford, Wareham, Cadbury, Cricklade, Winchester, and Wallingford in recent years have revealed the character of their defences and in some of them a regular street pattern which suggests that royal policy deliberately encouraged settlers who would form a genuinely urban community.

In such explorations the urban archaeology of the Anglo-Saxon period has made an excellent beginning, but as yet is hardly more than a beginning. There is every reason to expect that in the years ahead it will throw much new light on the towns of the late Old English period. In the meantime documentary evidence assures us of their capacity for corporate action. Each borough had its court, meeting thrice yearly in accordance with King Edgar's law; in 1018 the bishop of Crediton notified a mortgage transaction to the courts of all four Devon boroughs, Exeter, Totnes, Lydford, and Barnstaple. Exeter, in addition to its borough court, also had a guild, a voluntary association of townsmen chiefly for religious purposes; its regulations, however, include provision for a rudimentary form of fire insurance. The statutes of similar associations have survived from Bedwyn, Abbotsbury, and Cambridge. Those from Abbotsbury include the interesting statement that Urk, a housecarl under Cnut and Edward the Confessor, and founder of an abbey there, gave the brethren a guildhall in memory of himself and of his wife. A London guild which survived the Norman Conquest is thought to have begun as an association of men appointed by magnates who owned property in the city to look after their interests and keep them supplied with goods from the London market. Charters tell the same tale: they speak of messuages in Winchester belonging to the rural manor of Tisted, of one in Wilton belonging to Wylye, and of one in Hereford granted to the lord of Staunton on Arrow.

By the end of our period most villagers would have been within easy reach of a borough or port. Some of the boroughs were defended by stone walls, but the houses were built of more combustible materials. Thetford, burnt down by the Danes in 1004, was rebuilt only to be burnt down again in 1016.

*Houses*

Once destroyed by fire, the wooden foundations and walls of Anglo-Saxon houses are hard to detect. Often nothing survives but marks, visible in the subsoil, of the holes into which the builders fitted posts, beams, and planks. These leave a pattern which requires interpretation by the excavator, and he is always exposed to the temptation of finding just what he is looking for. Many archaeologists believe that the sunken huts described in an earlier chapter co-existed with larger timber buildings at ground level. This belief has been to some extent confirmed by recent research on the same sites.

At St Neots (Hunts) an excavation reported in 1933 revealed eight huts which the excavator assumed to date from the tenth or eleventh centuries. The inhabitants, according to him, "lived in almost as primitive a condition as can be imagined. They had no regard for cleanliness, and were content to throw the remains of a meal into the furthest corner of the hut and leave it there. They were not nervous about ghosts, since they did not mind having a skeleton sticking out of the wall of one of their huts. . . . It is almost certain that they were wretchedly poor serfs." This gloomy picture has been somewhat modified by the more recent discovery of substantial timber buildings at St Neots, one of them over 60 feet long. Similarly at Maxey (Northants) an excavation undertaken in the hope of finding larger buildings between the sunken huts already known there brought to light seven rectangular structures built of timber, wattle, clay, and thatch. They varied in length between 30 and 50 feet, and in width between 16 and 20 feet. These findings accord very well with the documentary evidence of a social system which included, side by side in the same village, cottagers of the lowest grade and more substantial farmers with an appreciably higher standard of living.

What of the landlord? At Sulgrave (Northants), best known as the ancestral seat of George Washington's family, excavation has brought to light an Anglo-Saxon manor house which seems to have been built early in the eleventh century. On the ground floor a cobbled porch led into a single-bay room screened by a cross-partition from the main body of an aisleless hall, 75 by 20 feet, which had a central hearth, side benches against the south wall, and a dais at the east end. The eastern-most bay was carried on stone footings four feet high. Beyond it stood a two-storied block, L-shaped or possibly T-shaped, containing two or three rooms on the ground floor and on the upper floor a chamber which extended over the end bay of the hall. Associated with this complex was a free-standing tower or bell-house, a composite structure of stone and timber. It is clear from this example that by the late Saxon period, if not earlier, the dwelling of a rural thegn could exhibit a noteworthy degree of sophistication.

In the second quarter of the tenth century a new hall, 60 feet long and 28 or 30 feet wide, was built in the royal manor of Cheddar (Som), superseding the hall which had been used in Alfred's reign. Massive posts, up to two feet square, were set at eight-foot intervals and presumably connected by plank walling. A chapel and what may have been a corn-mill were added to the site. Later still, perhaps in the reign of Ethelred II, the nave of a new and larger chapel was built round the older one.

Archaeology in future years will doubtless tell us more about the pursuits and surroundings of the Anglo-Saxons in the later phase of the Old English state. It is less helpful when we turn to examine the social structure. Here we must rely chiefly on written sources.

# Chapter XIII

# THE SOCIAL STRUCTURE IN THE LATE OLD ENGLISH PERIOD

One result of the unification of England under a single crown was to make it impossible for a Northumbrian warrior to be sold into slavery by his Mercian captors, or a Kentish woman to be carried off and held as a slave in Wessex. Warfare between the smaller kingdoms had ceased to provide a constant supply of slaves. But the class was still recruited from above. A free man might fall into penal servitude, either directly as a punishment for law-breaking, or because he had incurred a heavy fine which he found himself unable to pay. Poverty, again, and fear of starvation might drive an innocent man to sell himself and all his family. When he does this he must put his head between his master's hands and be handed a bill-hook or an ox-goad in token of his new condition. This was the ceremony to which a Northumbrian lady referred when she set free "all those people whose heads she took in return for their food in the evil days."

## Slaves and the Economics of Slavery

It was still not uncommon for slaves to be bought and sold. We hear of such transactions taking place at the church door in Bodmin, where the portreeve collected toll on the sale. In calculating the price, a woman was sometimes valued at half a pound, and a man at a whole pound, or eight times as much as an ox. When a personage named Ælfric tried to enslave one Putrael, a well-to-do Cornishman, on what ground is not recorded, Putrael by a fee of 60 pence to Ælfric's brother induced him to intercede with Ælfric and persuade him to accept eight oxen as the price of freedom for himself and his family. Five other Cornishmen with their sons and grandsons obtained King Edgar's leave to defend themselves by oath against an evil-doer who had asserted that their fathers had been serfs of the king.

Periods of social upheaval offered many chances of escape from thraldom. We have Archbishop Wulfstan's word for it that the Viking incursions enabled many a slave to change places with his master. Less violent in their operation, economic forces also pressed upon the slave-owner. "In twelve months," one writer told him, "thou shalt give thy slave men 720 loaves, besides morning and evening meals." This, if really provided, was no meagre ration, no negligible item in the household expenses. No wonder many masters found it worth while to set their slaves up as self-supporting or partly self-supporting tillers of the soil. The church encouraged them to do so, not only from religious motives – to free men from a recognized evil like slavery was a charitable action, and the emancipator would expect the emancipated to pray for him – but also because the serf with a plot of ground and a dwelling of his own became liable for Peter's Pence and other ecclesiastical dues.

### "Coliberti"

From the middle of the tenth century onwards testators frequently provide by will that all their *witetheow* men, their penal slaves, shall be set free. On the face of it this clause would release even those who had incurred the penalty only a month or two before the testator's death; if so, they were lucky to escape so lightly. Other wills make no distinction between penal and born or purchased slaves; they merely direct that "half the men" on a given manor or "all my men" shall be freed. It is usually held that the "men" in these cases were slaves. And when an East Anglian lady desires that all her men shall be set free, "both in the household and on the estate," we may reasonably assume that the first group are domestic slaves; but what of those on the land? The men to whom another East Anglian testatrix bequeaths their homesteads (*toftes*) are certainly settled on the land, for she calls them *landsethlan*. Another testator desires that the men to whom

he grants freedom shall have all things which are in their possession "except the land."

The truth is that men "freed" in batches like these, *coliberti*
as they are called in Latin documents, may be settled on the land,
but they are still only half-free. Sometimes the ceremony of
manumission was performed at a cross-roads, implying that the
freedman might go wherever he would and choose a new master,
but more often he remained, perhaps by choice, on his master's
land, subject to more or less burdensome dues and services.

About the middle of the tenth century a rich and highly connected widow named Wynflaed made a will disposing of her unfree dependants, her livestock, and lands of which some belonged
to her in her own right and some were leased from the minster at
Shaftesbury, where she appears to have taken the veil. One of the
slave women, exceptionally, is given freedom to choose her own
mistress; others, including a seamstress and a weaver, are left to
various members of her family. She also owned a number of penal
slaves, some of them with wives and children. She frees two
dozen or more of them by name and expresses the hope that for
the good of her soul her children will release any others there may
be. Two of her Somerset estates, Chinnock and Charlton Horethorne, appear to have been leaseholds, for at neither does she
make a bequest of land, and she expressly states that Chinnock
will belong to the nuns of Shaftesbury after her death, but she
adds that she herself owns the stock and the men. The slaves and
livestock she leaves to her daughter-in-law, but the occupants of
the rented land (*gebura the on tham gafollande sittath*) are to go
with the estate to the minster. Similarly at Charlton Horethorne
she frees two men and one woman but leaves the rest of the men
and stock to her daughter, "except the freedmen." The implication is that she had stocked these estates with men and oxen,
and that both alike remained her property. The men are clearly
of servile status, and those who have not been freed may presently
be sold off by her heirs or removed to some other estate like the
half-dozen serfs on the royal manor of Bensington (Oxon) who
were uprooted by the ealdorman of Mercia and transferred bodily,
with their offspring, to an estate under other ownership five miles
away. The freedmen, however, pass with the land, either to the

next leaseholder or to the owners of the estate. In practice they have security of tenure, but the fact that they have it by express stipulation, and not as of right, shows how much their lot depends on grace and favour.

Wynflaed's will, taken in conjunction with the two East Anglian wills already cited, proves that the "men" disposed of by the testators were not all slaves, but included farmers of servile antecedents who by law, if not always in practice, were tied to their master rather than to the estate. They owed him rent for their holdings. To such "men" Wulfgeat of Donington bequeaths a year's rent as a gift.

## The "Cotsetla" and the "Gebur"

The lord who meant to turn his slave into a freedman had to decide what he wanted from him: rent, service, or some of each. If the continued need for service was uppermost in his mind he might call the man "work-worthy" and describe his holding as "work-land" or "earning-land." He could stipulate for unpaid labour on the demesne one day a week throughout the year. In such cases he might allow the freedman enough timber to build himself a cabin, and with it a few acres of land. If this proved insufficient for his support, the cottager might hire himself out for wages on one or more of his free days. This freedman of the lowest class is called in the mother tongue a *cotsetla*. We meet him first under this designation in 956, when King Edwy makes a grant of 15 hides at Milton (Berks) and throws in six *cotsetlan*.

For a number of reasons – pressure of growing population, the consequent drive to expand tillage, a desire to reward good service, a greater need for money than labour – the lord may see fit to create larger holdings, of perhaps a yardland or more, and let them to rent-paying farmers. The rent-payer is the *gafolgelda*, and we remember here that where King Ine had spoken of the *gafolgelda* and the *gebur*, Alfred the Great classed both together as *ceorlisc* men. We remember, too, that Alfred's treaty with Guthrum had equated the English *ceorl* with the Danish freedman. But the vaguely generic *ceorl* is being displaced in this context by the more specific *gebur*. The *gebur* is not a boor, any more than the

217

*Note:* The categories in the following table are not mutually exclusive, e.g. a *gebur* might also be a *gafolgelda*, and every *ealdorman* would also be a thegn. Those marked* are probably all included in the genus *ceorl*.

| | Middle Saxon<br>*c.* 650–*c.* 850 | Late Saxon<br>*c.* 850–*c.* 1066 |
|---|---|---|
| Slave | *theow* | *theow*<br>*thraell* |
| Unfree or half-free cottager | *?esnewyrhta** | *cotsetla** |
| Freedman occupying a farm | *gebur** | *gebur**<br>*leysing**<br>(Latin)<br>*colibertus** |
| Rent-paying tenant | *gafolgelda** | *gafolgelda** |
| Free farmer | *geneat*<br>*?syxhynde* | *geneat*<br>*dreng*<br>*radcniht* |
| Landed nobleman | *gesith*<br>*thegn*<br>*?twelfhynde* | *thegn*<br>*landrica* |
| Governor of one or more shires | *ealdorman* | *ealdorman*<br>*eorl* |

*ceorl* is a churl as we understand the words, though we may well believe that he has much to make him boorish and churlish. Wynflaed calls her rent-payers at Chinnock "*geburas* settled on *gafol-land*." There is a shorter way of expressing this. The bounds of twenty hides at Hinksey, Seacourt, and Witham (Oxon) granted to Abingdon abbey *c*. 956 are described as the bounds of the *geburland*, and in 963 the *gebura londe* appears in the bounds of Laughern (Worcs). Two persons at Bedwyn (Wilts) pay 300 pence each to be "done out of the *geburland*," given freedom, in other words, to go wherever they please. The monks of Ely kept an extremely precise record of the *geburas* on their Hatfield (Herts) estate and of the marriages which took their children off to other villages, sometimes more than a dozen miles away. It is reasonable to guess that their offspring, like the couple at Bedwyn, had paid or were liable to pay for being "done out of the *geburland*."

### The Custumal of Tidenham

At some date between 956, when King Edwy granted Tidenham (Glos) to the monks of Bath, and 1065, when they gave a lease of the manor to Archbishop Stigand, a custumal was drawn up, recording the dues and services of the tenants. Tidenham was a multiple estate at the confluence of the Severn and the Wye. It included dependant settlements at Stroat, Milton, Kingston, Bishton, and Lancaut. It also had ninety-five fish-weirs on the Wye and Severn, the great majority of them basket traps of the kind still in use today. The lord of the manor claimed every alternate fish caught, and while in residence had to be informed when any fish were to be sold. Sturgeon, porpoises, herrings, and sea-fish were at all times reserved to him. The services of the *geneat* – of whom more presently – are stated in very vague and general terms, but the more servile *gebur* was bound to supply wooden rods for making fish-traps and fencing for the manorial demesne. The rent for each yardland, of which there were 27 at Stroat, 14 at Milton, and 13 at Kingston (now Sedbury), was twelve pence, besides fourpence as 'alms' to the church.

The principal agricultural service of the Tidenham *gebur* takes the form of 'week work', labour performed on an unspecified number of days every week throughout the year. In each week he must plough half an acre, the seed for which he will fetch from his lord's barn, and a whole acre for church-scot for which he supplies the seed himself. He must reap an acre and a half, mow half an acre, and do work of any other kind that may be demanded of him. Besides the rent of his yardland, he must give sixpence and half a sester of honey after Easter, six sesters of malt at Lammas, and a ball of good net yarn at Martinmas. If he keeps pigs he must pay for mast and give three pigs out of the first seven and thereafter always the tenth. There is no need to labour the interesting points of resemblance and contrast between these services and those claimed in Alfred's day from the *ceorls* of Hurstbourne.

## The *"Rectitudines"*

To fill out the picture of manorial economy in the eleventh century we have an illuminating tract entitled *Rectitudines Singularum Personarum*, a text which has no surviving parallel before the Norman Conquest. It reads as if it had been prepared by Wulfstan, bishop of Worcester and archbishop of York, from memoranda left by Oswald, his predecessor in both sees. It shows clear signs of drawing on experience of a large estate in the west midlands, but the writer insists that no two manors are exactly alike, that services are heavy on some, lighter on others.

Since the obligations of the slave are limited only by what is feasible, they are not enumerated in detail, but the writer declares that a slave woman ought to have eight pounds of bread-corn, one sheep or three pence for winter food, one sester of beans for lenten food, and whey in summer or one penny. The male slave should have twelve pounds of good corn, the carcases of two sheep and a good cow for meat, and the right of cutting wood for fuel or building. The allowance of corn, if annual as some scholars believe, seems small, but perhaps it is seed-corn, intended to be sown on the plough-acre which the writer says every bondman on the estate ought to have, and it will no doubt be supplemented by the meals which the lord will give his slaves while they are working for him. They are also entitled to a "harvest-handful" and to be feasted at Christmas and Easter.

We hear also of slaves employed as swineherds, bee-keepers, and herdsmen, each of whom is entitled to his perquisites. When they die, all their belongings go to the lord.

In the writer's opinion the *cotsetla* ought to have five acres or more; anything less would be inadequate. This humble tenant pays no rent, but is burdened with heavy services. On some estates he must work for his lord every Monday in the year, and on three days a week in August. As a day's work he is expected to reap an acre of oats and half an acre of other corn, after which the lord's reeve or bailiff should give him a sheaf as his perquisite. He may be called upon to keep watch on the sea-coast and to perform services incidental to the king's hunting. He pays church-scot at Martinmas and Peter's Pence on Ascension Day "as every free man ought to do." This last phrase should not be construed as implying that he is anything but a serf; it is put in only as a re-minder – a rather pointed one – that being now so far emancipated as to occupy a cottage and a small holding, he incurs the normal obligations of a householder to the church, obligations from which the slave is exempt.

The lord who sets his man up as a *gebur* should provide him with two oxen, one cow, six sheep, and seven acres already sown on his yardland, besides all necessary tools for his work and uten-sils for his house. Both the land and the outfit remain the property of the lord, and will revert to him when the man dies. For the first year no rent is payable; thereafter the *gebur* must pay ten pence a year at Michaelmas, equivalent, we may note in passing, to the rent that Alfred's *ceorls* had paid at Hurstbourne. He must per-form week-work as ordered: on some manors for two days in each week of the year, and for three days at harvest and from Candle-mas to Easter. At Martinmas he must pay two hens and twenty-three sesters of barley, presumably for church-scot, and at Easter a lamb or twopence. From the time when ploughing is begun until Martinmas he must plough an acre a week and fetch the seed for its sowing from the lord's barn. He must also plough three acres a year as 'boon-work' at the lord's request, two acres a year for his pasture rights, and three acres a year as part of the rent of his holding: for these last he must provide the necessary seed-corn. Between Martinmas and Easter he takes his turn to watch at the lord's fold. He too, like the *cotsetla*, is liable for Peter's Pence. He must give sixpence to the swineherd when he drives the village herd to the woods, and must join with another man of his own condition to maintain one of his lord's hounds. The writer adds that on some estates the *gebur* pays rent in honey, on some in meat, on some in ale. It all depends on the custom of the manor.

The *gebur* of the *Rectitudines* has been described as a "man trembling on the verge of serfdom." To most of us he will seem well over the verge. He may have started life as a slave or fallen into slavery for one reason or another. If so, he has certainly gone up in the world, but his lord retains all the rights he had over him while enslaved, except the right of punishing him with the lash. If he is the younger son of a free husbandman too poor to keep him, he may be able to implead other free men in the hundred court, but he himself is in all probability justiciable in the court of his lord. These are matters of surmise; what is certain is that economically he is an utterly dependent being, possessing nothing that he can really call his own, and the only recognizable mark of his freedom is his obligation to pay a householder's dues to the church.

### The "Geneat"

Well above him in rural society stands the *geneat*. There is nothing servile in his condition. On some manors he pays his lord a rent and gives him a swine a year in return for pasture rights. He is expected to reap and mow on the demesne, to join with others in maintaining the hedge around the manor-house and in cutting and erecting the fences required when the lord goes hunting, to provide cartage service, to escort visitors, to entertain his lord, to keep guard over his person and his stables, and to ride on errands far or near wherever he may be directed. The Tidenham custumal says in much the same words that the *geneat* must work on or off the estate, whichever he is bidden, and ride and furnish cartage service and supply transport and drive herds "and do many other things." For agricultural service he probably sends his servants to lend a hand in the busy season or goes himself to superintend the labour of the humbler tenants. A law of Edgar couples *geneatland* with the lord's demesne as land from which tithe is due. In a later law the same king says that if a *geneatman* does not pay his rent by the appointed day the lord shall be forbearing and not exact any penalty; if, however, the *geneat* resorts to violence he may lose his life as well as his land. This sensational picture of a recalcitrant *geneat* barricading himself in his farmhouse and holding out there to the death does credit to the lawgiver's imagination, but can seldom indeed have been realized in practice. Normally the *geneat* is most in evidence when his lord requires the services of a horse-man. Thus when the bishop of Worcester complains of encroach-ments on his woodland, the defendant orders his *geneat* named Ecglaf to ride round with one of the bishop's clergy and identify all the landmarks which the priest will read out from the old charters of the estate. We may safely identify the *geneat* with the countryman of superior status who will figure in the Domesday account of many manors, particularly in the west midlands, as a *radcniht* or mounted retainer.

The author of the *Rectitudines* goes on to detail the customary perquisites of the manorial servants. The sower may have a basket-ful of every kind of seed he sows; the oxherd may pasture his cow and two or more oxen with the lord's oxen on the common; the cowherd is to have the milk of a grown cow for seven days after she has calved, and that of a young cow for a fortnight; the goat-herd ought to have a year-old kid, the milk of the herd after Martinmas, and before that his portion of whey. The shepherd is entitled to have twelve nights' dung at Christmas, one lamb, one bell-wether's fleece, the milk of his flock for a week after the equinox, and a bowlful of whey or buttermilk all through the summer. Any remaining buttermilk is for the cheese-maker, who – if the text at this point has not been misunderstood – can keep a hundred cheeses for herself. The overseer of the granary takes all the corn spilt at the door of the barn. Every tree blown down in the wood belongs to the woodward.

The *Rectitudines* ends with a cheerful allusion to feasting at Christmas, at Easter, at reaping, ploughing, mowing, at the making of hay-ricks, the gathering of wood, the making of corn-ricks, and other occasions of rustic revelry.

## The Reeve

In the same manuscript as the *Rectitudines*, and probably by the same author, is a tract called the *Gerefa*. It deals with the functions of the reeve, whom it depicts as literally a man for all seasons, a walking encyclopedia of country lore. The list of tools he is expected to provide runs to fifty items, followed by a further list of sixty-three necessaries, including bee-hives, beer-barrels, and candlesticks. "He ought never to neglect anything that may prove useful, not even a mousetrap." The most interesting part of the tract is its picture of the agricultural routine, which is given with the caveat that in many districts the work of the farm begins earlier than in others. In May, June, and July men must harrow, spread manure, set up hurdles, shear the sheep, make good the fences and buildings, cut wood, clear the ground of weeds, make sheep-pens, construct fish-weirs and mills. During the next three months they reap, mow, set woad with the dibble, thatch and cover the crops, clean out the folds, prepare the sheep-pens and pig-sties and ploughs. During the winter they plough, in frosty weather split timber, prepare orchards, put the cattle in stalls and the pigs in sties, set up a drying oven on the threshing floor, and provide a hen-roost. Finally in spring they graft, sow beans, set a vineyard, make ditches, hew wood to keep out the wild beasts, set madder, sow flax and woad, and plant the vegetable garden. "I have spoken about what I know," says the writer in conclusion; "he who knows better, let him say more."

## Ælfric's "Colloquy"

More had in fact been said earlier, and more imaginatively, by Ælfric, monk and schoolmaster at Cerne Abbey in Dorset. Nearly all abbeys at that time housed a number of oblates, boys whose not over-fond parents had placed them at a tender age in a monastery to be trained as monks. To help the oblates with their Latin, Ælfric composed a charming *Colloquy* in which each pupil in turn impersonates a labouring man and answers questions about his occupation.

First the ploughman describes himself as rising at daybreak in all weathers. After yoking the oxen and fastening the share and coulter, he must plough daily a full acre or more. He is accompanied by a boy who applies the goad to the oxen and is hoarse from cold and shouting. He fills the cattle-stalls with hay, carries out the dung, and waters the oxen. "It is heavy toil, because I am not free."

At the end of the day the oxherd leads the oxen to pasture and watches over them all night to guard them against thieves. In the morning he hands them over, well fed and watered, to the ploughman.

The shepherd leads his flock to pasture, with dogs to protect them from wolves. He shifts their folds, milks the ewes twice daily, and makes butter and cheese. (In fact this would usually be done by his wife.)

The king's huntsman cuts the throats of the prey his dogs have driven into nets. With hounds he pursues the stag, the boar, the roedeer, the she-goat, and sometimes the hare. The king feeds and clothes him, and occasionally gives him a horse or a bracelet for his trouble.

The fisherman uses fish-hooks and baskets. He takes eels, pike, minnows, trout, lampreys, and generally all freshwater fish. Sometimes he fishes the sea for herrings, salmon, dolphins, sturgeon, oysters, mussels, cockles, plaice, flounders, sole, crabs, and lobsters. He does not join the fishing fleets which go out whaling; lucrative as that is, he thinks it too dangerous. He could always sell more fish if the catch were larger.

The fowler uses nets, traps, lime, whistling, and hawks. He likes full-grown hawks because in winter they feed themselves and him. In summer he lets them fly to the woodland and fend for themselves; they would eat too much at home. In autumn he takes and tames their young.

The merchant imports purple and other dyes, gold and precious stones, wine, oil, silk, ivory, and bronze; at times also tin, sulphur, and glass.

Questioned about the value of his calling, the cook retorts, in strikingly twentieth-century terms: "If you try to do without me, you will all be cooks yourselves, and none of you will be a lord."

This leads in conclusion to the oblate's own diet. It includes meat, eggs, fish, butter, cheese, and beans. His drink is beer, or failing beer water. Wine is not for the young, but for the old and wise.

## Social Mobility

Enough has been said to show how wrong it would be to think of Anglo-Saxon society in terms of caste. Hungry men might enslave themselves for food in the evil days, but particular and collective acts of manumission provided frequent ways of escape from downright slavery into the mitigated bondage we call serfdom. At a given moment in any period some men are prospering while others less fortunate or less industrious are sinking in the social scale. Difficult as it might be for a half-free cottager to thrive, the more substantial *gebur* could sometimes find means to get himself "done out of the *geburland*." "It often happens," wrote Archbishop Wulfstan, "that a miserable slave earns freedom from a *ceorl*, and a *ceorl* becomes worthy of a thegn's rights through an earl's gift." A compilation put together by the same prelate or in his circle shows more explicitly how a *ceorl* might become a gentleman. "If a *ceorl* prospered so that he had fully five hides of his own land, church and kitchen, bell-house and fortified dwelling, a seat and special office in the king's hall, then was he thenceforth entitled to the rights of a thegn."

How could a *ceorl* acquire the five hides of property in land which qualified him to rank as a thegn? The patronage of an earl or other magnate was not the only way. Opportunities might well arise from the organization of farming in open fields. A lad would seek employment away from home and save a few pounds from his wages. When a cottage fell vacant he would apply for it and continue to work for wages while cultivating his plot in his free time, if necessary hiring plough-beasts from his neighbours. In six months he could buy a few sheep with the proceeds of his first harvest and use his right to graze them at no expense to himself on the common and the fallow field. In due time he might sell them at a profit. In this way he could build up some capital by the profit on his crops and stock till he felt strong enough to apply for a larger holding and become a full-time farmer. He might move again, or even more than once, each time to a larger holding until he reached the top of the agricultural ladder. We have no means of knowing how often this happened in the Old English period, but that it did happen sometimes is proved by a reference, in a charter issued by Ethelred II in 984, to eight hides of land formerly held by a *ceorl* ("rusticus") named Ætheric. The bounds identify this property with Leverton in the valley of the Kennet, and it is pertinent to recall that Berkshire is a county in which numerous charters vouch for the presence of open fields.

Again, a period of agricultural expansion, when more and more land was being ploughed up at the expense of the woods and pastures, could be as profitable to the working countryman as to his lord. An energetic, enterprising countryman would seize the chance of enlarging his holding and enriching himself, spurred on, perhaps, by a favourable bargain with the lord of the manor.

## The Freedom of the Town

Towns, as well as open fields, held out prospects of wealth and freedom. The security of boroughs and 'ports' naturally tended to attract a settled population. The burgesses or portmen would live chiefly by trade and handicraft, not agriculture. In some boroughs, it is true, an obligation to render agricultural service on the lord's demesne would linger on, and in others the burgesses would continue to cultivate the soil outside the walls on their own account. But their hallmark is the payment of a money rent for their houses. They are not serfs of the manor, and nobody will be so misguided as to call them *ceorls*. Their status is nearer to that of the *geneat*; it even approximates to that of the thegn.

## The Thegn

The word thegn has by this time ousted the older *gesith*. The *gesith* had been or had hoped to become a landed proprietor with men on his estate for whose good behaviour he was responsible, but he himself might well be the man of a higher lord. The same is true of the thegn who has acquired his position by gift of an earl or bishop, like that Eadric to whom Archbishop Oswald granted three hides at Tiddington (Wark), increased to five hides eight years later.

To the author of the *Rectitudines* the thegn was one who held his land by charter, subject to the three common dues of military service, the repair of fortresses, and work on bridges. Other obligations might be laid on him by royal edict, such as service connected with the deer-fence at the king's residence, equipping a vessel for coast-guard duty, acting as a personal bodyguard, paying church-scot and Peter's Pence, "and other things, many and various."

When a lady named Wulfwaru made her will, she divided her estate at Butcombe (Som) between her eldest son and her younger daughter in equal shares, and enjoined them also to share the mansion-house "as evenly as they can." If a five-hide thegn used his power of testamentary disposition to divide his property in this way between two sons, they would inherit his rank but their economic position would be little better than that of a *geneat*. In the late Old English period the rural population included numberless petty thegns distinguishable only in title from the neighbouring farmers. At the other end of the scale were rich men like Wulfric, the founder of Burton Abbey, whose will disposed of more than seventy villages in Staffordshire, Derbyshire, and six other counties. To run this complex he must have employed a small army of reeves and other officials.

### Ealdormen and Earls

In authority and influence even such wealthy nobles as Wulfric took second place after the ealdorman. From the time of Edgar, if not before, the ealdorman shared with the diocesan bishop the presidency of the shire-court. In time of war he called up the militia and commanded them in the field. References in charter boundaries to "the ealdorman's land" imply that certain estates were earmarked for his maintenance. He was also entitled to a share of the fines levied to the king's use in boroughs, hundreds, and the shire. In process of time he was appointed to govern not one shire as of old, but two or more. Towards the close of the Old English period his enlarged sphere of office found expression in a change of title. By analogy with the Norse *jarl*, the English *eorl* came to mean, not as originally any nobleman, but, at first in Northumbria and finally over the rest of England, the governor of a province which might be co-extensive with a former kingdom, a Wessex or a Mercia. At the same time it became normal for a son to succeed a father in his earldom, though his appointment still had to be confirmed, and could on occasion be revoked, by the king.

## Bishops

Thus by the end of the tenth century England was largely dominated by rich and formidably powerful lay magnates and churchmen. At his accession Edward the Confessor found the English church organized in two provinces. That of York had as its only suffragan St Cuthbert's old bishopric, transferred in 995 from Chester-le-Street to Durham. The archbishop of Canterbury's province comprised thirteen sees besides his own, namely, Rochester, London, Selsey, Winchester, Ramsbury, Sherborne, Wells, Crediton, Worcester, Hereford, Lichfield, Dorchester, and Elmham. The last-named, with jurisdiction over Norfolk and Suffolk, after going into eclipse under the Danish occupation, had been revived in the middle of the tenth century. King Athelstan had established a bishop at St Germans to look after Cornwall as a deputy for the bishop of Crediton, and in 994 Ethelred II had given the Cornish bishop full diocesan jurisdiction, but in 1027 Bishop Lyfing persuaded Cnut to let him hold St Germans as well as Crediton and the two sees were thenceforth held as one. Then, as now, pluralism was the obvious expedient for a church in financial straits. From 972 to 1016, and again occasionally after 1042, the archbishop of York, impoverished by Danish encroachments, held Worcester in plurality with his Northumbrian see.

## Functions of Lordship

In its latest phase Anglo-Saxon society was permeated from top to bottom by the concept of lordship. Not that there was anything new in this. Lords had been there from the beginning, and we have seen that from the end of the seventh century, if not earlier, kings were holding them responsible for the good behaviour of their men. At first they shared this responsibility with groups of kindred. The fact of kinship loomed large in primitive minds, and for centuries the kindred occupied a place in the foreground of law-enforcement as well as in personal relations. As late as Athelstan's reign (924–39) the citizens of London contemplated the possibility that a group of kinsmen might be powerful enough to frustrate them in the exercise of their legal rights. But much had occurred to loosen old ties, and three-quarters of a century later we find Archbishop Wulfstan complaining that a kinsman does not now protect a kinsman any more than a stranger. More and more the duty of supervision and protection was devolving upon the lord. It is a mere accident that the charter of 956 by which King Edwy gave the archbishop of York rights of secular jurisdiction ('sake and soke') over Southwell and the discontinuous group of villages appendant to Southwell has survived to give us the first unequivocal evidence for the existence of private courts of justice in England. There is no reason to believe that Southwell was in fact the earliest manor to hold a court of its own, and we know that in the following reign not single manors but whole hundreds with their courts were handed over to ecclesiastical magnates.

Protection was the obverse of the loyalty a lord required from his men. To him they looked for support when in trouble with their neighbours or the public courts. Cnut complains that some lords represent their free men as slaves and their slaves as free, whichever makes it easier to defend their cause.

The troubles of the ninth and tenth centuries gravely disturbed the social fabric and left behind a number of lordless men. Such men were an anomaly on which legislators cast a decidedly unfriendly eye. Athelstan commanded the relatives of a lordless man to settle him in a fixed abode and find him a lord in the assembly of the folk. He also penalized any lord who should provoke an appeal to the king by failing to redress a wrong done by one of his men. Every lord must stand surety for his men. To remain lordless, or to plot against one's lord, is to risk outlawry and death.

Where earlier laws had spoken of the landlord (*landhlaford*), the codes of Ethelred II and Cnut speak of the *landrica*, the land-ruler, or lord of the manor, and entrust him with multifarious rights and duties. He shares with the wapentake the money lodged as security by men under arrest, and with the king's portreeve the security deposited by any one who seeks to clear a thief. It is for him to see that the man charged with theft goes to the ordeal, and if the accused evades the ordeal, half the fine he incurs goes to the owner of the goods, half to the *landrica*. He sends his own reeve with the bishop's to collect the defaulter's tithe. It is his duty to suppress heathen sanctuaries. If a villager fails to pay Peter's Pence, the *landrica* must pay it for him and impound the villager's ox. We may think it highly unlikely that a government which employs the lord of the manor to collect a tax due to the pope will not also employ him to collect taxes due to the king.

These enactments assume that the whole country is parcelled out into manors, each under the jurisdiction of a *landrica*. They also take it for granted that every lordless man has by now complied with Athelstan's injunction to find himself a lord, and that as a rule the lord is the local holder of book-right. Over much of England this was true enough, but it was not so in the eastern counties. Here many a land-book had been practically nullified when its holder fell in battle, leaving no legitimate heir. Many charters no doubt went up in flames when the Vikings burnt down the monasteries where they had been deposited for safe keeping. Moreover, land had changed hands often and easily, not by charter or lease, but by the testimony of the wapentake. Under such disruptive impacts the fabric of English landlordship had collapsed. Where the manor survived, its lord might well be too poor and insignificant to give his men the security they needed. Athelstan's decree obliged the lordless man to put himself under somebody possessing 'sake and soke', to become what a later generation would call a sokeman of that personage, but – and this was its fatal weakness – it did not oblige him to seek a patron in or near his own village, nor did it tell him what to do if no one in the village possessed rights of sake and soke. It left him free to go far afield and make what terms he could with some magnate – any magnate – powerful enough to lend effective support if he got into a scrape, but too remote to interfere with the daily business of his life. And if his neighbour had done homage to the earl, he might well think it a clever move to place himself under the still more exalted patronage of the archbishop. It was a situation which might have been expressly designed to produce tenurial chaos, just such a tangled network of personal and manorial relationships as would confront the Domesday commissioners in the eastern shires and perplex them by its marked contrast with the more orderly, old-established society of the south and west.

Alfred the Great had remarked that a king required three classes of men with which to fashion a well-wrought kingdom. He needed men who work, men who pray, and men who fight. These three components of a well-ordered society all awaited Edward in 1042 when he succeeded to his father's throne. The tillers of the soil, from the slave to the comparatively free man who cultivated his farm and occasionally served his lord as a mounted retainer, were organized in clearly distinguished grades to support the landowners who administered the courts of manor, hundred, and shire, and manned the army in wartime. The men of prayer, in a hierarchy of their own, gave the society which maintained them all that it knew of art, scholarship, and religious faith. All looked up to the monarch as the tie which bound the edifice together. To his Norman successors Edward would bequeath a rich monarchy, a well cultivated land, and a social structure which despite certain weaknesses was more complex, more advanced, than they had known how to build for themselves at home.

# CHRONOLOGICAL TABLE

N.B. The character of the sources is such as to leave the earlier dates in this table uncertain or at best approximate. Many of them are still under discussion by scholars. Dates of ecclesiastical events are printed in italic.

547. Ida, k. of Bernicia.
552. Victory of the Gewisse at Old Sarum.
556. Ceawlin, k. of the W. Saxons in the Thames valley.
558. Ælli, k. of Deira.
*563. Monastery established on Iona by Columba.*
568. Defeat of Ethelbert, k. of Kent, by Ceawlin.
577. Battle of Dyrham; W. Saxon conquest of the Cotswolds.
593. Death of Ceawlin. Æthelfrith, k. of Bernicia.
*597. Augustine lands in Thanet.*
617. Edwin, k. of Deira and Bernicia.
628. Baptism of Edwin.
     Penda wrests the Cotswolds from the W. Saxons.
634. Penda becomes k. of Mercia.
     Death of Edwin.
635. Oswald k. of all Northumbria.
643. Battle of *Maserfelth* and death of Oswald.
656. Oswy, k. of Northumbria, defeats Penda.
658. Victory of Cenwalh, k. of Wessex, at *Peonnum*.
659. Wulfhere proclaimed k. of Mercia.
661. W. Saxon victory at Posbury.
*663. Conference at Whitby. Wilfrid bishop of York.*
*669. Theodore archbishop of Canterbury.*
671. Death of Oswy; accession of Ecgfrith.

672. *General council of the English church at Hertford.*
675. Wulfhere succeeded as k. of Mercia by Ethelred.
682. Centwine, k. of Wessex, completes the conquest of Devon.
685. Ecgfrith defeated and killed by Scots.
Aldfrith succeeds to the throne of Northumbria.
Rise of Caedwalla in Wessex.
688. Ine, k. of all Wessex.
690. *Death of Archbishop Theodore.*
704. Abdication of Ethelred, k. of Mercia.
Death of K. Aldfrith.
709. *Death of Bishop Wilfrid.*
716. Ethelbald, k. of Mercia.
726. Abdication of Ine, k. of Wessex.
735. *Death of Bede. York becomes a metropolitan see.*
756. Murder of Ethelbald. Offa succeeds him in Mercia.
757. Cynewulf, k. of Wessex.
786. *Papal legates visit England.*
*Lichfield becomes a metropolitan see.*
Cynewulf dies. Beorhtric succeeds as k. of Wessex.
789. Vikings on the coast of Dorset.
796. Death of Offa. Cenwulf succeeds as k. of Mercia.
802. Death of Beorhtric. Egbert becomes k. of Wessex.
803. *The see of Lichfield loses metropolitan status.*
821. Ceolwulf I, k. of Mercia.
825. Egbert annexes Kent, Surrey, Sussex, and Essex.
838. Egbert defeats the Cornish at Hingston Down.
839. Ethelwulf succeeds Egbert as k. of Wessex.
850. Dalriada and Pictland united under Kenneth mac Alpin.
858. Death of Ethelwulf. Ethelbald succeeds in Wessex.
860. Death of Ethelbald; accession of Ethelbert.
865. Death of Ethelbert; accession of Ethelred I.
Great Danish Army raids over England.
869. Edmund, k. of E. Anglia, killed by Danes.
871. Death of Ethelred I. Alfred becomes k. of Wessex.
874. Burgred, k. of Mercia, driven out by Danes.
876. Foundation of a Danish kingdom at York.
877. Danes occupy eastern Mercia.
878. Alfred defeats the Danes and accepts their surrender.
886. Alfred captures London.
899. Death of Alfred; accession of Edward the Elder.
909. *New bishoprics at Ramsbury, Wells, and Crediton.*

911. Æthelflaed Lady of the Mercians.
     Edward annexes London and Oxford.
918. Death of Æthelflaed.
919. End of Mercian independence.
924. Death of Edward the Elder; accession of Athelstan.
937. Athelstan defeats the Scots at Bromborough.
939. Death of Athelstan; accession of Edmund.
946. Murder of Edmund; accession of Edred.
954. End of the Danish kingdom of York.
955. Death of Edred; accession of Edwy.
959. Death of Edwy; accession of Edgar.
960. *Dunstan, archbishop of Canterbury.*
961. *Oswald, bishop of Worcester.*
963. *Ethelwold, bishop of Winchester.*
973. Coronation of Edgar.
975. Death of Edgar; accession of Edward.
978. Death of Edward 'the Martyr'; accession of Ethelred II.
1002. Marriage of Ethelred II to Emma.
1013. Invasion by Swein of Denmark.
1014. Death of Swein.
1016. Death of Ethelred II.
1017. Cnut recognized as king.
1027. Cnut visits Rome.
1034. Duncan I, king of all Scotland.
1035. Death of Cnut. Harold Harefoot regent.
1037. Harold Harefoot king.
1040. Death of Harold.
1042. Accession and death of Harthacnut.
1043. Coronation of Edward the Confessor.

# SELECT BIBLIOGRAPHY

Excellent surveys of the period as a whole will be found in Peter Hunter Blair, *An Introduction to the Anglo-Saxon Period* (Cambridge University Press, 1956) and D. P. Kirby, *The Making of Early England* (Batsford, 1967). R. I. Page, *Life in Anglo-Saxon England* (Batsford, 1970) covers a wide field and is attractively illustrated, as also is D. M. Wilson, *The Anglo-Saxons* (Pelican Books, 1971), the best short introduction to Anglo-Saxon archaeology.

In *Lucerna* (Macmillan, 1964) and in *West-Country Historical Studies* (David and Charles, 1969) H. P. R. Finberg studies in detail several of the main problems in early English history.

Henry Mayr-Harting, *The Coming of Christianity to Anglo-Saxon England* (Batsford, 1972) is a full and fair discussion of the various influences at work in the Conversion.

B. Colgrave has edited and translated the more important Lives of the early saints: *The Life of Bishop Wilfrid by Eddius Stephanus* (Cambridge, 1927), *Two Lives of St Cuthbert* (Cambridge, 1940), and *Felix's Life of St Guthlac* (Cambridge, 1956). Bede's indispensable *Ecclesiastical History of the English People* has been translated by L. Sherley-Price (Penguin, 1955).

The Anglo-Saxon laws are conveniently studied in F. L. Attenborough, *The Laws of the Earliest English Kings* (Cambridge, 1922; reprinted New York, 1963) and A. J. Robertson, *The Laws of the Kings of England from Edmund to Henry I* (Cambridge, 1925). Both of these contain the original texts with translations into modern English. So does *Anglo-Saxon Wills*, ed. Dorothy Whitelock (Cambridge, 1930).

F. M. Stenton, *The Latin Charters of the Anglo-Saxon Period* (Clarendon Press, 1955), is a masterly introduction to these problematic texts. Their contents are made accessible by H. P. R. Finberg in *The Early Charters of the West Midlands* (1961, 2nd edition 1972) and

*The Early Charters of Wessex* (1964), and by C. R. Hart in *The Early Charters of Eastern England* (1966). These books cover the charters of fifteen counties, and the series, which is published by the Leicester University Press, is to be continued.

Vol. I of *English Historical Documents* (Eyre and Spottiswoode, 1955) provides English translations, with valuable introductions, by Dorothy Whitelock of very nearly all the more important sources for early English history from *c.* 500 to 1042, beginning with the Anglo-Saxon Chronicle.

F. W. Maitland's subtle and brilliantly written *Domesday Book and Beyond* (Cambridge University Press, 1897, 1907; Fontana reprint, 1960) starts from the principle that the way to early English history leads backward from the Norman period, and it suffers from the defects of that principle. Many of its conclusions have been shaken by the work of later scholars, but it remains a highly stimulating discussion of the fundamental problems.

F. M. Stenton's *Anglo-Saxon England* forms the second volume of the Oxford History of England. First published in 1943, with a second edition in 1947, it has been for a whole generation the most authoritative work on the period as a whole. Unfortunately the third (posthumous) edition, 1971, is inadequately revised, but it remains a classic of historical scholarship. Stenton's other contributions have been collected under the title *Preparatory to Anglo-Saxon England* (Clarendon Press, 1970).

The most recent examination of the Anglo-Saxon social structure and the rural economy in this period will be found in the seven chapters contributed by H. P. R. Finberg to Vol. I, Part 2, of *The Agrarian History of England and Wales* (Cambridge, 1972), which gives full references to the original sources. By kind permission of the Cambridge University Press the relevant sections of these chapters are repeated in this book, but without the footnotes.

# INDEX